And They Found No Witches

And They Found No Witches

A True Police Story

Tom Alessi

Cover design by M.E. Parker
HIT patch by Michael McAuliffe, RPD (Ret.)
ISBN: 0692406689
ISBN 13: 9780692406687
Library of Congress Control Number: 2015910441
Tom Alessi, Naples, Florida

Introduction

In the closing months of 1990, the Rochester Police Department (RPD) in upstate New York was rocked by back-to-back controversies. The chief of police was arrested for embezzlement in October of that year. He was charged with stealing money designated for use in narcotics investigations. What began as an audit in the department's property room led to the chief's aide—and close friend—going to the FBI with allegations of theft by the chief and himself. In an effort to secure a deal from the Justice Department in any forthcoming prosecution, the aide agreed to wear a concealed body wire and tape-record what he hoped would be incriminating conversations with his boss. In less than one month, enough evidence was obtained to make an arrest. In that same short period, other conversations were captured on tape. These conversations would help provide the basis for even more discord within the department.

Shortly after the arrest of its highest-ranking officer, a second and more devastating sequence of events occurred that would usher in the darkest era in the history of the RPD. These events would split the department in two and cause a morale problem that would last for years to come. As a result of a second but parallel investigation conducted by the FBI and the RPD, five members of the Vice Squad would face federal civil rights charges.

This is the true story of what happened to the members of a specialized street-drug enforcement unit. I was the sergeant in charge of the Highway Interdiction Team (HIT) from its inception in April of 1988 until it was disbanded in October of 1990. My life and the lives of several other police officers were turned upside down by the investigation. This event brought about the end of several careers as well as the end of effective street-drug enforcement in the city of Rochester, New York.

With the US Justice Department—and its unlimited resources—and our own agency targeting us, these officers and I were faced with a difficult decision: we could succumb to the overwhelming indictment the federal prosecutors had hoped to steamroll us with, or we could fight back. Some of us were offered options: plead guilty to a reduced charge, testify against our codefendants, and we would receive minimum sentences. You will see what happened before, during, and after the investigation and trial, as well as who helped us and who turned their backs on us.

In conversations I've had with people both on and off the job, I've found the ordeal generated more questions than answers. Usually it was because of a lack of background information on the part of the person to whom I was speaking. In some cases, people thought the two investigations were actually one, and that my colleagues and I were somehow involved in the allegations directed at the chief of police and his aide. Also, because the chief was named in *our* indictment, and eventually pleaded guilty, people who don't understand the system assumed the government must have been justified in their attempts to put us away. My late sister one day said to me, "You must have done something wrong. They indicted you."

Chapter One sets the stage for what unfolded after the arrest of the chief of the Rochester Police Department. It is important to understand what position certain people were in at a particular time so as to appreciate their roles in the investigation. For some, their personal or political agendas were more important than our careers, our reputations, or even the truth. For over two years, my codefendants and I had to remain silent while the news media portrayed us as rogue cops who had run amok. Long before any of the government's arguments were heard, we were convicted several times over in the court of public opinion. From the "pulpit prosecutors" of the minority community, who attempted to turn the case into a racial issue, to the editors of the local newspapers, the general public and our fellow officers were subjected to a barrage of allegations and assumptions. And the fact that ours coincided with the Rodney King case didn't do much to endear us to those who were screaming for our heads on a stake.

Being a police officer today is more difficult than ever before. Many people believe that it's due to the increased levels of violence on the streets of America. Most cops will tell you (usually off the record) that given the proper tools of the trade, they are ready, willing, and able to deal with the criminal element that pervades our society. The truth is that the greatest obstacles faced by police are the ever-increasing demands of administrators who find it necessary to bow to pressure from self-serving politicians and various segments of the community. After a while, it becomes an endless cycle—the worse the bad guys get, the more the police have to find new and effective ways of dealing with them. When those methods are questioned, and cops are punished for doing their job, the less inclined they are to try to make a difference. This creates an environment in which experienced officers don't want to risk losing their pensions, or going to prison, for what they believe is an ungrateful citizenry and criminals learn just how much they can get away with. Before long, the veterans retire or transfer off the street to a desk job, usually working days. Then along comes the next batch of rookies looking to save the world with their aggressive approach to law enforcement, and the cycle begins anew. In the end, it's the good people of the community who lose, and most of them never even know why. In this case, it was the good people of Rochester, New York.

"For better or worse,

most people's lives seem

to turn out rather

differently from what

they had expected."

Oliver North, 1991

One

"**C**hief Gordon Urlacher has been arrested. Deputy Chief Rickard, Capt. O'Brien, and Sgt. Mark Blair have been suspended. Sgt. Tony Cotsworth is the acting commanding officer of SCIS until further notice." That was the incredible announcement Capt. Tom Conroy made as he and Sgt. Mark Gerbino walked into my office.

Until that moment, it had been just like any other day for me at work. I was a sergeant in the Rochester Police Department's Special Criminal Investigation Section, otherwise known as the Vice Squad. As one of five supervisors working under Capt. Jim O'Brien, I was in charge of a specialized street-drug enforcement unit. The Highway Interdiction Team, HIT for short, was a federally funded project that focused on low-level street dealers and their operations. Conroy, the commanding officer of Internal Affairs, also advised me that HIT was to suspend all activity. He instructed me to send the patrol officers who made up the majority of the unit back to their respective districts. I had no way of knowing that the news I had just heard signaled the beginning of a nightmare for me, several of my fellow officers, and for the most part, the department itself. What I would soon learn was that the interim police administration along with City Hall and the federal government would bring that nightmare to life in the form of a joint investigation. The date was October 18, 1990, and would soon become known throughout the regional law enforcement community as Black Thursday.

It took a while for the shock of Capt. Conroy's visit to my office to wear off. Not only had the chief of police been arrested, but my immediate supervisor, Capt. O'Brien, had been suspended. He had been relieved of his badge and his weapon and was escorted out of the Public Safety Building along with Sgt. Mark Blair. What made the situation even harder to bear was that nobody told us why. When I asked Conroy if he could elaborate on the news he just delivered, all he said was "No." I looked to my good friend Mark Gerbino, who was trailing right behind Conroy, for an answer. Even a shrug of his shoulders to indicate his own lack of knowledge would have helped. Mark never even looked at me. It was as though he was concentrating on the captain's every move. Since he didn't work for Conroy, and never said a word during the entire visit, brief as it was, I had no idea why he was even there. The remainder of the day was spent trying to find answers or to give them. Members of SCIS were coming to me to see if I knew what was happening. I felt helpless because I could not even comfort them with a reason for the chaos all around us. It wasn't long before the phones started ringing and members of the news media were added to the growing list of those wanting to know what the hell was going on. What had started out as a fairly quiet day was quickly turning into a three-ring circus on the mezzanine floor of the police department. Soon, FBI agents both local and out of district were crawling all over our offices. What was really strange was that many of the feds were working with members of our own department. Not that we hadn't ever worked with federal agents on cases before, but this was different. The RPD personnel weren't people from the specialized units typically associated with a joint investigation. These were investigators, sergeants, and lieutenants from all over the police department. The day ended as many of the following ones would—with a lot of questions but few answers.

Three days later, on a Sunday, I went to a popular gin mill where a good friend of mine, Joe Laudisi, tended bar. The place was packed and very loud. After fighting my way to the bar, I indicated my drink preference to Joe by pointing to a bottle of Pinch. It's my favorite brand of scotch, and it was kept on an upper shelf, waiting to be utilized on one of *those* days. After loading me up, Joe pointed out a spot in the bar behind me. When I turned around, I saw Mark Gerbino and another city cop talking to two women. Between the music and the noise from the crowd, it was not very conducive to carrying on a conversation, but I figured I would at least be able to find out from Mark what had happened the previous Thursday. I made my way over to the foursome and stood next to Gerbino where I waited for him to finish speaking to one of the women and acknowledge my presence. The usual, friendly greeting I expected never materialized. Instead, after what seemed like an intolerable and uncomfortable wait, the only words my good friend spoke to me in the time it took me to finish my drink were, "So, you're working six to two, huh?" A highly unusual question since I had pretty much worked those or some variation of those hours since our downtown sections days in 1982. Something was definitely wrong. I drained my glass and went home.

Less than one month before Tom Conroy's announcement, our department, along with the local FBI office, initiated a joint investigation into possible corruption in the office of the chief of police. This investigation stemmed from an audit conducted in the property clerk's office. Large sums of money were missing from their evidence envelopes and had been replaced with strips of plain paper. It was learned that a veteran Vice Squad officer had taken the money to support a gambling habit. The money had been confiscated during drug investigations and was either evidence or money to be seized under state or federal forfeiture laws. With authorized access to any arrest packages, the veteran cop would take out the property sheet that included confiscated money. He would then go to the property clerk's office and sign out the cash without being challenged, and return the envelopes with blank paper. Most departments today use clear plastic envelopes, but ours were plain manila ones that hid the contents. It had been the officer's intention to replace the money with the expected winnings from his bets. Unfortunately, his losses outnumbered his wins, and the cash was never returned.

Gordon Urlacher was appointed chief of the Rochester Police Department in 1985 and brought his close friend Officer Roy Ruffin to that office as his aide. Urlacher had been the commanding officer of the downtown patrol section prior to his promotion to chief and was pretty much liked by most who knew him. He had a reputation as a good-time Charlie and could frequently be seen around town enjoying himself with his usual circle of friends. When the candidates for chief were announced, many people viewed Urlacher as a dark horse. While he may have done a good job as the captain of a patrol section, it was hard for some to believe he would be considered for the top administrator's position. One of Roy Ruffin's duties was to disburse money for various reasons. This money was kept in a safe in the chief's office. Usually once a month, I would have to withdraw cash in $2,000 increments from the federal grant money used in day-to-day operations of my unit. This money was used for undercover drug buys and for payments to informants. I would sign the cash out of the chief's office and document the withdrawal in my records. As I gave the bills to my officers, those transactions would also be recorded in my books, as well as in the records maintained by each team. Very often it was Roy Ruffin who initially gave me the money. There had not been an audit of the chief's office in the past five years. Now that a problem had been discovered in the property room, Ruffin feared that the auditors would move their investigation from the basement of the Public Safety Building to his office on the sixth floor. He had good reason to fear such an audit. In a short time to come, he would admit to stealing money from the chief's safe. The irony of it all was that there never was any intention to scrutinize the methods by which those funds were disbursed.

Officer Roy Ruffin, close personal friend and aide to Chief Urlacher, had been taking money for his own use from the safe in the chief's office. Now he lived with the fear that outsiders would soon be probing the financial records, and he would be left to explain the discrepancies. Roy needed a plan. If it's true what they say about the best defense being a good offense, then what better plan than to point the finger of guilt at the man in charge. After all, Urlacher was ultimately responsible for the contents of his safe. Within a week of the arrest for the thefts in the property room, Ruffin went to the FBI and told them that he and the chief had stolen $58,000 over the past several months. The actual amount of money stolen would eventually grow to $300,000 before the investigation was completed. But Roy hoped to convince the feds that it was his boss who took the majority of the missing money. It was Roy's intention to negotiate a deal with the government whereby he would assist them in gathering evidence against Urlacher in exchange for leniency. And he would gladly make restitution for an amount of money federal agents would later determine he should plead guilty to stealing. Besides, since investigators were brought in from outside Rochester, he would be dealing with agents who had not had the opportunity to observe Ruffin on a regular basis. How could they know that he and his wife enjoyed a lifestyle that belied his patrolman's salary of less than $36,000? It was not uncommon for Roy to fly to Las Vegas and watch a championship fight from ringside seats. In spite of his wardrobe and his spending habits, could it be that Ruffin's new friends in the federal building would believe that his income was supplemented by his wife's phone company job and occasional modeling assignments? Perhaps they would think that because Roy was an accomplished pool player whose skill with a cue stick was well known, his extra income must come from tournament winnings. The thirty-nine-year-old Ruffin had done well for himself after fourteen years in the RPD. With a prestigious job in the chief's office and a home in a fashionable section of Rochester known as Corn Hill, he found himself in an enviable position. But as an article in the *Democrat and Chronicle* on October 21, 1990, related, Ruffin's friends said he felt pressured to better his family's lifestyle.

Anyone that has been in this business knows that the best evidence you can have against a suspect is either his actions on video or his words on audio. Roy agreed to wear a body wire for the government in the hope of engaging his good friend, Gordon Urlacher, in an incriminating conversation. In the end it would be those taped conversations that would result in a guilty verdict at Urlacher's federal trial. In less than one month, the FBI felt they had enough evidence on the chief of police, and on Thursday, October 18, 1990, Urlacher was summoned to Mayor Tom Ryan's office. Waiting for him were Dep. Chief of Administration Roy Irving; FBI agents Gene Harding and Robert Langford; Monroe County District Attorney Howard Relin; and Asst. US Attorney for the Western District of New York Dennis Vacco. At approximately 2:00 p.m., Chief Gordon Urlacher was arrested and taken into custody. He was suspended from duty with pay. Part of the chief's defense was that it was Ruffin alone who was responsible for the missing money, and that Urlacher spoke the condemning words captured on tape only in an attempt to trap his aide. The jury didn't buy it. Urlacher was convicted and sentenced to four years in federal prison. He would leave Rochester for his tour in "Club Fed" maintaining his innocence as he had since his arrest. In March of 1992, after admitting to stealing "at least a hundred dollars," Ruffin pleaded guilty to a misdemeanor charge of embezzlement. But Roy's fate would have to remain on hold for a while. It would be another five months before his sentencing. The government sharks were already engaged in another feeding frenzy, and they still weren't finished with Gordon Urlacher.

During the time Ruffin wore a hidden microphone for the purpose of snaring the chief, he had numerous conversations with other members of the police department. Some of those conversations were the grumbling gripes and bitches of officers who felt that Ruffin would relay their "concerns" to Urlacher. I think it's safe to say that none of them ever figured on having their words immortalized for all time in the form of transcripts that would one day be used as evidence against other police officers. One member of the RPD who had unwittingly been caught on tape was a narcotics officer by the name of Earl "E. J." Lergner. Much of what Lergner had to say to Roy Ruffin on October 12, 1990, provided fertile ground for the conspiracy seeds others had sought to plant. And he wasn't alone. There were others from SCIS who voiced their opinions on both the personnel and the operations of our unit. Some officers who provided technical support for Narcotics and Intelligence didn't care for certain supervisors. They shared their opinions with people in the federal building who felt contempt for those same bosses. It wasn't long before plans were made at the federal level to investigate SCIS.

By 1990, E. J. Lergner had been in the Vice Squad for approximately thirteen years. He had seen administrations, as well as numerous supervisors, come and go. In the old days he was one of a dozen or so officers who made up the two-man teams responsible for handling drug-related investigations. Back then, the office consisted of three separate units: Narcotics for drug cases; the Enforcement Unit worked gambling and prostitution; and the Intelligence Unit monitored organized crime activity. Some officers would rotate in and out of the different units, but for the most part, people who developed an affinity for a particular type of work would stay in their desired field. The operative word here being *stay*. Barring retirement, promotion, or pissing off the wrong person, officers could stay in Vice as long as they wanted. The perks associated with such an assignment were well known. Plenty of overtime, a take-home car, and the ability to pretty much come and go as you pleased. As long as you and your partner were producing what, at least at that time, passed for acceptable results, nobody bothered you. Over the years, E. J. Lergner became proficient at developing and managing wiretap investigations. This was back when marijuana was sold out of inner city "smoke houses," and heroin was a prolific problem. LSD was somewhat limited to the college crowd, and cocaine was still a few years away from exploding onto the scene. While the issue of drug use and trafficking warranted its own unit in the RPD, it certainly didn't generate the cacophony we were hearing from a concerned population ranking it nearly the number one problem in our country. As far as Lergner was concerned, he would have been quite happy to be left to work his wiretaps and other in-depth investigations. But the times were changing, and soon it would be time to start paying more attention to the people at the bottom of the drug-dealing food chain and less to the ones at the top.

In 1985, Capt. Tom Conroy was the commanding officer of SCIS. Shortly after Urlacher became chief, he was replaced by Capt. James O'Brien. O'Brien had most recently been the commanding officer of a patrol section on the city's east side. He had turned down two previous requests to take over Vice. But due to mounting pressure from the mayor's office with respect to the ever-increasing drug problems and Conroy's lack of productivity in dealing with them, Urlacher's third approach to O'Brien was more along the lines of an implied order to take over the unit. Years later, Conroy would tell FBI agents that he advised the chief not to give the job to O'Brien, because O'Brien would have to be kept on a short leash. No reason was given for Conroy's opinion of his successor.

Jim O'Brien didn't waste any time in making the changes he felt were necessary to keep up with the current issues relative to increasing narcotics problems. What had been three units was reduced to two. The Enforcement Unit was eliminated, and its members were absorbed into either the Narcotics or Intelligence Units. It was felt that since most of the gambling activity in Rochester was controlled by what was at that time a considerably reduced organized-crime influence, the Intelligence Unit should take over that responsibility. The Tactical Unit, which operated within the Patrol Division, was given the task of dealing with prostitution. Whereas Conroy didn't concern himself much with the operations of the Narcotics Unit, Jim O'Brien considered it the flagship of SCIS. Times had indeed changed, and it was now time for a new approach to the enforcement of the state's drug laws. While it was still necessary to conduct complex investigations such as wiretaps, it seemed as if overnight, blatant street-sales of dope had become such a prevalent problem that something had to be done to address the concerns of citizens in every section of the city. As a patrol sergeant in 1985, I had been quite aware of the ever-increasing number of circumstances where uniformed officers found themselves involved in drug arrests not really sure what to do about that mysterious substance they were certain was illegal. Usually it meant calling a supervisor who would then attempt to reach someone in Narcotics. In many instances, the attempts were futile because the narco guys were too busy working on some investigation and couldn't break away for what was probably only a misdemeanor arrest. Some patrol officers viewed the Vice cops as prima donnas, and this situation didn't do much to enhance the relationship. But any ill feelings on the part of the street cops were usually stifled since it was the desire of many of them to someday transfer into the Vice Squad. The drug problem that existed in 1985 along with the change of command in SCIS led to radical changes in the way narcotics officers did their job—changes that E. J. Lergner would not welcome.

In the spring of 1987, the Monroe County Drug Task Force was established. Most of the surrounding police agencies, along with the sheriff's department and the New York State Police, sent representatives to work with RPD narcotics officers in a collective effort to address drug problems within their respective municipalities. Rochester was the host agency, and the task force was housed in our public safety building. Besides some minor logistical problems, such as floor space for accommodating additional bodies and their related equipment, there was the problem of some very large egos all in the same room. It's bad enough when diverse personalities from your own department work together. People who have been making their own cases for years but every now and then don't see eye to eye either work it out themselves or have a supervisor settle things. Now add cops from several agencies who are also used to doing things their own way, and you've got a recipe for potential conflict.

One of the new task force members was Dan Varrenti, an experienced narcotics officer from the Irondequoit (pronounced E-ron-da-quoit) Police Department. I had gone through the academy with Varrenti in 1979 but never really associated with him after graduation. As our careers progressed within our respective departments, I would often read accounts in the local newspapers of the many drug arrests or investigations Dan had been involved in. It soon became obvious that he was making a name for himself and was considered to be an excellent narcotics investigator by many people in the business. Of course, the nature of the cop beast being what it is, some felt that Varrenti couldn't begin to measure up to their own skills and experience. E. J. Lergner was just such a person, and in the months to come, he would often express his feelings on the subject. One occasion happened to be on October 12, 1990, just six days before Chief Urlacher's arrest. Lergner ran into Roy Ruffin and, while talking into Roy's hidden microphone, ranted and raved his way through his grocery list of complaints regarding certain members of SCIS.

The Monroe County Drug Task Force was under the direct supervision of Sgt. Tony Cotsworth, who had extensive experience as an investigator and a boss in Narcotics. Regional drug task forces are common throughout the country. Basically they consist of a host agency, such as RPD, and various surrounding municipal departments. As was the case with our task force, it may also include the county sheriff's office and the state police. Other agencies send representative officers who bring information relative to drug activity in their local areas. Then more assets from the larger task force can direct their enforcement efforts to the represented municipalities. In addition to increased drug interdiction for those agencies, they also received a percentage of any asset forfeitures from the arrested drug dealers.

Capt. O'Brien, or O. B. as he was commonly known, used a hands-on approach in his role as commander, which is to say he would often be involved in cases generated by both the Narcotics and Intelligence Units. But when it came to decisions regarding drug investigations, O'Brien would often defer to Sgt. Cotsworth's experience. While it was Tony's expertise that determined what direction a case might go in, it was Jim O'Brien's authority that determined if it would go at all. Both Cotsworth and O'Brien soon developed a good working relationship with Dan Varrenti. He was knowledgeable and displayed an enthusiasm for the job that they may have considered a refreshing change. Not only was Danny a likeable person, but he also proved to be a good target for the relentless, albeit good-natured, ball breaking that the captain and Tony regularly engaged in.

Shortly after Jim O'Brien assumed command of SCIS, Tony Cotsworth switched places with Sgt. Mark Blair as the supervisor of the Intelligence Unit. O. B. had brought Blair up to the squad from the patrol section where they had previously worked together. Cotsworth was looking forward to the more relaxed change of pace his new environment would afford him. He had been the only supervisor in the Narcotics Unit, and in spite of the overtime money he was making, working both day and night got old after a while. Now he was able to let his personnel do their work and keep him informed on the status of their investigations. This arrangement had lasted for about a year when it was decided that Cotsworth and Blair would revert back to their original supervisory positions. Tony made it clear to the captain that if he returned to Narcotics, he did not wish to pull double duty as he had done in the past. Cotsworth requested from O'Brien an additional supervisor to work nights. The boss agreed, and the posting for a second sergeant in Narcotics was sent throughout the department. Now all they had to do was wait for the stampede of applicants to come through the door. In the meantime, Sgt. Cotsworth would oversee the daily (and nightly) operations of the newly established task force.

Two

For some people, becoming a police officer is a lifelong dream, but it wasn't something I had always wanted to do. Growing up in Rochester, the one ambition I remember was to become a veterinarian, thinking what a great job it must be. Play with animals all day and get paid for it. As I got a little older and realized how much education it required, I didn't think I would ever overcome my dislike for school enough to reach that goal.

Rochester is the third largest city in New York. With a variety of lower-, middle-, and upper-class neighborhoods, it is the home of Eastman Kodak and Bausch & Lomb with a strong Xerox presence. When I was young, the economy was good, unemployment was low, and it was a great place to live. But with no marketable skills and no plans for college, I enlisted in the marine corps for four years right after graduating from high school (a minor miracle in itself) in 1967. While in the service, I married my high-school sweetheart. And five months before my discharge in 1971, I became a father. I had hoped to go to college using my VA benefits. The only problem, besides trying to feed my family with my monthly allotment checks and a part-time job, was finding something interesting enough to study. I had been trained as a jet-engine mechanic in the marines, but there wasn't much demand for those skills in upstate New York. I enrolled in a liberal arts program at Monroe Community College and spent the first few semesters taking all elective courses. During that time I met a number of people studying criminal justice. By the time I started giving the idea of a career in law enforcement any serious thought, my wife and I decided it would be best if I left school and helped her provide a decent existence for our family.

In 1972, I went to work for the Rochester Telephone Company. My brother-in-law got me in under Equal Employment Opportunity Commission (EEOC) guidelines, which apply to gender as well as race. I was to be one of a handful of males working among approximately one hundred females. I began as a clerk in the final accounts office and later became a residential-service representative. It didn't take long to realize I would never be able to make a career of sitting at a desk all day while customers called to blame me for every conceivable problem with their telephone service. And there wasn't much hope for advancement without a college education. During my four years at the telephone company, I gave more and more thought to becoming a police officer. When my job became unbearable, I decided to go for it. I quit Rochester Telephone and returned to MCC to study criminal justice in 1977. Given my track record in academics, and realizing I had a long way to go toward an uncertain future, I was, at the least, apprehensive. Scared as hell was more like it.

It's amazing how much different school can be when you're there because it's something you want as opposed to required attendance. I found most of the related subject matter fascinating and managed to absorb much of it from just listening in class. Being rewarded with A's and B's for the first time in my life felt good and made me realize just how much of an opportunity I had wasted as a kid in school. Once again I made a number of acquaintances at MCC, and many of them were police officers from agencies in Monroe County. I lived in a neighboring county and figured I may as well try to get hired by the local sheriff's office. Some of my classmates suggested taking any civil service exams that came up as practice before taking the one in my county. One of those classmates was an officer in the Rochester Police Department. Bob Duffy had been with the RPD for about two years when we met in school. He often told me of the fun and excitement he enjoyed as a city cop and suggested taking the city test myself.

Since the exam for my county had not even been announced yet, I thought why not? I took the city test in August of 1978, and a short time later I took my county's civil-service exam. With only one semester to go before graduation and no employment prospects, it was time to start biting my fingernails. I had been working in the school bookstore for extra money and was beginning to wonder if I had wasted my time pursuing a degree I would never use. As the end of the year drew near, I was notified that I had passed the city exam and would be advised of further processing dates. I continued with the stages of getting hired, such as a physical agility test, medical exam, and psychological testing. During this hiring process, I moved my family into Rochester where we rented an apartment from my wife's grandfather. We had hoped to save enough money for a down payment on a house if and when I ever got a decent job. When we moved from Ontario to Monroe County, I notified the post office to have our mail forwarded. There were still no results from the Ontario County Sheriff's test. It would be another two years before I learned that every piece of our mail except my test results had been forwarded to our new home. They had been returned to the civil service office. As it turned out, I scored 100 percent on the test and was told I would have definitely been hired had I responded. Old man fate had changed the road signs on me. You can be sure it wouldn't be the last time.

In early February of 1979, I received a phone call at the bookstore. It was from the recruitment office of the Rochester Police Department. The officer calling said the next academy class was scheduled to begin on March 12 and that a job with the RPD was mine if I was still interested. The reality of my good fortune wouldn't sink in until several hours after I hung up the telephone. For the past eight years since returning home from the marine corps, I had been troubled that I did not have a clue as to how I was going to earn a living. I had seen so many people just settle for any job that came along and end up hating every day they went to work for what would probably be the next twenty or thirty years. Much like my telephone company job.

Two exceptions were Bob Fraser and Jim Briggs. They were two good friends of mine from high school who became union electricians. Occasionally we would get together at a local drinking establishment and conduct random field tests of the beer supply. Invariably, the two skilled workers would begin talking shop, and I'd end up talking to the bartender. They would rattle off the names of guys they had worked with over the years, and I could sense their attitude of belonging to a family of coworkers. I had nothing in common with two of my closest friends. Now I was about to enter a new family of my own.

I was exactly five months shy of my thirty-first birthday when I reported to the police academy. As I entered the room, I was pleasantly surprised to see my former MCC classmate, Bob Duffy. As it turned out, Officer Duffy, the person who had most influenced my decision join the city police department, would be one of my class counselors. Duffy and Officer Dick Farrell of the Irondequoit Police Department would be overseeing our group of shiny new cops-to-be.

For the next three months we would be subjected to the usual rigors associated with initial police training. I had two things going for me. First, after returning to MCC and developing a new attitude toward academics, I was actually looking forward to learning all the new material coming my way. Second, with four years in the marine corps behind me, the quasi-military environment of the training was a walk in the park. Spit and polish was second nature to me. There are four awards given out at the end of training: academics, physical fitness, marksmanship, and best all around. I managed to take the award for marksmanship.

While in the academy, we received instruction on the workings of the department's Special Criminal Investigation Section. Sergeant Bob Wiesner and Investigators Eric Larson and Mark Gerbino were the guest speakers. Wiesner would one day become my boss, but all three became good friends. Many years later, two of them remain close while one chose to turn his back on me.

Upon graduating from the academy in June and completing another twelve weeks of field training, I was permanently assigned to the

Genesee Section. One of seven districts in the Patrol Division, Genesee covered the southwest area of Rochester where I worked third platoon (the 3:00 p.m. to 11:00 p.m. shift). It was here that over the next three years I would acquire the basic skills of police work. I, along with one of my academy classmates, Bob Urtis, learned from some of the best cops in the department. Men like Lieutenant Lou Genovese and Sergeant George Ehle, two seasoned veterans, helped us acquire the instincts that can't be taught.

After responding to everything from barking dogs to homicides several times over, often involving the same people (except the homicide victims), it was time for a change.

In July of 1982, I transferred to the newly established Downtown Patrol Section. I worked in the Crime Suppression Unit, usually in a proactive mode. Our hours were normally 8:00 p.m. until 4:00 a.m., Tuesday through Saturday. The hours were subject to change depending on special situations. My new commanding officer, Capt. Gordon Urlacher, had impressed upon our sergeant, Charlie Loray, the need to liberate the downtown area of both male and female prostitutes. It seemed they were especially bothersome to local government officials who would have to pass by the assortment of hookers, he-shes (transvestite prostitutes), and chicken hawks (young male prostitutes) as they entered City Hall for their Tuesday night council meetings. My unit was given the unpleasant task of discouraging these undesirables from plying their trade. What made it unpleasant were the methods by which we attempted to complete our goal. Posing as customers and trying to convince these characters of our desire to pay them for their services was not my idea of a party.

Like the very first time we tried to pick up a male prostitute. Typical of my luck, I got to go first. Using one of our own vehicles and dressed in street clothes, I cruised around City Hall trying not all that hard to look appealing. It didn't take long before I caught the eye of who I thought was a likely candidate. Having picked up female hookers before, I thought this venture would take the usual couple of minutes to get an offer of sex for a fee. In a business where time is money, once they feel sure you're not a cop, the pros can negotiate the terms of the deal, collect the money, render services, and be back out on the street in a matter of minutes. When the customer turns out to be an undercover cop, steps two, three, and four are replaced by arrest, transport to jail, and paperwork. With my luck holding true to form, the guy I picked up was not a working prostitute. He was looking for someone to have a meaningful relationship with. I knew it was going to be a bumpy ride when he suggested we take a drive to the lake where we could walk along the beach. Our prearranged signal for the backup cars to move in for the arrest was to tap on the brake pedal a few times after the offer was made. Twenty minutes later, *my* backup must have thought I was falling in love. Since it was obvious this lonesome dove was more interested in picking out furniture than in making money, I began accusing him of being an undercover cop. I told him the whole time we were in the car together he must have been waiting for me to make him an offer so he could arrest me. I pulled to the curb and reached for the door on his side, telling him to get out. He became so flustered at the thought of losing his new playmate he blurted out, "OK, OK, I'll do it all. Cock, balls, and ass for five dollars." Thank you, Lord! I pulled my gun out from under my left thigh and stuck it in his face. In sum and substance I told him our beach date was off because he was going to jail.

In addition to prostitutes, we would also set up details where we targeted suspects for car larcenies, burglaries, and pickpockets. Whenever manpower shortages dictated, we would work in uniform and take calls for service. All in all it was a good assignment, and it provided me with additional experience many officers in patrol don't get.

When the Downtown Patrol Section was created, officers from other sections were assigned to its four shifts. Some of these people I knew but had never worked with. Others I was meeting for the first time. Two officers, Lou D'Angelo and Bill Bartell, would not only be my coworkers, but they would also become close friends whose loyalty would prove invaluable in the years to come. One new acquaintance was Officer Mark Gerbino. He had prior experience in the Narcotics Unit, and in a short time we became good friends. Mark and I spent many nights working together in a patrol car or an unmarked vehicle cruising around downtown in search of evildoers. He talked about his days in the Vice Squad and the things he experienced working undercover. He had been involved in one of the city's most notable drug investigations that resulted in a shoot-out at the airport. When it was over, one undercover cop was shot, and a Lebanese heroin dealer was dead. I had never given much thought to working Vice, and it was probably because I didn't really know anyone who did. On rare occasions while working in patrol, I would assist on a raid of a drug house. That usually just meant covering the perimeter of the building while the guys with the long hair and beards had all the fun. The more Mark would talk about what a great assignment it was, the more intrigued I became with giving it a try. I figured if I didn't like it I could always return to uniform work.

When I first joined the police force, I never thought about moving up in rank. First, you have to have at least three years as a patrol officer before you're eligible to take the sergeant's exam. With the test given every two years (if the list from the previous test isn't extended), and with bad timing, your three-year anniversary could be just after an exam is given. That would make it five years before you could take the next test. Then, depending on how well you score, you may or may not be reachable on the promotion list. There are only so many openings, and often times, people "die" on the list when it expires. Then you start all over again. I've always admired the people who had several years of service and kept taking the exam until they got promoted. I was lucky. I passed the first one I took after my initial three years of service. I was also fortunate that there was a lot of movement within the department, and dozens of officers were promoted over a short period of time. On the down side, as the chances of making sergeant increased, the more they decreased for me ever getting to the Vice Squad. Narcotics personnel were either officers or investigators. Sure enough, though, my time came, and I was among the group of newly appointed sergeants in the city council chambers waiting to be sworn in on December 12, 1985. Standing in line with us, waiting to take the oath of our new rank, was my old friend and class counselor, Bob Duffy.

My first assignment as a new boss was in the Lake Section. This area was, at the time, one of the seven patrol sections. In days to come, that number would be reduced to six with the merging of the Highland and Atlantic Sections. Lake Section is bordered on the east by the Genesee River and extends north from downtown approximately five miles to the banks of Lake Ontario in the community of Charlotte. It was not uncommon to be at the lower end of the section and get a call for a bar fight, or worse, an officer in trouble, in Charlotte. That was when you really got to see how fast a police cruiser could get from point A to point B.

I was in charge of the fourth platoon, the overlap shift, and like my assignment in the Downtown Section, we worked 8:00 p.m. to 4:00 a.m. When I first took over, the platoon was on a regular work wheel like the rest of the section. At that time the wheel was four days on, two days off, four on, two off, five on, two off, with everyone's days off staggered. This meant sometimes we would have an abundance of officers on what would typically be slower nights and a shortage of manpower on Friday and Saturday nights. It also meant there would be nights when some of my officers would be working while I was off. This situation lasted for a few months until Capt. Bob Wiesner was named the new commanding officer of Lake Section. Wiesner was more inclined to employ a proactive approach to police work than was his predecessor. He allowed me to change my platoon to a straight five-two wheel with Sundays and Mondays off. This provided adequate coverage on the weekends and insured that the whole platoon worked together. Capt. Wiesner had Vice Squad experience and was in favor of using covert details in areas where we might see a rash of crimes such as burglaries or car larcenies. My platoon operated much like the unit I worked in downtown. While I was happy with my assignment as a patrol sergeant, I couldn't help regretting that my promotion meant I had virtually no chance of ever getting in the Narcotics Unit. Or so I thought.

Like most cities, Rochester has its share of bars and restaurants frequented by members of the law-enforcement profession. Some are typical "cop bars" where rookies and old timers alike go nightly to unwind. Others are used less often for large gatherings such as promotion or transfer parties. It was at just such a party that I ran into Officer E. J. Lergner in early 1987. I had met him sometime before and learned that he, too, had been in the marines. Every now and then we would compare notes about our respective tours of duty. At this particular get-together, E. J. informed me there was about to be a posting for an additional sergeant in Narcotics and that I should put in for it. A short time later I submitted my transfer request and was interviewed, along with numerous other applicants, by Capt. Jim O'Brien. I didn't think I had a chance of getting the job, because it hadn't been all that long since I got my stripes. I figured there must be plenty of sergeants who worked in Vice before getting promoted and would be favored for their prior experience. Either that or someone else would get it just because he knew the right people. It's amazing, but when Old Man Fate is determined to really screw up your life, all the rules for what should happen go right out the window. One night while working my normal shift in Lake Section, Sgt. Tony Cotsworth of Narcotics contacted me and asked if I could meet him for coffee. We met at a nearby restaurant where he conducted a second interview and informed me that no one had the inside track for the position. Tony said Capt. O'Brien had more or less left the choice up to him since it was Cotsworth who would have to break in and work with the new sergeant. He answered all my questions and advised me that he still had other people to interview. From then on, all I could do was wait.

Three

The massive transfer list came out in October of 1987. It was three pages of the names of officers moving in and out of different patrol sections, as well as some specialized assignments. One of the lines on the last page read, "Sergeant Thomas Alessi: From the Patrol Division, Lake Section Fourth Platoon, to the Special Criminal Investigation Section." It had been five years since my old friend Mark Gerbino started me thinking about working drug cases. After believing for so long that the good fortune of being promoted to sergeant came at the expense of such a desirable assignment, I would now get to experience the benefits of both worlds. When I reported to SCIS on my first day, Capt. O'Brien called me into his office to explain just what he expected of me. He made it clear that I would not be making any undercover drug buys myself. Basically, I would be overseeing the officers who had that responsibility.

In the beginning, I worked days with Sgt. Cotsworth. I would ride along with him on raids and various surveillance operations. Tony taught me most of the things I needed to know about the drug-enforcement business. I learned the different types of drugs that were available, where they were sold, and who sold them. After my breaking-in period, I would go out with the different teams of investigators while Tony involved himself with a host of other things that demanded his attention. Very often he would meet with members of the other local departments that made up the task force. Sometimes it was a question of selling the merits of pursuing a particular target to the DA's office or to the chief, if spending an inordinate amount of money was an issue. It had been explained to me from the beginning that I was brought up to the unit to be the night supervisor. I knew working the day shift was only temporary. In the meantime, I learned the operation of the office itself and what other offices in the Public Safety Building I would be interacting with. It seemed that a good part of working days meant numerous trips up and down in the elevator to different floors in the building. It didn't take long to remember why I enjoyed working nights. During the day there were bosses everywhere.

Parking around the Public Safety Building was a nightmare. And trying to get things done in the street was a real pain. In patrol, if I needed to get somewhere fast, it was just a matter of flipping on the lights and siren, pulling into the opposite lane, and aiming my blue and white cruiser at oncoming traffic. Anyone who has ever driven an emergency vehicle with lights flashing and siren wailing knows that a motorist can be driving right in front of you and not be aware of your presence. It's much easier to get the attention of someone looking through their windshield and seeing an assortment of lights bearing down on them. Unlike the driver in front of you who finally does look in the rearview mirror and just slams on the brakes, drivers who see you coming head on are quite eager to pull over and let you by. For the next few months, I continued to work days with Tony. Unlike when I first came on the job and didn't know anyone in Vice, by now I had worked with some of these guys in patrol before they started working dope cases. That made things a lot easier for me being a new guy and a boss with no experience in drug enforcement. At least in my prior assignment, where some of the people who worked for me were rookies, there were very clear lines of distinction between the roles of officers and sergeants. It's much easier working within the boundaries of your own expertise, and when someone had a question or a problem, I knew the answer, or I knew where to find it. In my new environment, things were much different. With very few exceptions, the things we got involved in on a daily basis dealt with the state's drug laws. I made it clear to the people I worked with that I had no intention of trying to tell them how to run their investigations, especially since they were the experts and the smell of dry cleaning fluid from my uniforms was still fresh in my memory.

Prior to my arrival at the Narcotics Unit, the Rochester Police Department had applied for a federal grant to be used for drug enforcement. Eventually, our city was one of seventeen selected to receive money from Washington to combat street sales of narcotics. By the spring of 1988, all but the final stages of the grant process had been completed, and it was relatively certain that the money would be forthcoming. Capt. O'Brien advised me that I would be the project director of the grant. Anyone in the business knows police projects have to have cute little names. Usually it's an acronym made up from the first letters of a multiword name like Street Crime Reduction Unit, or SCRU. Get the idea? Well, ours was no different—our specialized unit would be called the Highway Interdiction Team, or HIT. Some of the people involved with the unit at its inception suggested Street and Highway Interdiction Team. Nice try, guys. I could just see us running around the city with SHIT on the front of our raid jackets and ball caps. The structure of HIT was unlike anything our department had tried before, at least on a permanent basis. The plan was to have one sergeant and four full-time members of the Narcotics Unit as the core of the squad. In addition, we would bring up to the unit, in thirty-day cycles, one uniformed officer from each of the six sections of the Patrol Division, the idea being that our guys knew the dope business, and the patrol officers knew the local dealers. It also provided a reward for beat cops who were busting their humps every day in the neighborhoods. Try catching dope dealers while wearing a uniform and driving a marked police car. They don't exactly stand around waiting to get popped while you park your law-enforcement billboard on wheels and walk up to them. It's frustrating for the good street cops who spend their nights racing around answering calls while drugs are being sold and consumed all around them. At the beginning of each month, I would address the new group of patrol officers assigned to HIT and explain the do's and don'ts of their temporary job. Along with this was a spiel that one of the regulars dubbed my "plumbers and carpenters" speech. I told the temporary people that police work was all I knew; I didn't know carpentry, plumbing, or anything else, so don't do anything that would cost me my job, because this is how I pay my bills. I also told them it was "payback time" (them being paid back) for all those nights they had to drive past known drug dealers unable to give them proper attention. Another consideration was the decent people who lived in these neighborhoods. They would see the police driving up and down the streets while dealers sold their poison in what had become an open-air market. In talking to citizens, we learned they honestly believed the police were inept and couldn't do anything, they were corrupt and didn't want to solve the problem, or maybe the boys in blue just didn't care. Something had to be done to turn things around in these areas where people were afraid to walk the streets or let their kids play outside.

Sergeant Joyce Walsh had come on the job about three years before I did and was currently assigned to the 3:00 p.m. to 11:00 p.m. shift in Lake Section. She had been working in Lake during the last two years I spent there, but we never had much to do with each other. Part of the reason was that she had had a prior relationship with my friend Mark Gerbino, and according to him, she burned Mark pretty good. When he and I worked downtown together, Mark had told me that Joyce's father hated him and offered to give her money for a down payment on a house if she broke off the relationship. The next thing Mark knows, he's out, and Joyce is shopping for things to put in her new house. I never heard any other version of the story, and because he was a friend of mine I had no reason to disbelieve Mark. I think because of what Gerbino had told me, I had an automatic dislike for Sergeant Walsh and steered clear of her when we worked in the same section.

One night at a transfer party, I noticed Joyce sitting at the bar. What happened next was probably a combination of the way she was dressed (tight jeans and form-fitting sweater was a far cry from her uniform) and the amount of beer I had consumed, but the fact she had ripped my buddy's heart out was the farthest thing from my mind. We talked for a while, and before long I was staring at the taillights of her car as

I followed her home on what was the first of many nights we would spend together.

By February of 1990, I was less than two years into my second marriage and had contributed more than my share to bring about its demise. In fairness to my first wife, and the mother of my two children, we had been married for eleven years and then her husband became a cop. Usually, police officers get married after they're on the job, and the new spouse pretty much knows what he or she is getting into. Marriage number two was a huge mistake, and now here I was about to set up housekeeping with yet another woman. When Joyce asked me to be a full-time houseguest, I couldn't help remembering what Mark Gerbino had told me about her father. Even though she had given me a totally different version of how her relationship with Mark ended, she also said there was a good chance her dad would disown her if she lived with a man she wasn't married to. I had not even met Bill Walsh until I was living with his daughter, but it didn't take long for us to become good friends. In a short period of time I grew close to the whole family. When our schedules allowed, we would eat dinner at Joyce's parents' house. Her father would often take her younger brother to a nearby bowling alley for something called Rock and Bowl, and we would meet them after work. There was never a shortage of things to talk about with Joyce's dad. He was retired from the Rochester Fire Department, and an important focus of his later years was staying abreast of the local and national news. Bill was very opinionated and didn't mind sharing his views on a litany of subjects, whether you wanted to hear them or not. Fortunately for me, I agreed with most of the positions he took.

My relationship with Joyce was going smoothly in spite of the aggravation associated with my previous marriage. Unlike the transition from my first one, this was shaping up to be a real battle. Those headaches aside, things at work were going great. Capt. O'Brien had decided who the four full-time members of HIT were going to be. In addition to me, the team would include Investigator Bill Morris, Investigator Scott Harloff, Officer Greg Raggi, and Officer Roy Hopkins. It was up to us to make the new project a success. We would also be the ones to lead the patrol officers, who were assigned to the unit every thirty days, around the city in search of the Merchants of Death, as we sometimes referred to dope dealers.

Billy Morris had been in Narcotics the longest of anyone else in the squad. He and Scott Harloff had been partners for a while prior to the formation of HIT, and like his three veteran counterparts, he had been drafted into this venture with some reservations. Morris had been used to making his own cases and, like most narcs, was always searching for the biggest dealers to take down. For several years before the Monroe County Drug Task Force was established, Billy had been partners with Officer Dave Monk. They were responsible for some of the biggest and most successful drug cases in the department's history. With the creation of the task force, and new people coming into the Vice Squad, several changes were made with respect to which officers worked together. Monk had announced his retirement, and Morris was paired with Scott Harloff. Greg Raggi and Roy Hopkins had been working together for some time already. I had not really known Billy Morris prior to my new assignment. Other than seeing him on a few raids I had participated in while in patrol, I knew him only by reputation. He was tall and thin with long, salt-and-pepper hair and a full beard to match. On one of the raids Morris was on, he happened to walk up behind a uniformed lieutenant who mistook him for one of the suspects. Lt. Lou Genovese (my former mentor from Genesee Section) delivered a kick that shattered one of Billy's knees. His surgery and rehabilitation proved to be more successful than the lawsuit he brought against the department and the lieutenant.

Billy's partner, Scott Harloff, had moved to Narcotics from the Intelligence Unit. Harloff, in his thirties when I came into the squad, was a large, imposing figure whose nickname was Stain because of his sometimes beet-red complexion. Scott's thinning hair was somewhere between white and blond, which made his face stand out even more. He and Roy Ruffin had worked together in the Intelligence

Unit back in the days when the local mob faction was divided into the A-Team and the B-Team. These two cops would follow organized-crime figures around, recording their movements and associates. Harloff and Ruffin became close enough friends that they were in each other's weddings.

Greg Raggi and I had gone to grammar school together. We played on the varsity basketball team in eighth grade at Blessed Sacrament. After graduation, Greg went on to Bishop Kearney, a Catholic high school. I took the entrance exam for BK, but at the last minute I changed my mind and went to Monroe, a public high school. I think the fact that in 1963 the Catholic school was divided with boys on one side and girls on the other side influenced my decision considerably. Greg is built like a bull. He wore his hair short with a close-cropped, neatly trimmed beard. A tough guy back in school, Greg was now known and respected in the department for his ability to handle himself when shit hit the fan. Raggi had been in the Vice Squad for more than ten years when I got there. His partner was Officer Roy Hopkins. Hoppy, as Roy was commonly known, had been in the unit for only a couple of years. He had come from Genesee Section where he worked the midnight shift. Roy had been one of Sensabaugh's Raiders, which consisted of anyone who worked for Lt. John Sensabaugh, a legend in the department long before he ever retired.

John Sensabaugh came on the job in the early sixties and shortly after that had his ass handed to him in a fight. He vowed it would never happen again and started lifting weights. It didn't take long for the future lieutenant to become an imposing figure with a barrel chest and big arms. By the time I met Sensabaugh, he was the lieutenant on the midnight shift in Genesee Section. He had a reputation for wanting to be in the middle of confrontations and being very supportive of his men. Most times he could be seen with his ever-present pipe in his mouth, and he reminded me of General MacArthur. There was more than one officer who transferred from another unit just to work for Lt. Sensabaugh.

Roy was the only black officer who was a permanent member of the Narcotics Unit when I arrived. Many times black or Hispanic cops would be temporarily loaned to the unit to make drug buys in predominately minority neighborhoods. For those of you who are not accustomed to buying dope in the more depressed areas of your hometown, suffice it to say it's not easy for pasty-faced white boys who aren't known to the dealers to just walk up to a drug house and make a buy—that is, without getting ripped off or killed. For this reason, it was necessary to employ the services of the department's minority officers. That's not to say dope wasn't bought from white dealers. It was. But percentage-wise, the majority of the work we did was in the inner city. Sometimes a minority officer would be temporarily assigned to the unit if a long-term operation was planned and a new face was needed. Often it would be someone fairly new to the job without much exposure on the street and who worked on the opposite side of the city from the operation. In most cases, officers would be used on what was normally their time off, which meant being paid overtime. In any event, none of the officers picked for the job ever complained. Why should they? They got extra money, a little change of pace, and some experience that may benefit them in the future. Of all the minority cops used in this fashion, a black officer, Kenny Mann, was the best. Nicknamed Hawk for his resemblance to the character in the TV series *Spencer for Hire*, Kenny eventually earned a full-time assignment in SCIS and proved to be a real asset to the unit.

Roy Hopkins wouldn't be in the HIT Squad very long. In the spring of 1988, his wife died, and, with two boys to raise by himself, Hoppy found it necessary to transfer to days. In November, Officer Mike Mazzeo replaced Roy as the squad's permanent member. Mike had come up to the unit the previous August. Before that, he had rotated through HIT as a patrol officer from the Maple Section. I knew Mike before he became a police officer. He was a civilian evidence technician in the RPD and was trying to get hired as a sworn officer. Prior to going to the Vice Squad, I worked a part-time security job at a local department store. Mazzeo had been working there part time as well, and we became good friends. Eventually, Mike did become a police officer, and sometime later as a boss in Narcotics, I was given the opportunity to choose one patrol officer for a permanent assignment in Vice. I remember calling Mike from my car phone and asking him if he was interested. Driving toward the Public Safety Building, I reached for my phone. "Mike, it's Tom," I said. "Hey, what's up?" he asked. "I'm about to step into a meeting with Captain O'Brien where I can pick one guy from patrol to come to SCIS. You interested?" There was a pause on the other end of the line. For a minute I thought we had been disconnected. Then Mazzeo responded, "Oh, man. I've got a good shot at going to Mounted." He was being considered for an opening in the Mounted Patrol and wasn't sure which job to choose. "Buddy," I said, "I just found out, and you were my first thought. I have to give O. B. a name in about thirty minutes." Remember what I said about Old Man Fate when he really wants to screw up your life? Michael chose Narcotics. It was a decision he would live to regret. Raggi and Mazzeo worked well together, and Greg proved to be an excellent mentor for his novice partner.

With the combined experience of the full-time members of the group and the strength in numbers provided by the rotating patrol officers, we began racking up big numbers in arrests and seizures. This was evidenced by the first month's statistics. In April 1988, a month of twenty workdays, HIT was responsible for one hundred arrests. While this may not be an impressive number in larger police departments, let me put it in perspective: in the entire year of 1987, the Narcotics Unit had made fewer than two hundred arrests. All things considered, we didn't do too badly for an eleven-man squad in four weeks. While everyone was smiling over the success of this new drug-fighting machine, I could see the potential for problems with putting up big numbers. Clogging up the already overburdened court and jail systems was among the top concerns. But heading the list was the number of citizen complaints we could expect just from the number of contacts with people on the street. While we may have arrested a hundred people in the first month, we probably had negative contacts with three times that number of suspected dope dealers, customers, or anyone who happened to be in the wrong place at the wrong time.

At the time HIT was developed, the Rochester Police Department had a policy known as the Three-in-Eighteen Rule. This meant that any officer in the department who received three complaints for excessive force in eighteen months would have the complaints kicked back to their captain, and the incidents would be scrutinized a little more carefully. The idea was to identify a pattern of behavior of the officer in question. When this policy was first adopted, many officers who worked in the rougher sections of town felt hamstrung. Given the times, and the fact that our department actually encouraged citizen complaints, some cops decided they weren't putting their hands on anyone. "You're under arrest. Get in the car. No? OK, have a nice day." It wasn't quite that bad, but it did make a lot of cops second-guess themselves. That can be costly in this line of work. The significance of this policy was not lost on the permanent members of the newly formed HIT Squad who could envision three complaints in one day, let alone eighteen months. These concerns were voiced to Capt. O'Brien who in turn relayed them to Chief Urlacher. It was decided that because of the frequency of contacts expected by members of HIT, complaints originating from those contacts would be red-flagged by Internal Affairs. This was nothing more than a way to let IA know that a specialized unit was involved in a large number of contacts on a regular basis. This was not unusual given that when people are arrested on drug charges, the only recourse many of them have is to say they were beaten or that the cop stole the offender's property, or both.

When HIT first began in the spring of 1988, nobody in the Narcotics Unit wanted to be one of the four full-time officers involved in the project. After all, why give up the freedom to work in two-person teams and be responsible for just yourself and your partner? To make it a little more palatable, Capt. O'Brien said the people picked could rotate back to general investigations in about twelve to eighteen months. As part of the changing face of SCIS, other specialized units were created to address particular problems. The Jamaican Organized Crime Unit (JOC) was formed to focus on the ever-increasing problem of Jamaican posses (gangs) who had entered the country illegally and had set up numerous, widespread drug networks. Bob Urtis, who had left Genesee Section long before me to go to Narcotics, worked in JOC. A Hotel/Motel Unit was developed to handle dope dealers who would travel to Rochester, conduct business in a short period of time, and return to wherever they came from. This unit would also watch the airport, bus depot, and train station.

Bill Morris was the first permanent member to leave HIT. He returned to general investigations in June of 1989 and was replaced by Officer Ron Runzo the following month. Greg Raggi also returned to general investigations and was replaced by Officer Brad Goater. In May of 1990, Morris was assigned to the Hotel/Motel Unit. Ron Runzo was a twenty-year veteran who had worked in the Mounted Patrol for the past several years. He experienced a terrible tragedy when his seven-year-old son, Dustin, was killed in a motor-vehicle accident, and Ron was contemplating retirement. Dep. Chief Terry Rickard wanted to give Runzo a change of pace by letting him rotate through HIT as one of the patrol officers. Not having known Ron, I thought, "Great, just what I need: a twenty-year slug looking for a place to hide." Nothing could have been further from the truth. Ron was a breath of fresh air. He was like a first-year rookie who couldn't get enough of the job. Runzo was such a positive factor in the unit that his first thirty-day assignment was extended—twice. After three months, Ron was transferred to SCIS and made a permanent member of my unit.

With the new replacements aboard, we continued to make record numbers of arrests. It seemed that at least once a month our unit would score a large seizure of dope, money, or both. We were receiving a lot of media exposure for the effect we were having on local drug operations. It had been two years of jumping out on street corners to scoop up dope dealers, or knocking off drug houses with search warrants. The time went by quickly, and the initial fears of being hung out to dry on personnel complaints had pretty much faded. We were constantly being praised for our success. In June of the previous year, we received an award from the city. Everything was going fairly smoothly in spite of the occasional personality flare-ups, which may have been due to the jealousy of other Vice Squad members who felt we were getting too much recognition.

Given the first nine months, 1990 was shaping up to be another bad year for Rochester's drug dealers. But October was just around the corner, and the tide was about to turn in their favor.

Four

The concept of the Highway Interdiction Team was unlike any other drug-fighting initiative ever attempted in the Rochester area. The main difference was the volume of low-level dealers that were targeted on a continuing basis. In the past, the Vice Squad would periodically conduct street sweeps of known offenders, hitting them in various areas of operation. This required the combined use of all SCIS personnel along with officers from the Tactical Unit and any patrol officers from the section where the raids were being conducted. Usually there would be a few arrests made and, together with whatever dope, money, and weapons were seized, would constitute a reason for noteworthy publicity. Afterward, the Vice Squad would go back to doing whatever it was they were doing before they put on the cattle drive, and, for the most part, would be out of sight of the public and the uniformed cops. Thanks to the number of patrol officers who complemented the regular members of HIT, we didn't need the Tactical Unit. We also didn't have to take any other uniformed people away from their assigned patrol duties. What had been done only sporadically in the past with respect to multiple arrests and seizures was now being done on a nightly basis. Also, what made our tactics so effective was that instead of grabbing someone off the street and bringing them back to our office for processing, we brought all the necessary paperwork with us. Everything we needed to make the initial arrest was in the trunk of one of the cars. All information pertaining to arrested suspects, as well as any contraband, was kept separated in individual files. Since the only paperwork needed to lodge someone in the Monroe County Jail was a prisoner data report, we would call for a patrol officer to transport our suspect(s) and the jail copy of the PDR downtown. Within minutes of making the arrest, we would be back in our cars and headed for the opposite side of the city. After several arrests were made, we would return to the office where the remainder of the necessary paperwork would be completed. Crime reports, court papers, property custody reports, etc., would be compiled in separate packages. Often times, the work would be finished before our 2:00 a.m. shift ended, and since the temporary officers had no other assignments in SCIS, and there wasn't enough time to return to the streets again, I had two choices: I could make them sit in the squad room and watch television for the remaining hour or so, or I could let them secure (go off duty). Each group that came up to the unit was advised that because of these circumstances, I didn't expect them to submit an overtime slip for anything less than an hour. I told them that since there would be nights they would not get to eat dinner or they might be held over to complete their work, I had no problem letting them secure early. They also knew just being there was its own reward. Section captains used the selection of their personnel to HIT as a "bone" for good performance in their patrol duties.

This new concept in attacking the drug problem in Rochester provided another significant benefit. With few exceptions, every officer who rotated through the program (more than one hundred in two and a half years) had no previous experience with the types of narcotics sold and consumed all around them. After leaving HIT and returning to their respective patrol sections, these officers now had a working knowledge of the local drug trade. They were taught how to conduct the different chemical tests of cocaine, heroin, and marijuana, eliminating the need to reach out for a narcotics officer every time they encountered these substances. This enabled good, aggressive street cops the opportunity to make numerous misdemeanor and felony drug arrests. This not only enhanced their statistics but had a major impact on the drug trade in our city. Accordingly, the number of drug-related arrests by uniformed officers skyrocketed. And for the most part these were arrests that would not have been made otherwise. The training these officers received in our unit enabled them to go that extra step when their instincts told them dope might be involved. They possessed new knowledge of their legal limits when it came to searching a vehicle suspected of containing contraband. Our success was so well known that departments from as far away as Pennsylvania asked to have their officers rotate through HIT. The program also helped eliminate much of the animosity felt by some street cops toward the Narcotics Unit. Unfortunately, the publicity we were receiving on an almost daily basis caused some cops to resent us. And these were members of SCIS.

When HIT was first conceived, Capt. O'Brien knew it would take experienced narcotics officers who knew the streets and the players they would be attacking. Greg, Scott, Billy, and Hoppy were all natural choices for the job. They had a well-established track record for working the heavily drug-infested areas of Rochester. They knew they had been "volunteered" for their new assignment, and while they weren't crazy about the idea of having their routines changed, they accepted the task. This was somewhat tempered by the fact that O'Brien said they would have to endure their new duties for only about eighteen months, at which time they would be replaced by other members of the Narcotics Unit. E. J. Lergner was quick to openly verbalize that nobody was going to make him jump out of a car and chase dope dealers off street corners. It appeared he felt this type of work was beneath his level of expertise and seniority. He also seemed to enjoy rubbing it in to those who had been chosen to do it. Over the years, Greg and E. J. had had their differences on more than one occasion, and most people knew there was no love lost between them. Raggi wasn't the only member of SCIS Lergner disliked.

When Lergner began his conversation with Roy Ruffin on the Friday before Chief Urlacher was arrested, he had no way of knowing his words were being recorded by a government-owned body wire. Although some of it was inaudible, the following excerpts are from a transcript of the conversation:

Lergner: I tell you, between you and strictly…

Ruffin: Yeah, between you and me…

Lergner: Between you and I, I think there's enough…there's [inaudible] down there today that [inaudible] but the chief has got enough information that…to do something about those assholes down there.

Ruffin: But he knows what's going on, so that's why…ya know…

Lergner: Let me tell ya. A subordinate comes to the boss and says [inaudible] and the boss says, "I don't want to hear this shit." What good are they? They're…then those guys continue and…and…and the guys that are trying to be honest are getting…pushed…fuck it…get away from me. They don't want nothing to do with that. That's what's going on down there. That's the problem.

Ruffin: Well, that's the thing with Tony. Now, they've done and…squeezed him out. Right? He's not part of anything. Right?

Lergner: Basically. Cause the captain found that Varrenti would do anything he said, no matter what.

Ruffin: Varrenti's his man. Even though he's not an RPD guy.

Lergner: I don't trust him. He's gonna get somebody killed. He's fucking incompetent. He's incompetent.

Lergner: We're in big trouble right? Between you and I…we're in big trouble.

Ruffin: That's something I'd like to run by the chief. This…well, you probably talk to him some, but ya know I think…

Lergner: Yeah, but he moves too slow. But he does…I would never dare say to the chief, "Chief, things are so bad that if we don't get a change of command down the line a little bit, ya know…it's gonna hit the fan again. It's just a matter of time."

Lergner: You know…we see what he's doing. We're getting destroyed. We used to be the best [inaudible]. Now people

	laugh at us. They don't want to come near us. They don't want to work with us.
Ruffin:	Because of O. B.?
Lergner:	O. B., Varrenti, and shit like that.
Ruffin:	Remember you blew up last year? That's when they sent you over to the federal building for a year.
Lergner:	Oh yeah, he tried to shitcan me…Jim did. Oh yeah. I blew up. I told him…I says you can't continue with this…kind of shit you just did.
Ruffin:	You see, my thing is to protect the chief. Yeah. So that's why…ya know…I'm just trying to find out things… ya know…that ah…you know…cause I'm sure O. B… Rickard [reference to Dep. Chief Terry Rickard]…the time I was down there, I never saw Rickard in the Vice Squad. He's down there all the time now and I'm sure he knows everything.
Lergner:	Sure.
Ruffin:	You think there's some stuff going on?
Lergner:	I used to…ya know. You just don't know it all.
Ruffin:	They got a whole clique.
Lergner:	Oh, we'll get fucked. I'm telling you Roy you listen to what I'm telling ya. You got a few years left to go in this department. If the chief don't do something about what's going on down there…with some of those people, whether it's a month from now or six months from now or a year from now. Something's gonna happen down there that'll make this thing with Blair seem like baby shit. You remember what I tell ya. Remember what I'm telling ya. It seemed fucking…that this chief will take a fucking atom bomb.
Ruffin:	No shit.
Lergner:	See, I'm all over the chief and the captain knows that. He's real resentful. He's real resentful. I mean I never told

	him that cause he can tell. You know my remarks…I'm a pretty outspoken guy.
Ruffin:	Well, you got a reputation. They said you'd lock up your own brother if he broke the law.
Lergner:	I would. Now, I'd break my ass for [inaudible] totally and do the report system right so our reputation stays good and he lets them do anything they fucking want to.
Ruffin:	Was that when…like when you got sent over you didn't…you have a blowout or something? The way they were doing things or something?
Lergner:	Yeah. Yeah. What happened was…they just fucked up a couple of major cases and I ran my mouth pretty good on this. I says you can't do something like this. We're gonna eat shit. We're gonna end up eating shit, and that's when the captain decided he was going to keep Varrenti there. Now, Varrenti had shit for experience and he said the captain said that he's done that. I'm keeping him here and you guys do it that way or else. [Inaudible] you just want another guy that's gonna say [inaudible] go kick in the doorway without a warrant or do this, that, or the other thing. Ah…[inaudible] if that's the kind of guy you want. That's [inaudible] out of line. You wait. You know as well as I do, you check some of those Internal Affairs records. You can see some guys that had the living shit kicked out of them.
Lergner:	If a guy wants to fight with you, if a guy wants to do this, that's fine. If he tries to resist, that's fine. Bring him in, sit him down in the little rooms in the Vice Squad and beat the living shit…
Ruffin:	That ain't O. B. doing that shit?
Lergner:	No. No and ah…O. B. he's [inaudible]…
Ruffin:	Is it everybody doing it or just particular guys?
Lergner:	Particular guys. Certain guys. It's Morris.

Ruffin: Greg Raggi…I heard he was bad.

Lergner: It was Harloff.

Ruffin: But it's just like you said that you work with guys in there that you don't think are [inaudible]…

Lergner: It never used to be like that. You know you could tie it down to those three guys I specifically stay away from. The most dangerous is Morris. The most dangerous is Morris.

Ruffin: Is he as vicious as Raggi? Cause I heard years ago from when Grande [reference to retired vice sergeant, John Grande] was down there that Raggi is vicious.

Lergner: Greg is vicious in a different way cause Greg [inaudible] if there's a couple of guys they don't kick the shit out of a guy. Morris [inaudible] if there's five or six guys there cause Morris is a coward.

Ruffin: [Inaudible] beat him, beat him half to death.

Lergner: Being kicking him in the balls, kicking him in the head.

Ruffin: That's a shame.

Lergner: What are you gonna do? I mean that's the way they…

Lergner: That's the way they stay in business with the [inaudible] mentality. O. B. has destroyed our respectability. O. B. has destroyed all of our, our ability to [inaudible] to go over to the DA's office now and ask for appropriate help.

Ruffin: Since O. B. took over down there [inaudible] started getting bigger and bigger.

Lergner: If I were the chief of police…

Ruffin: What would you do?

Lergner: You see, the chief of police is never going to turn around tomorrow and transfer O. B. cause it will look real bad.

Ruffin: He has to clear it through the mayor.

Lergner: Right.

Ruffin: You see, the mayor thinks O. B. is doing a great job because of that big drug situation, but he don't know O. B.

Lergner: That's right, the shit's going to hit the fan on Monday. The chief pretty much knows two or three guys down there that are a problem. Those guys and a couple of command officers. If he could change those people.

Ruffin: Well, who should he change? O. B. and Cotsworth [inaudible].

Lergner: He'll never change. I don't believe he can get away with changing O. B. right off the bat, but if he can get away with moving maybe Cotsworth around, he can get another sergeant in there and then you'd see a party you never saw before if he got a way to get rid of [inaudible]. You'd see a party. There would be a party.

Some people go through life without having even their smallest wishes come true. E. J. Lergner had to wait a mere six days to see some of his fulfilled. The following Thursday, while Gordon Urlacher was being arrested, Capt. O'Brien and Dep. Chief of Operations Terry Rickard were suspended from duty and escorted out of the Public Safety Building. Two and a half months after Black Thursday, the remaining names on Lergner's wish list would be scratched off. Perhaps it's true what they say about being careful what you wish for. Instead of returning to the good old days in Narcotics, Officer Lergner retired from the Rochester Police Department on November 30, 1991.

Five

One week after Chief Urlacher's arrest, Greg Raggi and Bill Morris were transferred from SCIS to the training academy. The building formerly used for initial police and fire recruit training had been relegated to being used for firearms and some in-service training. Formal classroom instruction for new police and fire recruits was now conducted in a separate area of Monroe Community College. The old academy building was located out near the airport and, since it was geographically isolated from the rest of the department, it was an ideal spot to segregate someone from the general police population. Raggi and Morris were told they were to develop a new training manual for narcotics investigations. At the time, Scott Harloff had already been temporarily reassigned to the Central Investigation Division located on the fourth floor of the Public Safety Building. On October 25, the *Democrat and Chronicle* ran an article that said the police probe included brutality cover-up charges and civil-rights violations. The article stated that three officers were possibly the targets of an investigation that expanded well beyond the scope of the case against the chief. With no names being mentioned in the paper and the recent repositioning of Raggi, Morris, and Harloff, it was not hard to guess who the subjects of the overworked rumor mill were. Acting Chief Irving picked two new lieutenants, Mike Berkow and my old friend Bob Duffy, to ramrod the police department's part of the investigation. And speaking of new lieutenants, on November 30, 1990, Joyce Walsh traded in her sergeant's stripes for gold bars when she was promoted to lieutenant.

All through November and into December, everyone in SCIS tried to keep busy in spite of the changes occurring almost daily. Capt. Vincent Faggiano was selected to replace Capt. O'Brien, and two more sergeants were added to the Narcotics Unit. Up to that point, Tony Cotsworth, Eddy Wegman, and I had been the only RPD sergeants in the unit. There had not been any discussion among the supervisors as to the need for additional bosses, but for some unknown reason they were just assigned. Even though Capt. Faggiano assured everyone during one of our staff meetings that nobody had been brought on board to replace anyone, Wegman and I had our doubts. Faggiano was a good guy and a respected boss in the department, but it was becoming increasingly obvious that someone else was calling the shots. Mike Mazzeo, Ron Runzo, Brad Goater, and I were all that remained of HIT. We would work with other members of the unit on various cases, but with the investigation of our officers going on all around us, it was getting harder every day just to come to work. It didn't take long for the word to get around that several officers from the Patrol Division were being called into Internal Affairs for questioning. It was soon learned that many of these officers were also subpoenaed to testify before the federal grand jury. The common denominator? Over the past two and a half years, they had all rotated through HIT.

Tensions and tempers were being stretched to their limits. On any given day, a team of investigators made up of RPD and FBI personnel would walk into our office unannounced and roll out entire file cabinets on handcarts. On one such occasion, when pressed for an answer as to what they were looking for, an investigator from our department replied, with a notable tone of disgust in his voice, "There were crimes committed here," and continued with his task of gathering evidence. An atmosphere of *us* versus *them* had developed, and we weren't even sure who *them* were. Nobody knew exactly who was being looked at or for what. One day, a miniature surveillance camera was discovered hidden above the drop ceiling in the squad room and was quickly disabled. Could this really be happening? Who installed this thing and on whose orders? We used to have a saying: it's not paranoia if they're really out to get you. At about the same time, I received written notice ordering me to report to Internal Affairs on December 14, 1990, where I was to be questioned on my knowledge of any misconduct by members of SCIS. Great, it was bad enough my whole unit was in complete turmoil, but now I was getting dragged into whatever was infecting the department. Over the past eleven years, on the few occasions I had been summoned to IA, I never found it necessary to have a union representative accompany me. But this was unlike anything I had ever experienced. Every day, rumors had someone new being targeted for a blindfold and a last cigarette. I was advised to take a rep in with me. I called Ron Evangelista, the president of the Rochester Police Locust Club, which is the department's union. Ron agreed to meet me for my 10:00 a.m. appointment.

On Friday, December 14, we were told that Acting Chief Roy Irving was coming down to speak to us about the ongoing city/federal investigation. Hopefully, we would be given some explanation for all the cloak-and-dagger activity that surrounded us. Evangelista called to say he would be delayed, and I notified IA that we would be up as soon as he arrived. In the meantime, I would at least get to hear for myself what the acting chief had to say. When Roy Irving and his entourage got there, we were all herded into the Intelligence Unit for what would become known as his "10 Percent Speech." He began by slapping a yellow legal pad down on the nearest desk, demanding that anyone who didn't want to work in SCIS should put their name down, and he would arrange for their transfer. For those old enough to remember the television show *Mr. Peepers*, try to imagine Wally Cox, the show's star, in an angry rage. Irving, who is short and bald with big ears and wire-rim glasses, was a tough-sell as the irate boss of bosses. He was trying to convey his anger about veteran members of our unit telling officers called to testify that they should not say anything. The speech earned its title because Irving said 90 percent of the unit was composed of good cops, but there was that 10 percent who were trying to impede a narrow and focused investigation. No names were mentioned, so everyone looked at each other trying to figure out what percentage people were in. Nobody put his name on the "I don't want to work here anymore" list, and the acting chief returned to his newly acquired office. Ron Evangelista met me shortly after Irving departed. Content with the thought that I must be part of the 90 percent because I had not told anyone what to say regarding the investigation, we proceeded to Internal Affairs on the sixth floor.

The formal name for Internal Affairs is the Professional Standards Section, and it had evolved over the years through various administrations. The problem was that if you were talking to a cop from another department, especially out of town, they didn't know what it was, so it was just easier to say Internal Affairs. Regardless of what name people chose, its primary function was to investigate police officers. Whether a complaint originated from a citizen or within the department, the job of the people in IA was to determine if the officer in question was guilty of the allegation. Many officers believe it is indeed the *desire* of those in IA to prove them guilty. While I don't feel that to be the case, some investigators (or headhunters, as they are often called) do approach their job with a where-there's-smoke-there's-fire attitude. It used to be that when a patrol officer was up for promotion to sergeant, he or she would be assigned to IA for a period of time to gain some administrative experience. Now the office is made up entirely of sergeants, most, if not all, of whom requested the assignment. The majority of street cops just can't understand why anyone would want a job investigating other cops.

The interview rooms in Internal Affairs aren't exactly decorated for the purpose of bringing cheer into one's life. A tape recorder sits in the middle of a plain table surrounded by chairs, and a video camera stares at the guest of honor from one end of the room. To ensure nothing is missed, a stenographer also records the interviews. Ron and I were directed to just such a room and told that Sgt. Juan Rodriguez and Sgt. Kurt Kirstein would be joining us. After a brief wait, the two men entered the room. Rodriguez walked up to me and said, "Before we get started, I have to give you this." He handed me Personnel Order #P-90-409. The one sentence that made up the text hit me in the face like the back of a coal shovel: Sergeant Thomas Alessi is suspended with pay from the Rochester Police Department effective 0900 hours, December

14, 1990. The signature at the bottom of the page was that of Acting Chief of Police Roy Irving. Getting punched in the solar plexus is the best analogy I can make as to how I felt at that moment. I felt the air go out of my lungs and my knees get weak. I couldn't believe what I was reading. This must be a mistake. No matter how many times I read this little piece of paper, the words didn't change. I was being suspended. When I finally regained my senses and asked what the hell this was all about, Rodriguez said he couldn't tell me. What? You just turned my world upside down and now you won't even tell me why. What the young sergeant did do, however, was take my service weapon along with my badge and police identification. With my mind racing, trying to figure out just what it was someone thought I had done to deserve this, I asked to have the interview postponed. My request was denied. I was told I had to answer their questions then and there or I could be fired in accordance with departmental policy.

What had been scheduled as an interview (at least in my mind) had suddenly transformed into an interrogation. In the beginning, Rodriguez and Kirstein wanted me to describe the personnel structure of HIT. They also wanted to know what our primary duties were. Then their interest turned to work hours and supervisory responsibility. I was asked when and under what circumstances members of my unit worked less than an eight-hour shift. I knew what they were getting at. I made no attempt to hide that even though our "regular hours" were 6:00 p.m. to 2:00 a.m., we would often secure early. Trying to explain the reasons for this to a couple of Remington Raiders from the Rat Squad was truly an exercise in futility. One of the reasons I cited was that the full-time members of the group would sometimes be called in early to assist on other cases. By the time our normal shift was almost over, we would have been at work well beyond eight hours. Also, when the group had made multiple arrests during the night and all related paperwork and processing had been completed, there was nothing left for them to do but watch television until 2:00 a.m. Basically, it was no different than when officers are cut loose early from in-service training. Something that was practiced by bosses in every section was now being cast as some sinister plot. Letting my officers go early under these circumstances was apparently cheating the department out of labor it was entitled to. Next, I was questioned about the number of times I wasn't with the squad when they were out busting dope dealers. Again I attempted to illustrate the reasons I wasn't with the group every time they left the office. The final topic of conversation had to do with overtime. My examiners wanted to know if I was aware of anyone in my unit who made it a practice of putting in for overtime pay without having earned it. Specifically, the questions had to do with people going to court and having assistant district attorneys sign overtime slips for other officers who weren't even there. I explained that if I had ever thought that to be the case, I would have brought it to the attention of Capt. O'Brien. The questioning officially ended at 12:22 p.m., and I was excused. Evangelista and I left the room and I returned to SCIS. I went directly to Capt. Faggiano's office to see if he could answer some of my questions. To my surprise, and apparently his, Faggiano had not even been advised by the chief that one of his sergeants was about to be suspended. I went to my office and called Joyce. I told her what had happened and asked if she could pick me up since I had been relieved of my departmental vehicle. During the ride home, I stared out the window and wondered what the future held for me. As much of a shock as getting suspended had been, it was only the beginning of a long and painful journey, both professionally and personally. Shortly after we got home, I learned that Scott Harloff had been suspended the day before I was. I thought back to the October 25 article regarding the police brutality and cover-up issue. Could they be going after Harloff for that? If they were, how bad did they think things were? Something wasn't right. Scotty isn't exactly the warm and fuzzy type, but brutality…where was this coming from? Answers to this and many more questions were still a long way off.

Six

Christmas of 1990 was less than two weeks away, and while most people were getting into the holiday spirit, I found myself trying to figure out just what I was supposed to have done to get myself suspended. It's a little difficult to plan a defense strategy when you haven't been told what you're accused of. With Joyce working the midnight shift (the downside of promotion is usually a transfer to the most undesirable work schedule), I spent a good deal of time alone. It wasn't much better during the day while she was sleeping. I've never needed much more than five or six hours sleep, and since I had worked afternoons for the majority of my career, I was used to staying up well past midnight. I found it impossible to stay interested in anything for very long without my thoughts drifting back to the events of the past few weeks. When was someone going to tell me what happens next?

At one of our get-togethers, Jim O'Brien told us he'd been out doing a little Christmas shopping when he received a message to call Lt. Frank Frey, the commanding officer of Internal Affairs. Frey told O. B. the administration was "contemplating" serving him with departmental charges. Remember Black Thursday? O'Brien had been suspended and removed from the Public Safety Building, and, like me, he was never told why. In his usual style, O. B. told the lieutenant that if in fact he was to be served with charges, they could be addressed to *Mr.* James O'Brien and sent to him at the University of Alabama where he was enrolled in an accelerated master's program. When the bewildered lieutenant said he didn't understand, O. B. informed Frey he had submitted his retirement papers to Albany, and as of January 7, 1991, he would no longer be a member of the Rochester Police Department. After twenty-five years of service, O'Brien knew the writing was on the wall, and there would be no returning to the career he loved. Besides, his wife had been haranguing him for years to pack it in and move the family to Florida. It looked as though her wish was about to come true.

I contacted Union President Ron Evangelista to see if he had any answers. He got back to me a day or two later, and if getting suspended wasn't enough to rock my world, his rendition of the conversation he had with Acting Chief Irving certainly was. Ron told me the departmental charges I was facing had to do with letting people go home early. He said, "They're looking to take your stripes." What? There hadn't been a sergeant demoted in twenty years, and they wanted to bust me for something bosses did all over the department? This was nuts. Evangelista went on to say he had asked the chief if he would let the disciplinary process run its normal course. What Ron told me next astounded me. He said the chief told him that if I went before a hearing board and was found not guilty, Irving would overturn the verdict, find me guilty, and fire me. Why did this man hate me? My immediate reaction was that he believed I had actually done something much worse, but this was the only way he could get me. But that can't be, because I hadn't done anything. A few days after my conversation with Evangelista, I received my departmental charges in the mail. For letting people leave early, I was charged with three separate violations of the RPD rules and regulations. They were outlined as follows:

Charge I. Violation of Section 1.1; Obedience to laws, ordinances, and rules. Specification I: From April, 1988 through October 1990, as Commanding Officer of the HIT Team, you did make or cause a false entry in the business records of the city when you indicated on such records that members of the HIT Team worked eight (8) hour duty tours when you knew that they did not actually work the full eight hours. These actions constituted violations of section 175.05 (1) of the New York State Penal Law, falsifying business records in the second degree.

Hmm, that's a misdemeanor in New York. Well, they came right out with a fastball.

Charge II: Violation of section 5.1 (c); Altering, delaying, or falsifying reports, to wit: Employees shall not falsely make or submit any type of official report or knowingly enter or cause to be entered any inaccurate, false, or improper information on the records of the department. Specification I (Worded exactly the same as specification I in charge I). Charge III: Violation of section 6.1; Command, to wit: Commanding officers shall insure that employees under their command perform their full duty. Commanding officers shall project an image of efficiency, effectiveness, and meaningful direction. Specification I: From April, 1988 through October, 1990, as Commanding Officer of the HIT Team, you failed to insure that members of the HIT Team perform their full duty, in that you failed to insure that said members worked full eight (8) hour tours of duty.

That's it? Thanks to Internal Affairs complaint #90-1605, I now knew what they wanted to chop my head off for. It was the why part I couldn't figure out. That question would be answered in the coming weeks. The scuttlebutt around the department indicated there were major problems in SCIS. There had to be more to this than just cutting people loose early. On the last two pages of the charges, there were five paragraphs that stated that I had until January 2, 1991, to respond to the chief in writing. Failure to do so would constitute an automatic plea of guilty, and a penalty would be imposed. I went on to read that I was entitled to a hearing, and that I could have either an attorney or a union representative with me. With Ron Evangelista's words regarding his conversation with Acting Chief Irving still fresh in my memory, I read the second-to-last paragraph: Any penalties after a hearing will be totally dependent upon evidence presented at said hearing and your employment record. I couldn't believe my eyes. I checked the envelope to make sure it was addressed to me. The letter was signed, "Sincerely, Roy A. Irving, Acting Chief of Police." Let's see. The evidence was that I freely admitted letting people leave early, and my employment record was eleven years of service with no disciplinary action. The Rochester Police Department uses a system of progressive discipline. For each successive offense, there was a corresponding level of discipline. Now the first time I have to be disciplined the chief tells my union president he wants to fire me.

By this time, it had become common knowledge that the patrol officers who had rotated through HIT were being called in and questioned about their tours of duty with my unit. Most people were ordered to the federal building and questioned by teams of investigators made up of RPD officers and FBI agents. These sessions were referred to as their "career interviews" because it was believed their career paths would be determined by their answers. Many of these officers were then subpoenaed to testify before the federal grand jury. Word got back to us that they were being questioned about numerous specific incidents that occurred during the time our unit was in operation. Right around the end of December, Joyce came home from work, and while she was changing out of her uniform, she pulled an overtime slip out of her bag. She held it up for me to see and asked, "Is this one of the guys that testified against you?" I looked at the slip and read the name of Jeff Anderson. I told Joyce he had been in the last two groups that came up, and it was felt he had said some unfavorable things about some of the permanent members. She replied, "Well, here's three hours overtime he'll never see." Then she tore the slip in half and threw it in the wastebasket. It was indicative of the attitude toward those who were believed to have passed their "career interviews" with flying colors. I never gave the incident another thought—that is, until several months later.

I was informed that if I pleaded guilty to all charges and specifications, I would receive as my punishment a demotion to the rank of patrol officer and a thirty-day suspension without pay. After considering all my options (all *one* of them), I figured a patrol officer with a job is better than an unemployed ex-sergeant. On December 31, 1990, I submitted my written response to the chief, pleading guilty to the charges against me. After not so thoroughly enjoying the Christmas and New

Year holidays, I met with the chief and Dep. Chief Bob Craig in Irving's office on January 2. Craig had most recently been a captain and CO of one of the patrol sections. He was brought up to replace Terry Rickard, who had been the deputy chief of operations until his suspension on Black Thursday. I was working in Genesee Section when Bob Craig was promoted to sergeant. He was assigned to the midnight shift under Lt. John Sensabaugh, and given the number of times I regretted his showing up on my jobs and using unnecessary force, I found it ironic that he was now passing judgment on other police officers. After discussing the terms of my punishment, Irving gave me my choice of patrol sections to work. I knew there was an investigator's test coming up in the summer, and I told him I might try that route. Since I'd never worked on the east side of the city, I asked for Goodman Section. It had a nice mix of people with enough action to keep me busy. The commanding officer was Capt. Mike Karnes, who was well respected as a good cop and a fair boss. As Dep. Chief Craig and I walked down the hall to the patrol major's office, I asked him if the department had any other charges in mind for me. He replied, "No, this should be it for you. Although, we don't know what's going to come out of State Street." This was a reference to the joint city/federal investigation going on in the federal building located at 100 State Street in Rochester. I told him I wasn't worried about that because I hadn't done anything wrong. Little did I know that even as we spoke, the administration's game plan called for a lot more than just burying me in a patrol section and letting me get on with my career. It didn't dawn on me at the time, even though I knew I had been slam-dunked on my first and only transgression. I should have known that with the progressive discipline system, there wasn't a whole lot left in the punishment category should any new charges come my way. Yeah, but what the hell, the DCO himself just told me I was all done. Funny how that phrase can have more than one meaning.

Two days after my meeting with Irving and Craig, Greg Raggi and Bill Morris were suspended. They had been kept on ice out at the old police academy since October 25. It had been rumored for some time that Greg, Scott, and Billy were the primary targets of the ongoing investigation. I couldn't imagine what these men had done to bring about a probe of this magnitude. Information was impossible to get since the acting chief put out an order shortly after Chief Urlacher's arrest prohibiting contact with any suspended officer. I figured with my luck I'd be up on charges again just for talking to one of them. Besides, I was starting to resent my former subordinates. Without knowing exactly what the scope of this investigation was, I thought it was their fault I was in trouble. Since Raggi had almost two months' vacation on the books, they made him use it all up in November and December, After all, why have someone on paid suspension when you can force them to burn up their vacation time? Greg returned to work on January 3, 1991, and the following day, two sergeants from Internal Affairs and a lieutenant from the sixth floor of the Public Safety Building were sent out to the academy to inform Raggi and Morris of their suspensions. When Billy offered to give Greg a ride home, the lieutenant advised them that the three command officers would do that because he did not want any further communication between the two suspended officers. After arriving at his house, Greg was ordered to surrender his department-issued equipment. Since he refused to allow his chauffeurs to enter his home, they remained in the driveway. His wife, Michelle, cried as she watched her husband collect the requested items, which symbolized his almost twenty-year career with the Rochester Police Department.

While Greg was trying to comfort his family and assure them everything would be all right, Billy Morris was at the Public Safety Building. Unknown to any of us, he had gone in search of Acting Chief Irving and Lt. Mike Berkow, who, along with Lt. Bob Duffy, were in charge of the investigation. Just like Roy Ruffin less than six months earlier, Billy wasn't about to wait for anyone to offer him a sweetheart deal. He had his own plan for surviving the shitstorm he felt sure was coming our way. Again, like Roy Ruffin, Billy Morris would soon admit to criminal conduct while performing his duties as a police officer. For the next three months there would be meetings and conversations between Morris's attorney, Larry Andolina, and the people involved in the investigation. Decisions had to be made as to the value and degree of Billy's cooperation. The US Justice Department assigned three federal prosecutors from Washington, DC, to our case. The lead attorney for the government, Michael Gennaco, was a thirty-seven-year-old graduate of Stanford Law School. Two assistants, Cathleen Mahoney and Jessica Ginsburg, would later join him. Andolina represented the Rochester Police Locust Club, as well as several other police unions, and had been retained by Morris early on in the investigation. As an assistant district attorney in 1979, Larry taught New York State Penal Law to my academy class. During his career, he had earned the respect of police officers and defense attorneys alike. He had also represented Gordon Urlacher. Now it was his job to protect the best interests of his newest client, Billy Morris, at least until Morris felt he no longer needed Larry's services.

On March 26, 1991, Morris drove his car to what would be the first of several clandestine meetings with Lt. Mike Berkow. What Morris didn't know was that the lieutenant brought something else to the meeting. At 7:30 p.m., just before Billy's arrival, Berkow activated the recorder attached to his body wire. Since Morris didn't know any of the government attorneys from Washington, he figured his best bet was to talk directly to someone he did know. Mike Berkow was from his own department and in charge of the investigation. Morris called the lieutenant and arranged the meeting. The purpose of the meeting was for Billy to find out just what he had to do to secure the best deal possible. Morris was in scramble mode and needed to plead his case to someone he thought might be able to help him. He was nervous, and he rambled on quite a bit, but it's important to understand just how desperate Billy really was. So desperate, in fact, that the conversation he was about to have with Berkow would take place without the knowledge of his attorney, Larry Andolina. As I listened to the tapes and read the transcripts, I could almost smell the sweat he must have been secreting as he attempted to minimize his own culpability, while at the same time trying to pick the lieutenant's brain. Following are excerpts from the transcription of their first meeting:

MB—Michael Berkow
WM—William Morris
UI—Unintelligible words

MB: Meeting with Billy Morris. Three, twenty-six, ninety-one [March 26, 1991]. It's nineteen twenty-seven hours. I'm gonna start the tape running before he gets here.

MB: Hey, hi, man, how you doing?

WM: Not bad, how you doing?

MB: Good, doing good, till that phone call.

WM: [UI] I'm sorry I didn't call. I just wanted to talk to you.

WM: I know you sat down with Larry.

WM: And [UI] Mike.

MB: Gennaco.

WM: Gennaco. Uhm. [UI] Larry had [UI] and I know he talked to you briefly.

What happens to me in terms of what we, we reach an agreement. I'm being very careful [UI] because I don't, I mean I suspect that when we talk to each other that you know, [UI] I don't even want to…no, that's not the point. I, I mean you guys [UI] I don't know whether to shit or go blind. Uhm, and I'm being very careful about, and I'm not trying to [UI] the fact that I'm guilty.

MB: Yes.

WM: …or, or anything. I just want to talk with [UI] I got a little wife and a, and a fifteen-month-old baby, and also have two children from past marriage. If I and you and Gennaco and everybody else reach an agreement and we decide that I'm gonna give you a truthful debriefing and cooperate proactively against whoever we need to cooperate against proactively, and we make a case, [UI] happens to me and my kids and everything else. I mean if I gotta get out of town, you gotta understand why this is a very difficult decision for me, I have to leave my other two kids here.

MB: Right.

WM: Uhm, you know it's not an easy thing to do. It's easier just to go to jail, to be honest with ya. If I have to go to jail because at least when I come out of jail my kids will be here if I have, if I have to go to jail. If I have to leave town, I mean and actually move away because, I mean not only will I [UI] those people that I gave you but the rest of the police department [UI]. You understand that. I mean, you think there are good guys now that are on your side of the fence and that I, I mean either way, I can't win. I mean my wife can't drive down the street. I can't drive down the street here and think I have any friends maybe, except, you know lawyers and jurors and two or three other people. I mean, I'm gonna be in a very bad situation, and my kids, you know, they're not reachable. I can't steal them and take them out of town. I can't kidnap them. I wouldn't do that anyway.

MB: Yeah.

WM: You know, logistically, I don't know. You know I got a house. I'm trying to sell my house. The house has been for sale since whenever. We've had one deal and finally we reupped the purchase offer one for sixty days and it's just…they can't sell it all, so I [UI]. Uh, you know there's two other people interested, and we've had no other purchase offers. I can go out of town, but it's, it's so difficult. It's a difficult decision to make with the kids. Uhm, that's what I've been debating. I haven't not gotten back to you for any other reason. Uh, you guys, I think someone's got, got to understand that. I can take my little one [UI]. I can take my big one; I mean my two big ones.

MB: [UI]

WM: ...and done something against the law, and if I don't, do I tell them I'm only gonna see them once in a while. It's not the same as "Come on over Friday night and stay until Sunday," it's now "Come on over for two weeks in the summer." You know, it's tearing me apart. I don't know...I'm trying to be loyal to the police department that's fucking me up the ass. That's basically how I look at it. I gotta lotta time to think. You might have been in one corner where no one wanted to suspend me, but when you didn't want to suspend me, everybody else...the more I think about it, the more...you know, I sat in that room with the door closed. How could I intimidate anybody [UI] closed door? Whoever wanted to come in that room came in that room with the door closed. I mean I don't understand how we did anything thing wrong.

MB: Right.

WM: This suspension thing has got me to the point I don't know, I don't care if I go back to work. That's...if you did, well, I'm not saying "you." I don't mean you personally. [UI]

MB: I understand.

WM: ...misunderstand. What the police department has done is it's taken away...I've been a policeman for twenty years. I don't have any other friends.

MB: Right.

WM: Now, if I'm suspended, I can talk to Greg and I can talk to Scott, but we're not the guys you want to talk about. I don't know if I want to go through the hassle of doing that. I still think, and, maybe I'm way off base but morally I don't deserve to go to jail. I don't. [UI] and I'm not going to debate that with you, but I don't. I think if I thought I'd done something that drastic that I morally needed to go to jail, I would have told Larry to take whatever offer you had given us to get the thing over. You know, I've done too many positive things for the police department, and I think, you know, knowing once, once you look at that they want to bury their heads in the sand and say this guy is an asshole [UI]

MB: All right. What did Larry tell you?

WM: Larry told me that, ah, the best deal I could make was a felony with limited jail time or no jail time. That's the best he offered me.

MB: Well, did he explain to you the different areas of value and all that?

WM: Yeah. [UI] but I mean it's, he explained it like, maybe I'm, maybe he hasn't told me everything and maybe he misunderstood you. Scenario number one is, I talk, I'm debriefed about Scotty and Greg, and I may not and probably won't be used as a witness because you're wherever you want to be with them people, and for that I would get a felony and jail time. Secondly, I talk about Tom Alessi and I talk about Jim O'Brien, and for my conversations I get a felony with minimal jail time in a halfway house. Thirdly, I do proactive work either wearing a, a wire or however this scenario plays out, and for that I get a felony, and Gennaco would go talk to the judge. Uhm, you know, if I go to trial, I'm gonna get a felony anyway, if I get convicted. If I don't get convicted, if I get a hung jury, if I keep one juror out, you gotta do me again. I don't deserve to get a felony and go to jail for ten years or two years pleaded. I don't deserve that. Uhm, I mean, if somewhere along the line maybe I'm missing the boat. What happened in Los Angeles is police brutality. [Reference to the Rodney King incident.]

MB: I want to refer to my notes here for a minute from when, when we talked to Larry, OK.

WM: And I probably shouldn't be talking to you, Mike, but I don't have anybody to talk to. I can't...

MB: I understand.

WM: I mean, you gotta understand when, what Larry's job to do is to defend me.

MB: Right. Well, you have to understand. I mean, you, you know, in a way, you put me on the spot because you call me and say, "Listen, I want to talk to you, but I don't want to tell Larry," Right? So...

WM: Well, you know why, because Larry, I think, I think Larry feels at this point that, that, you know, his, he's, he's backed up to the wall. He's backed up to the wall with the whole thing, and sometimes, you know, I'm not saying he's, he's probably the best lawyer in the world, and maybe, maybe I shouldn't talk and maybe I should just leave the thing up to Larry. But somewhere, I don't know why, you know I still feel a loyalty to the police department. You know, I've been a policeman for twenty years.

MB: All right. We met with Larry on February twentieth, OK? And, like you're saying, Mike Gennaco laid out three areas of your potential use. The first was the street-level incidents. You know what occurred. You're not needed for that. The second is the implication of the higher-ups. Helpful but not vital. And the third is the continued meetings and proactive. It is very important and helpful.

WM: No, I understand that.

MB: I couldn't tell, you know, I couldn't pretend to tell you how to do it but a lot of what happens is dependent upon what hap...what occurs in the end. You know how the information works, how [UI] in the end.

WM: I understand that.

MB: Uhm, the, you should put the suspension stuff out of your mind, and you should focus on the issue of "Am I going to jail? Am I going to trial?"

WM: Sure.

MB: …what's the best thing I can do for myself and my family? The other stuff is incidental. I, and, and, and here's [UI]. Am I going to, in trial, can I beat this? Because going to trial and losing is a bad proposition. I'm sure Larry went through the sentencing guidelines with you. And, all you have to do is get nicked for a couple of incidents. It doesn't matter, the statute requires substantial pain. It doesn't require injury, broken bones, bloody things, [UI] skull fracture [UI] requires I hit you. You say, "I hurt."

WM: [UI] OK?

As their conversation drew to a conclusion, Billy found he had been unable to nail the lieutenant down to giving him definite answers to his questions regarding his cooperation in the investigation. What he did know, however, was the more he gave, the more he would get (or in Billy's case, the less he would get for punishment). Billy Morris's character is best summed up by the following exchange from the same conversation with Mike Berkow:

WM: I don't give a fuck about anybody else or [UI].

MB: Right.

WM: I only care about me. And, and compared to what happened in LA, the thing that I'm [UI] have done I don't think is apples and oranges. That's, that's my own personal opinion.

For those who don't know, an informant is someone who provides information to law enforcement agencies. Their reasons for doing so range anywhere from a legitimate sense of civic duty to seeking compensation. The most common informants, or snitches, as they are often called, provide information for money. The amount of money is determined by the value of the information. Frequently, people who find themselves on the receiving end of criminal charges will trade information for favorable treatment. A major problem with some informants is that they will lie to get the maximum benefit from the agency they're working for. One method for determining the reliability of a new informant is to have him or her submit to a polygraph (lie detector) examination. This isn't done all the time, to be sure, but before an agency invests a substantial amount of time, effort, manpower, and/or money in an investigation, it certainly is a useful tool for establishing the informant's credibility. The logic here is simple: if the snitch is honest, there should be nothing to fear from taking such a test. Many people are aware from watching television that a polygraph can't be used in court to determine a person's guilt. But it can be a big help in preventing the proverbial wild goose chase.

On April 29, 1991, in the fifth secretly recorded conversation between Billy Morris and Lt. Mike Berkow, Morris is very upset. At some point in his negotiations since the first of the year, he had been given a copy of a cooperation agreement that representatives of the US Attorney's Office had put together for him. There was a paragraph in the document that required Billy to submit to a polygraph test if at any time his handlers felt it necessary. As you read the following exchange between Morris (the informant) and Berkow (the informed), keep in mind what I said about the motives and honesty of informants.

WM: I don't trust Relin at all. [District Attorney Howard Relin]

MB: OK, let me, let me, let me answer it to you specifically.

WM: I have information about people in his office.

MB: About people in his office?

WM: Yeah. I know you're looking at things over there and I have information about things over there. I...it kind of pissed me off and I think you knew it pissed me off a little bit; the first contract there was nothing about a polygraph in there.

MB: OK.

WM: No one ever mentioned polygraph until the day you mentioned it to me. It only made me upset because if I give you a truthful debriefing, I'll give you a truthful debriefing.

MB: No, it was there from the beginning. It should have been in the agreement from the beginning. Uhm.

WM: No, this is the first agreement that he faxed.

MB: Is this the one that said felony though?

WM: It may or may not have been, but this is what we believed the first contract was gonna be.

MB: OK.

WM: And, it's, and, and these subsequent contracts and I don't have a problem, I don't. I don't necessarily agree with the polygraph because I have never given one to anybody and I don't like them.

MB: Right.

WM: Well, we're not sure if he's telling the truth therefore the contract is null and void, I'm not happy about it, uhm.

MB: Let me see what I've got in this one, see this?

WM: And then during the meeting that, that Larry had with Gennaco and you, it was never mentioned, and the meeting that we all had together it was never mentioned.

MB: Right, but it, well, I don't remember if it was or wasn't.

WM: No. It wasn't.

MB: The second one but it, but it, it is definitely on the table, the feeling is, from everybody is that's it's gotta be there and the reason it's particularly there is like I was explaining to you, was the financial stuff.

WM: Now whose determination is it when a polygraph is given?

MB: Uhm, it would be myself, Gene, [FBI Agent Gene Harding] and, uhm, Duffy.

WM: So. If I give you answers that you think are truthful then…

MB: Yeah, we may never give one. Here it is, six, "Agrees to submit to polygraph examination [UI] concerning any information he provides as detailed in this agreement."

WM: I just don't like…what scares me about it, Mike, and it's not so much you scare me…

MB: Yeah.

WM: What scares me about it is if I fulfill every aspect of this contract...

MB: Right.

WM: ...and I take a polygraph...

MB: Right.

WM: ...who's to say whether I do good, bad, or indifferent on it? I don't want them to say, well, he did all he was supposed to do, but he was less than truthful on the polygraph, therefore, we're not gonna give him his deal now. And it's, it's an interpretation of a, of a machine and a man, uhm...

MB: Yeah, I don't know how to answer your question.

WM: ...that it could be used to renegotiate the contract.

MB: We're not going to use it to renegotiate the contract, Billy. I mean, it's just like you say, you're gonna give a full and truthful debriefing. Nobody is looking to fuck you, uhm, I mean...

WM: OK, and I'm not looking to fuck you, if I come on the team, I'm gonna...

MB: I understand that but, but we, we have to be concerned about the financial stuff, in particular.

WM: OK.

MB: Among other things.

WM: Sure.

MB: But a lot of things you can investigate and prove. I mean, if somebody gets beaten and there are six witnesses, you can prove it.

WM: I understand that.

MB: But a financial thing...

WM: I understand that.

MB: ...it's much more difficult

WM: I understand that it's information, I understand that I have information that no one else has.

MB: OK.

WM: I know that.

MB: OK.

WM: I mean, I know it and you know it and everybody else in the world knows it.

MB: That's the only reason you are getting offered a misdemeanor.

Negotiations over the level of Morris's cooperation went on for several more weeks before he actually started working for the government. When he was confident the best possible deal had been worked out, Billy Morris was ready to go into the recording business.

Seven

On February 1, 1991, with my suspension completed, I reported to Goodman Section's third platoon (3:00 p.m. to 11:00 p.m. shift) roll call. It had been only three years since I last wore a uniform, but it still felt strange. Maybe it was because I had to requisition all new clothing; together with the new boots I was wearing, I must have looked like some sort of time-warp rookie. My new coworkers all made me feel welcome, and some offered words of encouragement. I rode with different partners for the first few days until it was determined I had retained most of my basic patrol skills and could function alone. The hardest part of transferring to a new section is becoming familiar with the streets. People are pretty much the same all over. The names may be different, but every community has its assortment of lowlifes who have nothing better to do than hang on street corners devising new ways of getting something for nothing. Decent, hardworking people go to work every day to support their families. Kids play in streets, yards, and playgrounds. The people part of this job never changes. But the streets, with their intersections and dead ends, are all different. In addition to learning my new environment, I also had three years of changes in laws and departmental procedures to catch up on. It was a good thing. I needed all the preoccupation my mind could handle.

It didn't take me long to realize why I enjoyed working Narcotics as much as I did. When you're a patrol officer answering calls for service in a high-crime area, you spend a good deal of time documenting people's misery. Some working stiff comes home to find his house has been burglarized and everything of any value is either gone or destroyed. Sure, in some cases, through good investigative work or dumb luck, you might get to arrest the burglar(s). But you know damn well while you're filling in little boxes on the crime report that this victim is never going to see his property again. Then there were the victims who suffered physical injury. There are the random street muggings where an old lady would be beaten even after giving up her purse. Sign here, lady. Victims have a way of looking at cops that seems to say, "Why me and what are you going to do about it?" For all the good police work that gets done—and there's a lot of it—many of these crimes go unsolved. By contrast, it's very rewarding when your job is putting dope dealers away. Some feel that drug dealing is a victimless crime. Nothing could be further from the truth. From the casual user to the hard-core junkie, the negative effects of drug use ripple through our society: crime that ranges from shoplifting to murder; higher retail prices; lost productivity in the workplace; overburdened health-care facilities; higher insurance premiums; and domestic violence. Unless you get to deal with it, most people think there's no one else affected by another person's drug use.

The first two weeks of my new assignment were relatively uneventful. I came to work, took my calls, and went home. While I had nothing against the people I worked with, I wasn't particularly eager to socialize with them after the shift ended. Listening to some of them making plans to go out after work reminded me of happier times when I worked in the Genesee and Downtown Sections. Choir Practice, a popular term for off-duty drinking (and other assorted activities), was a common way to unwind with associates after work. The phrase came from the LAPD and was used to describe their after-work activities in Joseph Wambaugh's police novel, *The Choir Boys*. Every generation of cops can be credited with numerous war stories, some of which become legends heralding their exploits. Oftentimes at these after-work get-togethers, new life was breathed into old stories, ensuring their longevity. Many officers assigned to my platoon were new and had not rotated through HIT. They were not caught up in the investigation and went about their jobs without fear of being called into Internal Affairs or a federal grand jury. Having just gone through the wringer, I actually believed I could now enjoy the same benefits, especially since it was just a few short weeks ago the Dep. Chief Craig said I was "all done."

On February 17, 1991 (approximately six weeks after my meeting with the chief and his deputy), my platoon commander, Lt. Chris Piro, approached me after roll call and handed me an ominously familiar-looking document. It was an intradepartmental correspondence that read as follows:

To: Officer Thomas W. Alessi, Goodman Section
From: Internal Affairs Section
Date: February 15, 1991
Subject: Opportunity to be heard re: IA No. 91-0026

As a result of an investigation of violation of the Rules and Regulations/General Orders of the Rochester Police Department, by you, departmental charges are being contemplated.

Violations under consideration for incorporation into any such subsequent charges against you are: Rules and Regulations, Section 6.1; 6.2; and 6.3.

You have a right to be heard prior to the service of any such charges and to have counsel or representation of your choosing present. You are invited to appear in the Internal Affairs Section office on Tuesday, February 19, 1991, at 1530 hours to exercise this privilege if you so desire.

Your failure to appear will be construed that you do not wish to be heard or exercise this right and that the departmental proceedings shall proceed based upon this investigation.

Lt. Frank Frey
Commanding Officer, Internal Affairs

I stared at the paper in disbelief. My first thought was that it was a copy of the charges I pleaded guilty to on December 31. But this was

IA#91-0026—the "91" indicated 1991. This is something new. I felt sick to my stomach. For the first time, I began to think I wasn't just one small piece to a large puzzle. Prior to that moment, I was convinced what had happened to me was a question of being in the wrong place at the wrong time—like a bystander hit with shrapnel from a bomb blast meant for somebody else. I had rationalized that because I was the supervisor of HIT, the administration felt I should be held accountable for whatever it was they thought Bill Morris, Greg Raggi, and Scott Harloff had done. I guessed if they believed they had to charge me with something, it might as well be for letting people secure early. Now I was beginning to feel I would somehow be prominently figured into what Irving had called a "narrow and focused" investigation. It was narrow and focused all right—the chief had his sights focused on the narrow part of my ass. This time, things would be different. No walking into Internal Affairs and falling on my sword like I did before. Without formally declining my "invitation" to appear and be heard, I let February 19 come and go like any other day. Sure enough, the charges being *contemplated* found their way to me a couple of days later. Here we go again.

Charge I: Violation of Rules and Regulations, Section 6.1; Command, to wit: Commanding officers shall insure that employees under their command perform their full duty. Commanding officers shall project an image of proficiency, effectiveness, and meaningful direction. Specification I: As supervisor of the Highway Interdiction Team, you failed to provide meaningful direction to the members of the team, in that members of the team engaged in a continuing pattern of abuse of authority, including use of excessive force, which you either knew of or should have known of and which you failed to address appropriately.

Charge II: Violation of Rules and Regulations, Section 6.2; Supervisors, to wit: Employees who have been promoted or temporarily assigned to a supervisory position must provide a good example in both conduct and appearance, have a thorough understanding of the rules and procedures of the department, and shall assist and instruct subordinates in the proper performance of their duties. Specification I: As supervisor of the Highway Interdiction Team, you failed to assist and instruct subordinates in the proper performance of their duties, resulting in a continuing pattern of abuse of authority by Highway Interdiction Team Members, including use of excessive force.

Charge III: Violation of Rules and Regulations, Section 6.3; Subordinate Incompetency or Misconduct, to wit: Supervisors who either overlook, or condone and fail to take action on incompetency or misconduct on the part of their subordinates shall be guilty of neglect of duty. Specification I: As supervisor of the Highway Interdiction Team, you neglected your duty in that you overlooked or condoned and failed to take appropriate action on a continuing pattern of misconduct, including use of excessive force by Highway Interdiction Team members.

The last paragraph of the second page listed the penalty options in ascending order of severity. A reprimand, a fine not exceeding one hundred dollars, suspension without pay for a period not exceeding two months, a demotion in grade and title (been there, done that), or dismissal from the department. Let's see. Given the department's progressive discipline policy, what are the odds that if I'm found guilty (and we all know the laws of probability on that score) and I've already been demoted, that the chief will let me off with a two-month suspension? I had until February 28 to submit my answer in writing. With two days to spare, I forwarded my reply to Chief Irving. I entered a plea of not guilty to all charges and specifications. I'd bent over and grabbed my ankles once on December 31, and I'd be damned if I'd do it again.

This second set of charges had a profound effect on my attitude. The first time around, I was too shell-shocked to really get angry. Now I was pissed. All I wanted to do was get my career back on track. Leave me alone and let me do my job. But Irving never had any intention of letting my wounds heal. I had no idea what was going on with Raggi, Morris, and Harloff. What's more, I didn't care. I figured those guys screwed up big time, and now I was going to have to pay the price.

By the end of February, the remaining members of HIT had been transferred out of SCIS. Mike Mazzeo went to the Maple Section, Brad Goater was sent to Highland, and Ron Runzo transferred to the Downtown Section. Also, by this time, Danny Varrenti was informed he was no longer welcome as a member of the Monroe County Drug Task Force, and he returned to the Irondequoit Police Department. Other officers were systematically removed from the Narcotics Unit of a period of several weeks. Tony Cotsworth was all but stripped of his authority and was virtually barred from the office. Changes were occurring at breakneck speed, and nobody knew from one day to the next where they might end up working.

For the next two months, I came to work in the worst possible frame of mind. Every night as I rolled my patrol car out of the Goodman Section parking lot, I hoped the dispatcher would send me on a job where some asshole would give me a good enough reason to shoot him. One afternoon, I assisted a young officer from my platoon with a drug bust. As was the normal procedure, the suspect was transported to SCIS for questioning. I knew sooner or later the day would come when I would have to go back to my old unit for this very reason. It felt strange now, after having been a boss in Narcotics, to be standing outside the red steel door waiting for someone to answer the buzzer. I felt even more uncomfortable once I got inside. The suspect was put in one of the interview rooms where I talked to him for a while. After about fifteen minutes, I emerged from the room and, much to my surprise, found my old pal Mark Gerbino waiting for me. He had transferred back to Vice, and we hadn't spoken to each other since that strange night in the bar. Mark asked if we could talk before I left, and we went into what used to be my office. I'm not sure what he had planned to say, but I didn't give him the opportunity to begin the conversation. Since the day he blew me off, our relationship had changed, and my once good friend never even called me during my darkest days. Yeah, I know there was an order from the chief not to have contact with any of the suspended officers. So what? There were ways around that. "Mark, we were supposed to be friends, and friends don't turn their backs on each other. If it had been the other way around, if I had been the one ordered to participate in the investigation of a fellow officer who was a good friend, I would have approached you. Without compromising the investigation, I would have let you know that I was in a tough spot, and because we were friends, I would hope you'd understand. I would not have treated you as if you had leprosy." Mark's response in his own defense: "I saw your name on a list, and I was intimidated." Considering the conversation over, I walked out of the office and returned to my patrol duties.

Joyce and I had been planning a vacation for quite a while, and the Florida sun was just what I needed about now. With each passing day I became more and more bitter toward the administration for lying to me, and I was rapidly developing a hatred for anyone even remotely suspected of cooperating with the investigation. Joyce's father owned a condo in Ft. Myers, and we scheduled our time away for the first two weeks in May. I couldn't begin to guess what the future held for me with respect to my career, but I put all of my troubles on the back burner and enjoyed our vacation.

Feeling rejuvenated after two fantastic weeks of beautiful weather and total relaxation, I returned to work on May 20, 1991. It's amazing how therapeutic sunshine really is. For as miserable as I felt before we left Rochester, I came back feeling great. I was even ready to stand up to the latest set of charges against me. Did I say the sun was therapeutic? Hell, it must have been mind altering. There would no standing up to the charges. On Wednesday, May 22, I was a couple hours into my shift when my sergeant called me back to the office. Lt. Piro was standing just inside the rear entrance and met me as I came through the door. With a grim look on his face, Piro said, "Deputy Chief Craig and Major McGurn are waiting for you in the captain's office." With that all-too-familiar knot in my stomach, I walked into Capt. Karnes's office and saw the two members of the chief's command staff. Dep. Chief Craig was holding a sheet of paper in his hand and proceeded to read it to me. What? No "Hello, how's the family? How was your vacation?"

Without the slightest exchange of social graces, the DCO read aloud, "Officer Thomas Alessi is hereby suspended with pay until further notice." When I asked for a reason, Craig said he couldn't tell me. "OK, I know the drill," I said as I removed my service weapon from my holster and dropped it on the captain's desk. After carrying a revolver for so many years before we changed over to nine-millimeter Berettas, I was in the habit of not having the safety on. As I unpinned my badge from my shirt, I thought I should at least render my weapon safe. When I reached for my gun on the desk, Craig must have believed my second thoughts were more of a homicidal nature. He practically jumped out of his shoes to get to the fully loaded weapon before I did. I thought what a jerk this guy really was. I tossed my police identification card on the desk and walked out of the office. I met Lt. Piro in the locker room, and after changing back into civilian clothes, I gave him the combination to my locker. I told him the contents were all department issue and he could do whatever he wanted with it. At least this time I had my own car and didn't have to call for a ride home.

Eight

I woke up the following morning full of mixed emotions. I was angry, scared, and confused. Mike Mazzeo, who had been working uniform in Maple Section for the past few months, had also been suspended the day before. By this time it was pretty much a shared opinion that a federal indictment was hovering over the department like a storm cloud waiting to burst. But the scope of the investigation was still a matter of guesswork, and all most of us could do was wonder who would be named in the indictment. Perhaps the lack of contact with my fellow "suspendees" caused me to think I was merely being dealt with departmentally. Others might say, "No, Tom, you're just stupid." I called Ron Evangelista at the Locust Club office. He told me the club had been referring officers who were called to testify to a number of good attorneys. He also told me a handful of some of the best criminal-defense lawyers in the area had been held in reserve for the targets of the investigation. Ron suggested I give John Speranza a call. I had heard of John over the course of my career, but I'd never had any dealings with him. I called and made an appointment to meet him at his downtown office the following day. John Speranza is one of those people who, upon meeting him, impresses you before he even says anything. An impeccable dresser with a warm smile that says, "Don't worry, everything is going to be all right." He also has a vocabulary that makes you want to run out and buy a very big dictionary. We talked for a bit, and when I left his office I had the confidence that even though I would probably be named in the indictment, I now had a formidable partner. John told me he would make some preliminary inquiries and that I should wait until I heard from him.

My attorney wasn't the only person I met with on Friday, May 24. After I left John's office, I joined Bill Morris, Greg Raggi, Scott Harloff, and Mike Mazzeo for lunch at a restaurant near Lake Ontario. It was the first time all of us had been together since the suspensions began. When I arrived, somebody joked about my car. While I was in Vice, I drove a black 1988 Thunderbird. I was relieved of it back in December on the day I was first suspended. The following Monday, Gordy Santos, a friend I had met through Mazzeo, hooked me up with a 1981 Dodge K-Car for $1,800. Gordy owned a repair garage where he also sold used cars. Knowing the tough spot I was in, he let me pay a hundred dollars down and a hundred a month. Gordy has proven to be a true friend many times over the years. Billy commented more than once that he just couldn't get used to seeing me in that car. It was a nice day, and we sat at an outside table where we could enjoy the weather and the privacy. Well, at least privacy from the rest of the customers.

Joyce had cautioned me against meeting with my fellow suspended officers, but I felt an overwhelming need to commiserate with them. After all, this was unlike anything that had ever happened to any of us or even anyone we knew. To make matters worse, that day, Chief Irving issued a departmental order as a reminder prohibiting members of the police department from having contact with any suspended officers. The way I saw it, since we were being deprived of any support from our friends on the job, all we had was each other. During lunch, we talked about things such as which patrol officers had been called in for questioning. Some people were called in to Internal Affairs or the federal building as many as four and five times and grilled on HIT Squad cases they had participated in. We discussed the potential involvement of our union, the Rochester Police Locust Club, and how our attorneys would be paid for their legal services. But the most significant topic we covered was how we would love to see our persecutors pay for the hell they were putting us and our families through. Try to imagine being in the best job you ever had one day and then having your own people label you as a crook and banish you from the very world you had been a part of for several years. The more we talked, the angrier we all became. Most of us had been on the department long enough to know the dirty little secrets of the people responsible for our misery. It was real easy to conjure up evil thoughts and, in fact, verbalize the things we would love to do to them. I would even dare to say that possibly one or two of you reading this have engaged in "fantasy revenge" at one time or another. And all the while Billy's tape recorder was quietly documenting our tough talk.

What four of us didn't know was that Bill Morris was wearing a body wire and tape-recording our conversations. He had in fact recorded every conversation, via telephone and in person, with Harloff, Raggi, and sometimes Capt. O'Brien, since May 7. For the record, unlike some states where secretly recording a conversation you are participating in constitutes eavesdropping, that is not the law in New York. As long as one participant in the conversation is aware of the recording, it's perfectly legal. This was Morris's eighteenth recording, and it would prove to be one of the more significant ones.

What Morris had done over a period of several weeks was record conversations with some or all of us then meet later that night with his handlers at a confidential location to debrief them on the topics of conversation. Morris would also provide his version of events at specific locations where our unit had conducted narcotics operations during the months we had worked in HIT. Typically, Billy would meet with Lieutenants Duffy (my old pal) and Berkow from RPD, and Special Agents Gene Harding and Bill Dillon of the FBI. Since the first suspensions, the officers involved had to report to the chief's office for their paycheck every two weeks. Billy's debriefing of our lunch meeting must have really touched a nerve. On May 28, 1991, we were all sent letters from the chief. Mine read, "Dear Officer Alessi: Effective immediately you are not allowed access to any Rochester Police Department facility or vehicle. Commencing May 30, your paychecks will be mailed to your home. You will not be admitted to any police facility without my specific written permission. Roy A. Irving, Chief of Police." We had learned that a panic alarm had been installed on the sixth floor of the Public Safety Building. All that talk of "going out in a blaze of glory" captured on tape caused the administration to prepare in case we came charging off the elevator in some sort of maniacal assault on the chief's office.

What little doubt I now had as to whether I would be named in an indictment disappeared with the arrival of the day's mail. I received a letter from the US Department of Justice, Civil Rights Division. The first two paragraphs read as follows:

This letter constitutes an invitation to appear before the Federal Grand Jury for the Western District of New York sitting in Rochester. This letter is an invitation only and does not constitute an order or subpoena to appear before the grand jury.

This grand jury is investigating allegations of illegal conduct by members of the Rochester Police Department, specifically members of the Vice Squad, from 1986 to October 18, 1990. This investigation may result in a federal criminal indictment charging that the civil rights of various persons were violated. By law, the grand jury can indict any person who it believes to be guilty of a violation of federal law. You are a target of this investigation and these grand jury proceedings may result in the filing of criminal charges against you.

The "invitation" went on to remind me of my constitutional right against self-incrimination and my right to an attorney. The letter said the grand jury was scheduled to hear evidence on July 3, 1991. I thought to myself, "Hmm, great chance to ruin another holiday." I was to let them know by June 13. It was signed by Michael J. Gennaco, someone whom I would have the not-so-distinct pleasure of meeting very soon. Well, I better exercise that constitutional right of mine and call my attorney. John reaffirmed my instincts of definitely not going before the grand jury. In the meantime, the executive board of the Rochester Police Locust Club was deciding whether they were going to finance our defense. Ron Evangelista, the president, was corresponding with our attorneys. We received the full support of the executive board as well as the support of the majority of the total membership. While the details of just how the lawyers would be paid had yet to be worked out, it was an enormous comfort just to know they would be, and that most of our fellow officers were behind us. I say "most" because some favored the administration's view of us. Remember, nobody was allowed to talk to us, so it was like living in a vacuum.

Through the end of May and into June, Billy Morris continued to telephone Greg and Scott and record the conversations. There was another lunch meeting on May 30 that I was unable to attend. I did, however, make the following one on June 5, and Old Man Fate must have been sitting right beside me because of all the contacts with Morris and his body wire, this one would eventually help end my career with the Rochester Police Department. Remember when I related the incident where Joyce came home from work one night and tore up an overtime slip of someone believed to have testified against us? Now try to imagine seven people sitting around a table in a restaurant where there are several different conversations going on at the same time. Someone had asked me how Joyce was holding up through all this, and I said that she would get more cranked up than I would at times. Then I mentioned the overtime slip incident. Things would probably have worked out differently if Morris had been talking to someone else at that very moment, but as luck would have it, he heard me. That night at his debriefing, he volunteered the information to his deal merchants. I suppose I could have understood it if the wire had picked up that particular part of the conversation and one of those real sharp FBI guys read it in the transcription then used it against me. But it never came out on the recording. Billy gave them the information long before the tape was ever transcribed.

It really is amazing just how slow the days go by when they're not interrupted by eight or more hours of work. There is only so much puttering around the house you can do. By the second week of June, John Speranza notified me of a meeting he was scheduled to go to on the seventeenth at the US Attorney's Office. I told him I wanted to be there. After some discussion, he reluctantly agreed to my attending if I promised not to respond, and let him do all the talking. The day of the meeting, I met John at his downtown office, and we walked the short distance to the federal building on State Street. Waiting for us in a conference room were Lieutenants Duffy and Berkow and FBI Special Agent Gene Harding. Representing the US Attorney's Office, Michael Gennaco and Cathleen Mahoney from the Civil Rights Bureau of the Justice Department in Washington were also present. During the meeting, which lasted less than an hour, John and I listened to Mr. Gennaco briefly explain the case being built against "your client." The dialogue was directed toward my attorney as if I were the Invisible Man. The highlight of this little get-together came when they offered a deal. "Because your client's actions pale in comparison to those of Raggi and Harloff, if he pleads guilty to two felonies and testifies, we'll allow him to do twelve to eighteen months in federal prison." Of course on the other hand, John was advised that if I was convicted on all counts, I was facing thirty-three years in prison and $1.3 million in fines. It was all I could do to keep from biting the inside of my cheek to shreds. The whole time I sat there I was recapping the three years I spent in narcotics. What in God's name did these people think I did to deserve going to prison? We may not always have dealt with drug-dealing scum in the most gentlemanly fashion, but conspire to violate their civil rights? Give me a break. When the meeting was over, John, in his ever-gracious manner, thanked all those present and said he would be in touch with Gennaco's office. As we stood, Duffy, who was seated across from me, extended his hand for me to shake. I just shook my head in disbelief and thought to myself, "Pal, you've got a better chance of swimming to Canada." John and I didn't speak until we emerged from the federal building. Like I said before, I hadn't known him before this all began, and he sure as hell didn't know me, or he would never have asked me the question he did. With all sincerity he said, "What if I can get you a misdemeanor with no time?" I replied, "John, I realize you're probably used to dealing with people who really did what they are accused of, but I will never plead guilty to something I didn't do, and don't ever ask me that again." I think that was the real beginning of our attorney/client relationship.

On July 1, 1991, "the few, the proud, the suspended," as Mazzeo referred to us, all met at Greg Raggi's house for a cookout. Capt. O'Brien, Mark Blair, also now retired, and Greg's father, Lou, were there as well. Greg has a great house with an in-ground pool. And while the weather was a bit cool for July, it felt good to relax, enjoy some food, and catch up on unfolding events. O. B. and his family had moved to Florida, and he was staying with Blair while he was back in town. As usual, we discussed the investigation and expressed hatred for all those involved. Of course, Billy Morris was there with his electronic friend, "Mike," a.k.a microphone. A little while into the festivities, Morris made it a point to announce he was going to take a dip in the pool. He even joked about not wearing a wire. After all, how could he be wired if he was going in the water? Well, truth is, Billy had a small gym bag he'd stuck under one of the patio chairs, and his recorder stayed nice and dry while he swam. Morris took offense when O'Brien told him he was the odds-on favorite to be the rat in the group. (Strong call, O. B.) I should have picked up on that one. It really was a little too chilly for a swim.

About mid-July, Joyce received a telephone call at home from Internal Affairs informing her of an investigation regarding her failure to forward reports in a timely fashion. She was also ordered to report to IA on the twenty-second to give a statement relative to that investigation. Totally bewildered as she hung up the phone, Joyce said she had no clue what this could be about. I had never told her about my repeating the overtime slip incident at one of the lunch meetings. Better late than never. I explained to her that unless she had told someone else, it had to have been passed on to IA by someone at that meeting. The question was what do we do now? I could handle the battle I was facing, but now they were going after someone I cared about. We agreed on a plan whereby Joyce would deny any knowledge of the accusation. I told her to tell the headhunters in IA that she never tore up any overtime slip and if Officer Alessi said she did, they should take the matter up with him. By now it was apparent that someone in our group was cooperating, but who and to what extent was still a mystery. I told Joyce I would probably be called in soon after her denial. They didn't disappoint me. IA banged out a notice to me right after Joyce's testimony. I was to appear at 4:00 p.m. on the twenty-fourth. My appointment was at four because they also ordered Joyce back that day at 12:30 p.m. This time they were going to question her about any contacts she may have had with suspended personnel. Contacts? We lived together!

July 22 would prove to be even more significant. At 5:40 p.m., Billy Morris placed a call to Scott Harloff. It would be the last call he would ever make to Scotty. FBI Special Agent William Dillon monitored this particular call and it would be, from that day on, labeled Reel #54. That was the total number of conversations Morris recorded, and on this final one, he called his best friend to tell him he was a cooperating witness against us. The complete shock of the call didn't hit Scotty until after he hung up. Following are excerpts from the transcript:

Harloff:	Hello?
Morris:	Scotty?
Harloff:	Yeah.
Morris:	It's Billy.
Harloff:	Hey, what are you doing?
Morris:	I need to talk to you.
Harloff:	All right.
Morris:	Listen up and…
Harloff:	Yeah.
Morris:	Listen up, good buddy.
Harloff:	All right.
Morris:	I came in and I'm [pause] I'm cooperating.

Harloff: Are you really?

Morris: Yeah. I want you to know first. I don't want you to hear it from somebody else.

Harloff: OK.

Morris: I'm not trying to fuck you.

Harloff: Yeah.

Morris: And I'm not going to tell you anything. I just, on our friendship I want you to know first.

Harloff: All right.

Morris: None of this [pause] you know. I don't want you to hear it through Greg, or through a number of other people.

Harloff: Yeah.

Morris: You know, I didn't know if you'd talk to me or not, so…

Harloff: Well, I tried to talk to you. I tried to call you all week.

Morris: Just so you know what's up and you hear it from me. I'd, it's been going on for a while.

Harloff: Yeah.

Morris: So don't be surprised when you start hearing a lot of things. We've been gone since Thursday.

Harloff: Yeah.

Morris: And we're not coming back, so…

Harloff: Well, OK.

Morris: That's what's up. Just so you know, and I, you know, like I said, ah, [pause] I don't know, there's not a whole lot I can say, ah [pause] just take care of yourself and you'll be OK. You know that's all I can say. I don't want you to hear it from somebody else, because it, ah, no matter what you, you think, you're still the best friend I had. I wish you the best of luck and I mean that honestly, I'm not, I'm not blowing you off, or nothing like that. I, ah, of everybody in this thing I want you to be OK.

Harloff: Well…

Morris:	But that's coming, that's coming from my heart. It's, no one's making me say that or anything else and, you know, whatever happens, happens, but somewhere deep down inside I'm in, you know, I'm in your corner.
Harloff:	Yeah.
Morris:	Whether you think so or not.
Harloff:	I, I would guess it ain't going to do much good for me, I mean, you know, but, ah, whatever.
Morris:	I can't tell you what to do or not to do, see, that's, I mean, that's one of the instructions I got before I called you...
Harloff:	Yeah.
Morris:	...or because they wouldn't let me call you unless, you know, I, I agreed to do it a certain way, and I, I can't tell you what to do or not to do.
Harloff:	Yeah.
Morris:	Just take care of you, and Debbie [Scott's wife] and the kids, and worry about your own self, that's all.

The call ended a few moments later with Scott still in such a state of disbelief that he actually thanks Morris. In all that self-serving dialogue of Billy's, not once did he ever offer his "best friend" even the slightest hint of an apology. It didn't take long for the identity of the government's informant to get around. It would still be a long time before we knew just what Morris had told his new friends to cinch his deal.

Armed with the identity of the rat in our group, Ron Evangelista and I walked into Internal Affairs on July 24, 1991, with the rest of my plan to protect Joyce all laid out in my head.

Some people may not agree with what I did next, and unless they have been in a similar situation, they certainly couldn't understand my reasoning. For me, it had been a forgone conclusion that my law-enforcement career was coming to an end. Now it was a matter of my survival and the survival of those I cared about. I was now in a battle with my own department, and I couldn't care less about the rules. And for the record, Evangelista had no idea what I was about to do.

This time Sergeants Jerry Connor and Kurt Kirstein would be my interrogators. Joyce had already given her statement regarding contacts with suspended officers. At first I was asked about any contacts I'd had with suspended officers. Finally, they got around to asking me about the overtime slip—I told them it never happened. Believing they had my voice on tape relating the whole thing, I said, "Sure, I said it, but it never happened. I just made it up to see if anyone in the group was cooperating and would use it against me." Well, these two just looked at each other like Dumb and Dumber. I guess they were expecting me to deny any knowledge of the incident. I thought since it was only Joyce and me in the room when it happened, they couldn't prove otherwise. I left their office thinking we had dodged a bullet. We hadn't. The next morning we awoke to the ringing of the doorbell. An RPD investigator and an FBI agent personally served Joyce with a subpoena to go before the federal grand jury on Monday, July 29. Understandably, she was concerned. I told her to stick to the version she gave Internal Affairs and everything would be fine. But things don't always work out the way you plan. I drove Joyce downtown the day of her appearance and parked in a nearby ramp garage. It was a warm summer day, and I waited on a bench while she walked across the street to meet Bob Brennan, her union-appointed attorney, prior to her testimony. I enjoyed the sunshine for almost an hour before I saw Joyce returning. At first I didn't notice the strange look on her face when I asked her how it went. She replied, "I did it."

I said, "I know. How'd it go?"

"No, I mean I told them everything," she answered. "The overtime slip. The story we made up for Internal Affairs. Everything."

"That's it then. I'm all done," is all I said. I knew in a very short time I would be joining the ranks of the unemployed. Joyce never made it in to the grand jury that day. Instead, prior to what would have been her appearance, Michael Gennaco and other investigators questioned her about the overtime slip incident. At first Joyce maintained our version. But they didn't believe her. She was told she was going into the jury room and that if she stuck to her story, she would be charged with perjury, fired from the RPD, and sent to federal prison. Joyce could no longer call their bluff, so she told them the truth. She was granted immunity from prosecution and given a letter to that effect signed by Gennaco. She was allowed to return to Internal Affairs where she recanted her previous untruthful testimony. Finally, Joyce testified before the grand jury at 9:00 a.m. two days later on the thirty-first. Mayor Thomas Ryan wanted her fired. Chief Irving explained to him that termination would not be the appropriate punishment for her first (known) transgression, so when they charged her with three separate violations of the rules and regulations, it was decided she would be suspended without pay for forty-five days. Joyce knew better than to fight it, and they agreed to take the time out of her compensatory time bank. This bullet she did manage to dodge. Even though her Internal Affairs career history shows the suspension as a final disposition, the truth is she never lost a day from her comp bank. Some people are just lucky, I guess.

And the hits just kept on coming. August 8, 1991, I received a letter ordering me to appear in Internal Affairs on August 12 (my birthday, how nice) regarding HIT Squad drug-testing procedures and the filing of official departmental and court documents. I had no clue what this could be about. For this round of chitchat, I drew Sergeants Connor and Rodriguez, but this time I brought my attorney with me. Whenever someone gives a statement in IA, they have you sign a form that basically says you must answer the questions or be fired. Remember December 14, 1990, when they wouldn't let me postpone the interview after telling me I was suspended? To know John Speranza is to love him. By this time he was very concerned about my rights against self-incrimination because we didn't know what would be in the forthcoming indictment. Without boring you with the whole transcript, the following is a brief exchange prior to any actual questioning:

Examination by Sergeant Connor:

Q. Did you sign this advisement form?

A. Not yet I haven't.

Mr. Speranza:

Sergeants, we do have the form here, and I am going to proceed to have him sign the same. Prior to, just very briefly on the record, and this may be implicit in this hearing, but we understand this to be a compelled hearing. We understand that by law he's under a full grain of transactional immunity here with respect to the dissemination of anything he testifies to directly, derivatively or collaterally to any prosecutorial agency of either the state or federal governments. Is that an accurate statement that I've spread on the record this morning?

Sergeant Connor:

It's quite wordy. I'll have to think about that for a minute. Are we saying that he's giving a statement under duress?

Mr. Speranza:

Yeah. He's here because he's compelled. And he recognizes that. He's here giving the statement because it's part and parcel of his obligation and duty as a public officer. And at the same time, however, he understands that he is not waiving or abrogating in any way any of his fifth-amendment privileges against self-incrimination as a result of his particular status here. That being the case, of course, we would understand that nothing that he says in any way could be used against him criminally, as I've said, not to be repetitive, not only state, but of course with regard to the pending federal matter that everyone knows is now under investigation. So, predicated on that basis, which, as I say, is implicit in the law, as I understand it—and the particular case that I'm alluding to is a case called Matt, M-a-t-t, versus Larocca, L-a-r-o-c-c-a. It's at seventy-one New York second, one-fifty-four. So, perhaps I'm being redundant in articulating this, but,

nonetheless, I want to make sure we have a clear understanding
as to precisely the parameters and scope of the hearing.

Sergeant Connor:

OK, I understand that. Sergeant Rodriguez?

Sergeant Rodriguez:

No comments.

And so it went from there. From the looks on their faces after John's remarks, I don't think they had a clear understanding as to precisely what
planet they were on, let alone what the hell he just said. When all was
said and done, it was worth the price of admission just to see Speranza
put them through their paces. Apparently, based on something Morris
had said during one of his debriefings, they were looking into my guys
using presigned supporting depositions for field testing of narcotics and
whether I had knowledge of it. It really didn't matter, because the administration had a litany of charges they were going to throw at me.
That's why on this very same day they were drawing up charges against
me relative to my appearance on July 24 when I gave my made-up version of the overtime slip incident. Knowing the end of my career was
close at hand, I pleaded not guilty. I figured what the hell—why plead
guilty just so they could fire me? If they wanted my head on a platter,
they were going to have to work for it. I wasn't going to just give it to
them. I would receive a notice two weeks later that a hearing on the
matter was scheduled for January 16, 1992. It's also why I was back in
IA on August 19. This time it had to do with a raid on a drug house
in Genesee Section I had participated in on January 15, 1988, three
months before HIT was established. Guess who else was on that raid?
Bill Morris. The details of this particular incident will be described a
little farther on, but suffice it to say it was one of the highlights of a
Morris debriefing.

Nine

August 29, 1991, would prove to be another pivotal day in my rapidly changing life. That's when the grand jury handed up the long-awaited indictment. The United States of America V. Scott David Harloff, Gregory Robin Raggi, Michael David Mazzeo, Thomas William Alessi, James William O'Brien, and Gordon Frederick Urlacher. Nineteen counts containing over seventy-five overt acts all in violation of Title 18, US Code Sections 241, 242, 371, 666, and 924(c). A big production in the form of a combination city/federal press conference was held. Chief Irving and his underlings, along with Dennis Vacco, Assistant US Attorney for the Western District of New York, and an assortment of federal agents were all gathered for the news media. Using large posters, all the key points of the indictment were displayed for the cameras. Prior to the announcement of the indictment, our attorneys had requested that they be notified so arrangements could be made to surrender their clients for arraignment. Looking back, I'm surprised Vacco didn't insist on parading us single file in shackles past the reporters. Our arraignment was postponed until September 3, following the Labor Day weekend. Holidays are such special memories.

The two surprises were Urlacher and O'Brien. The former chief was named in our indictment because the leaders of this crusade believed that he and Captain O'Brien plotted to bury any complaints that may have arisen from the actions of HIT. Nothing could be further from the truth. Remember the Three-in-Eighteen Rule? If an officer had three complaints within eighteen months, they would be more closely scrutinized. When we were given our marching orders back in April, 1988, we all had concerns because of the sheer volume of people we would be dealing with. We had asked that consideration be given to differentiate our complaints from those of the Patrol Section. Besides, complaints were investigated by Internal Affairs, not the chief of police. Urlacher would have been involved in the final disposition, but whenever somebody wanted to complain about a cop, they walked into IA. And considering the number of people who didn't appreciate us interfering in their chosen lifestyle, IA entertained a fair number of complaints. That whole office would have had to be in on that conspiracy. The former chief hired Larry Andolina to represent him. Larry was the attorney for several police unions including the Rochester Police Locust Club. He was also Billy Morris's lawyer until he was fired when Morris decided to work for the government. O'Brien, who had since moved to Florida, told his wife, Cindy, that when the indictment came out, he would go back to Rochester to stand with us in court. The only problem was he thought he'd be there as a friend showing support for his former subordinates, not as a codefendant. The indictment consisted of twenty-nine pages and enumerated allegations spanning a thirty-four month time period. The first three pages included the introduction and the first count. Count I alone contained seventy-three overt acts. It said that between January 1988 and October 1990, while we were "then law enforcement officers with the Rochester Police Department, while acting under color of the laws of the State of New York, did willfully combine, conspire, and agree with one another and with persons known [guess who] and unknown to the grand jury, to injure, oppress, threaten and intimidate citizens of the United States and inhabitants of the State of New York in the free exercise and enjoyment of the right and privilege secured to them by the Constitution of the United States, to be free from the deprivation of liberty without due process of law, which includes: (1) the right to be secure in their persons and free from the intentional use of unreasonable force by one acting under color of law; (2) the right not to be compelled to be as witness against oneself; and

(3) the right to be kept free from harm while in official custody and detention.

It was part of the plan and purpose of this conspiracy that HIT would patrol areas of Rochester where drug trafficking was suspected to take place, and that HIT members would unjustifiably strike, kick, beat, assault and threaten persons who were detained or arrested by the HIT Squad.

In furtherance of this conspiracy and to accomplish its plans and purposes, the conspirators, while acting under color of the laws of the State of New York, committed the following overt acts, among others, within the Western District of New York."

The rest of the nineteen counts and corresponding overt acts were outlined in the remaining twenty-six pages of the indictment. We were listed by name with a variety of accusations attributed to each of us. For those not familiar with the law as it pertains to conspiracy, you need more than just two or more people conspiring to do something illegal. There must be one or more overt acts in furtherance of the conspiracy. For example, if three people agree to kill someone, it's not a crime. If one of them goes out and buys a gun for that purpose, then the conspiracy is born with that overt act. And if they succeed and are caught, whatever they did that directly led up to the killing could add up to several acts. Of the seventy-three overt acts listed in the first count, twelve were attributed to me. Six accused me of striking and assaulting suspects. The other six were simply because I was a supervisor at the scene when someone else did the striking, and I failed to intervene and take disciplinary action. All of the acts under Count I constituted violations of Title 18, US Code, Section 242 as a conspiracy. Counts III, IV, and VII were basically the same as alleged in three overt acts of Count I, but I was charged as an individual. Count XIII was the same incident as Count IV but made a separate charge because I carried a firearm, namely, my service weapon. Count XVIII was another conspiracy charge accusing us of embezzling funds from the government. This they said we did because HIT was operating with federal grant money and because we secured early sometimes and I didn't dock our pay. Count XIX was the same as XVIII but charged each of us individually instead of conspiratorially.

So that's it—all the waiting and wondering came down to this. After two and a half years of taking hundreds of drug dealers off the street—not to mention the amount of dope, guns, and drug money we took out of circulation—I was about to be prosecuted for striking and assaulting a grand total of five people and failing to stop others from doing the same. Well, at least I could take comfort in that they didn't think I had murdered somebody. My codefendants were also credited with a variety of assaults. Some were accused of taking drug money and planting evidence. O'Brien and former Chief Urlacher were charged with using their positions of authority to cover up our almost three-year reign of terror. Apparently, Morris had done a pretty thorough job.

As you can imagine, the following day, August 30, the local newspapers had a field day with the story. The *Rochester Times-Union* front page in large bold type read, "Cop charges raise question: How did the system fail?" Related front-page articles read, "Indictment triggers call for more civilian oversight," and "Feds moved after hearing from police, not public." The editorial on page six was titled "A badge of dishonor. If the charges are true, rogue cops betrayed the law and the public." On the front page of the local section, the large bold type read, "Urlacher: Indictment 'ridiculous.'" A reporter had tracked down the ex-chief at his mother's house. Urlacher was described as friendly, polite, and in good spirits. "The indictment as it relates to me is...what's a good word...is ridiculous," he said. The article went on to say the first overt act of Count I claims the former chief "vehemently opposed" a plan to videotape drug arrests. Urlacher's response, "So what?" O'Brien was included in this opposition in the form of an overt act in the indictment. This apparently was part of their big cover-up. What the reporter didn't know was there never was a *plan*. A suggestion had been made by someone on high to videotape drug arrests, and O'Brien's opposition came about as several questions, which he shared with Urlacher. Namely, who was going to do the videotaping? Not our guys—we had enough problems securing raid locations with the number of people we had. Would operations be compromised by having non-Vice personnel possessing sensitive information as to targets and locations? Which operations would be videotaped? All of them? If not, why some and not others? If they don't tape *all* of them, departments with a policy of videotaping interviews and interrogations leave themselves open to criticism for the ones they don't tape. "What did you do, beat the confession out of my client?" Don't get me wrong—I'm not against audio/video documentation. When a bad guy confesses to a crime, he can't say, "They never read me my rights. I asked for my lawyer, and they just kept questioning me. They promised me I could go home if I confessed." As I said earlier, I consider it to be "best evidence" to have a defendant's voice or actions on tape. But if you're going to do it, you better do it every time. Apparently, the sixth-floor experts on narcotics investigations considered any objection to their videotape proposal a cover-up.

September 3, 1991, the Tuesday following Labor Day weekend, we all appeared in federal court for arraignment. We had put together a regular Dream Team as far as lawyers go. Some of the best criminal-defense attorneys in the business were representing us: John Speranza (me), John Parrinello (Harloff), Anthony Leonardo (O'Brien), David Rothenberg (Raggi), and Carl Salzer (Mazzeo). After hearing from the prosecutor what a menace to society we were, Judge Michael Telesca ordered that we surrender any and all personal weapons. Of course, the newspapers were kind enough to report we were forced to surrender our weapons while they also printed our pictures and home addresses. I asked my lawyer if the newspaper was responsible if some dope dealer we had busted did a drive-by shooting while I was out mowing the lawn. You can guess what his answer was. After being released on a $50,000 signature bond, we enjoyed a visit to the FBI office where we were photographed and fingerprinted. That done, John and I returned to his office. He advised me that there was a lot of work to be done: countless meetings between lawyers and numerous motions to be filed. At this point things were pretty much out of my hands. All I could do was wait. I didn't know it then, but I, along with my codefendants, would be waiting for almost a year and a half.

Ten

My antagonists in the Rochester Police Department had not forgotten about me. I was served a new set of charges dated October 25, 1991. These were three separate charges stemming from my appearance in Internal Affairs back on August 19. It seemed that Mr. Morris had given his handlers a different version of a raid we had been on in 1988. Again, I won't bore you with the details of the charges and specifications, but they basically said I lied in my statement to IA, I used unnecessary and excessive force, and I was aware of other officers at the scene using excessive force but didn't report it. The raid was at a drug house at 65 Prospect Street in Genesee Section. We had hit the place a couple of times before and always had a problem because of the heavy steel fortifications on the doors and windows. I remembered this particular raid very clearly. Greg Raggi injured his leg when he fell through the rotted floorboards on the porch. I knew what I had done while I was there, but more importantly, I knew what I didn't do. I had until November 5 to respond. They make it real convenient for themselves. The letter said "If your answer is not received by the above date and time, you will be deemed to have pleaded guilty to these charges and a penalty will be imposed." (Like that's not going to happen anyway.)

I submitted my answer on October 28, 1991. It was very simple, one page with three lines in which I pleaded not guilty. My attorney, John Speranza, on the other hand, doesn't do anything simple. His "answer" was in the form of a request for bill of particulars and demand to produce. It was seven pages of legalese that asked for detailed information relative to all charges and specifications against me. One paragraph in the bill of particulars read, "With respect to Charge II, Specification I, state whether you have information or evidence in any file or which you should be aware of through the exercise of reasonable diligence that Officer Alessi or any other police officer acted in accord with inclusive but not limited to the mandates and requirements of Penal Law Article 35 entitled Justification." What? I hoped he didn't expect Irving to read and understand this. In the demand to produce, one of the ten paragraphs read, "Officer Alessi demands that the City of Rochester, et al, disclose to him the following: Any results or reports, typewritten and/or handwritten of physical or mental examinations and of scientific tests or experiments or copies thereof which are material to the preparation of Officer Alessi's defense or are intended for use by the city, et al, as evidence-in-chief at the hearing." Now I knew why these guys go to school for so long and why they charge so much. It's too bad it was all just a waste of paper.

I received another letter from Chief Irving dated December 23, 1991. I'm convinced they time these things around the holidays just for the negative psychological effect. Remember the story I told in IA back in July to protect Lt. Walsh? This letter was to inform me of the date and time, as well as the location, of my hearing relative to those charges. It also advised who the hearing officers would be: Major John McGurn had been designated as Hearing Board President. This is the same major who, along with Dep. Chief Bob Craig, suspended me back on May 22 when I working in Goodman Section. Gee, I wondered if he'd be wearing his unauthorized back-up gun on his ankle like he usually did. (Unlike some departments, RPD prohibited the carrying of back-up guns.) One of the hardest things to swallow about this whole witch hunt was that some of the people running it had done a lot of things over the years they shouldn't have done. More about that later. My former Lake Section captain, Bob Wiesner, and one of my former Downtown Section partners, Sgt. Bill Benwitz, were designated as his assistants. The way it works is the chief picks three command officers, and I get to exclude one. I submit the names of three command officers I want, and he picks one to replace my exclusion. Benwitz was one of my three choices. Even with two of the three being my friends, I couldn't help flashing back to what Ron Evangelista had said a year ago about the chief overturning a not-guilty verdict and firing me anyway.

Three weeks later, I received another letter from the chief. It read in part, "It has become necessary to replace Major John McGurn as a hearing board member. Major McGurn has learned that he was the subject of alleged threats made by you and others. He feels he no longer can be impartial in this matter." Then there were two captains from whom I was to pick a replacement for McGurn. He was referring to the "fantasy revenge" conversation at the lunch meeting Bill Morris had recorded eight months earlier. And McGurn just learned of it.

Irving's letter was irrelevant. There was no doubt as to the outcome. Since I had played this fiasco out as far as possible, and Lt. Joyce Walsh would be the star witness against me, I figured why put her through that grief. On the day of my hearing, John Speranza and I reported to the sixth floor of the Public Safety Building where the proceeding was to be held. John inquired as to what options, if any, I had at this point. He was told I could either quit or be fired after my hearing. Speranza figured if I quit, I would lose any right to an appeal. Besides, I didn't want to give them the satisfaction. We also knew the primary battle would be fought in federal court. If I lost there, my job would be a moot point. The chief agreed to let me plead guilty to misconduct instead of untruthfulness. As the finishing touches were put on my plea agreement, I waited in the hallway. Irving came up to me with a Styrofoam cup of black coffee. "You look like you could use this," he said as he handed me the cup. For a split second I pondered what I could possibly have to lose if I threw it in his face. Without a word, I took the coffee and drank it. I'd be damned if I was going to come all this way just to have him break me at the very end. I typed up a written plea of guilty to a violation of Rules and Regulations, Section 4.1, Conduct, and we left the building.

Once again it was time to wait for the other shoe to drop. I didn't have to wait long. Irving sent me a two-page letter dated January 24, 1992, in which he outlined my horrific disciplinary record, and how just when he was placing some faith in me and giving me a second chance, I was already a player in another incident (with specific reference to the overtime slip situation). He went on to say what a discredit to the department I was and how he could have fired me the first time. The final blow came in the last sentence of the fourth paragraph: The penalty imposed upon you, based upon the present charge and upon your past disciplinary record, is termination from the Rochester Police Department, effective immediately. That was it. After almost thirteen years as a police officer, it was over. It's strange how even though when you know something bad is coming your way, the impact is no less severe when it finally happens. I was standing in the kitchen with the letter in my hand with so many things going through my mind that I had to sit down and collect my thoughts. The first was how would I make a living, especially with no marketable skills. I remembered what I had gone through just to become a cop. Returning to school to get my degree. Going through the academy and field training. I knew I had some money coming from built-up comp time and unused vacation, but that wouldn't last forever. As it turned out, my former-wife's lawyer pulled a fast one on the city accounting office and managed to scam half of the money owed me, about $4,000.

The day I received my letter of termination, I went to the supermarket for something Joyce needed. As I walked through the door, I saw Russ Coriddi waiting in one of the checkout lines. He had recently been promoted to captain and was thought of as a rising star and a good guy. We had worked together back when he made investigator and transferred from the Tactical Unit into the Genesee Section. I always considered Russ a friend. As I walked into the store, he called me by name and waved. For no reason other than still being in shock, I just nodded and kept walking. A few moments later while I was trying to find what I came for, Russ approached me in one of the aisles. He said he got out to his car in the parking lot and thought about the way I treated him. He came back into the store to confront me. Russ asked if he had done something to offend me for me to blow him off the way I did. I explained to the new captain about receiving my letter of termination that day, and that I really wasn't up to dealing with former work associates. I started out by asking him what we should talk about, his career or mine. I had not seen or talked to Russ since my suspension. Besides, he was bound by the chief's order not to have any contact with me or my codefendants. He told me how all along the administration kept telling the rank and file to be patient and wait until the indictment came down. Then everyone would see how bad it was. But when it finally did come down, the attitude of many RPD personnel was that they had been misled. Russ was a company man now, and I didn't begrudge him that. He had earned his new position. But even this member of the chief's staff thought the federal indictment, based upon its contents, was way out of line with what it was that many thought we had done. I've always been grateful that Russ didn't just get into his car and drive away that night.

On January 27, Chief Irving issued a written order to be read at all roll calls. In it he stated the department would not be making any comments on the upcoming trial of former Chief Urlacher. Department members were also prohibited from making comments or giving opinions to the press. He also made it clear that no on-duty officers were permitted to attend the trial unless responding to a subpoena related to their police duties. If anyone appeared as a defense character witness, it had to be on their own time, whether they were scheduled to be on duty or not, and, of course, it could not be in uniform. At the end of the order he added a reminder: "The prohibition against any contact with the suspended members of the department continues."

For the next four months, my attorney worked on an appeal to the civil-service commission. John submitted documentation that showed a number of officers brought up on departmental charges no less egregious than mine, yet their punishment ranged from five to sixty days suspension without pay. He had attempted to show that I had been dealt with in an arbitrary and capricious manner. On May 7, 1992, John was notified by one of the city's attorneys that the civil-service commission had unanimously rejected the appeal and upheld my firing. During this time, I had applied for unemployment insurance, but the administration saw to it that my application was denied. In April, I picked up a part-time job as a bartender in a little blue-collar gin mill in East Rochester, a suburb about five miles southeast of the city. Most departments, as well as New York State law, forbid police officers from working in alcohol-related jobs, but what the hell, I wasn't a cop anymore. It didn't pay much, but I still had some of the money I cashed out with, and the job gave me experience I would use later. All things considered, I was making the best of my situation. Unfortunately, my relationship with Joyce was on a downward slide.

One day I had to move her car to the other side of the driveway. I backed it up and heard something crash in the trunk. When I checked, I found a portable cooler with a half-dozen empty beer cans and a pair of her underwear inside. I removed the cooler and left it on the kitchen counter where she would see it as soon as she walked in the house. Over the previous several weeks she had been irritable and prone to picking fights for no reason. On one occasion she attended a police social function, which she said she absolutely hated to do, and didn't get home until 5:00 a.m. Knowing she wasn't that careless or stupid, I figured the cooler incident was her way of pushing things to the brink. I told Joyce I would make it easy for her and just move out as soon as I could find a place to go. Even that wasn't quite good enough. She asked why I couldn't go live with one of my relatives and sleep on a sofa if need be. I happened to run into a former HIT Squad member who had since retired from the department. Ron Runzo was living in a two-bedroom apartment in East Rochester, and when I told him of my situation, he offered to let me stay with him. On June 15, 1992, while Joyce was at work, I packed my things and moved out of her house.

Needing a change of pace, I decided to spend two weeks in Florida by myself. I gave Jim O'Brien a call to let him know I would be looking him up when I got there. O. B. invited me to stay at his house. I took him up on his offer, and on July 1 my former captain met me at the Ft. Lauderdale Airport. For the entire time I was there, I tried to think of anything but my future. Lying in the warm sun every day was the only thing that interested me. Besides, there would be plenty of time to deal with my problems when I got back home. The two weeks flew by.

Prior to moving out of Joyce's house, her sister Karen had offered to help me get a job at Kodak, where she was employed. I'd filled out and returned the application and was waiting for an interview. Karen had explained to me that the only job openings were in Plant Services, which basically meant I would be a janitor. But with no money coming in, except the little I made tending bar a couple days a week, at least it would be a steady paycheck and benefits. With no medical insurance, every day I left my apartment I reminded myself to be careful and not get hurt. When the day came for my interview, I thought it would just be a formality. Answer a few questions, sign here, and tell me when I start. What I found was an interviewer advising me that I was way overqualified for the position I was seeking. By the end of the interview, I was practically begging for the job. I was hired August 24 and shortly thereafter found myself assigned to one of their chemical factories, on the four to midnight shift, where I mopped floors and scrubbed toilets for seven dollars an hour.

Like a lot of cops, I had worked a variety of part-time jobs since I began my career. They were mostly security of one type or another. My first extra-money gig was security at a downtown McDonald's restaurant. Over the years, I worked the numerous festivals held each year in Rochester. And as I mentioned before, I worked retail security with Mazzeo up until I went to the Vice Squad. It seemed I was always looking to make extra money to pay for some of life's decisions like alimony, child support, and boats. The difference was that I always had my real job. Now I was faced with trying to support myself on seven bucks an hour.

All in all, it wasn't a bad deal. I worked alone with no on-site supervisor. I came in, did my job, and went home. Well, not right home. I had trouble sleeping for a while. I would lie awake in bed going over all that had happened over the past eighteen months. I began stopping at a nearby bar on the way home. J. G. Crummers was a sports bar about two miles from my apartment, with friendly people in a comfortable atmosphere. I would sit at the bar and talk to Dave, the bartender. My usual routine was two bottles of Budweiser and a scotch on the rocks. I had to settle for Johnny Walker Black at first, but the owners, John and Joe, won me over after I mentioned that I preferred Pinch. The following week there was a brand new bottle on the top shelf. Crummers was my favorite watering hole, and Max, bartender extraordinaire, always had an adequate supply of Pinch on hand.

In the fall of 1992, I started seeing a young woman named Denise. She was just coming out of a marriage and had two young children, Nick and Vanessa. While the relationship wasn't without its headaches, as most aren't, it did afford me companionship at a time when being alone would have been unbearable. Some of my codefendants thought the stress of starting over in a new relationship, especially with kids involved, while we were going through our ordeal would be worse than being alone. But they all had wives with whom they could share their misery, fear, and anger.

As winter approached, the reality of our trial loomed ever closer. A date was set for early January 1993 but was eventually moved to the nineteenth. Long before the year ended, we each began meeting regularly with our lawyers. O'Brien had to confer with Tony Leonardo by phone since Jim lived in Florida. And the attorneys would meet with each other frequently to discuss strategies. The heart of the indictment was a conspiracy charge. We all had to come out of this unscathed, and the legal brain trust we were counting on had to put a solid defense together. It was understood that Bill Morris would be the government's star witness. And, of course, we expected the prosecution to dig up as many "victim" drug dealers as they could. What we didn't know yet was how many and which police officers they would put on the stand. It wasn't until the first week in December that the prosecution handed over the discovery material. It amounted to more than six thousand pages of documents that Mike Gennaco, the federal prosecutor, would use to support his allegations in the indictment.

Just as my colleagues did, I spent hours in my lawyer's office going over all the material that had been turned over. John and I would read the documents over and over looking for areas to attack: inconsistencies in Internal Affairs and FBI statements, grand-jury testimony, as well as dates and locations of alleged incidents. I told John that among the materials we would be asking the police department for, we should include all my travel vouchers for the times I was out of town on police business. These were important because my payroll time sheets would indicate an eight-hour day whether I was out of town or not. Sure enough, while matching the various dates I discovered they had accused me of helping to violate somebody's civil rights on Troup Street in Rochester when I was actually at a three-day conference in South Carolina. If this had not been so serious, it would be laughable.

About a week before the trial began, I told my supervisor at Kodak what was coming. John Lesio was a good boss who had treated me decently, and I didn't want him to get caught off-guard. He was a little shocked to find out what I had managed, at least up to that time, to keep to myself. As it turned out, there would be just five of us going to trial. In December, Gordon Urlacher pleaded guilty to the indictment. A lot of people who don't understand how the system works asked why he would do such a thing if he was innocent. The former chief was already incarcerated on his embezzlement charge. If he had gone to trial on our indictment, they would have dragged him up to Rochester, but instead of going home every day like we did, he would have had to stay in a federal holding facility for the duration of the trial. He had absolutely nothing to gain by slugging it out in court. You can expect a person to endure only so much in the name of principle. Any sentence he received would be concurrent with his existing one. It spite of appearances, it was the smart thing to do. At the end of December, I took another bartending job at an upscale restaurant called Hemingway's. Because of my dedication to the floors and toilets of Kodak during the week, I worked my new job only on Saturday nights. The tips were good, and I worked with a friend of mine, Steve Ziogas. It helped move the time along, and before I knew it, January 19, 1993, was just two days away.

Eleven

On Tuesday, January 19, the first day of our trial, I awoke early, showered, shaved, and put on one of the new suits I'd bought for the occasion. Then I drove to a nearby Perkins restaurant. Anyone who knows me knows I tend to be organized and somewhat structured. I knew it was going to be a long ordeal and figured I may as well get a routine established. Prior to all the trial preparation, I had renewed my interest in physical fitness. I spent hours in the gym working out on machines and using free weights. I did not want all that hard work to go to waste, so I decided to maintain a healthy diet. My breakfast was a bowl of oatmeal with honey, along with black coffee and ice water. As I waited for my order to arrive, I looked around at the other customers and wondered what their days would be like.

I chose the most direct route downtown without using the expressway. With the weather as bad as it had been, I wasn't about to take a chance on getting stuck in rush-hour traffic because of an accident. I parked in a ramp garage a block away from the federal building. After turning the engine off, I sat there listening to the pinging sound of the engine cooling down. For some strange reason I remembered being in boot camp twenty-six years earlier. There is a part of the water survival where we had to jump off a twenty-foot tower into about fifteen feet of water. There was a sign on the stairs that read something to the effect of, "No recruit ever walks *down* these stairs." At that time I couldn't swim, and I wasn't real wild about heights. When it was my turn to jump, I was scared to death, but I had to do it, so I did. After about five minutes,

I pulled the keys out of the ignition and thought to myself, "It's time to jump again." I got out of the car and headed for court.

Having seen television coverage of high-profile court cases before, I expected the media to be there, so I'm not sure why I was so surprised to see antenna trucks from the various stations. As I waited for the light to change, I took in the scene unfolding before me. Reporters were stationed around the entrance to the federal building with their camera operators jockeying for position. Some were set up in fixed positions with tripods, while others were running up to be the first to shove their camera in the face of an oncoming participant. As I got closer to the building, I noticed a couple people give me a double take or point me out to their partners. Here they come. I felt like the Good Humor Man walking onto a playground full of kids with money in their hands. I had dealt with most of these people before. My unit had received a good deal of news coverage over the years, and I had a pretty good relationship with the media. I always thought police officials looked foolish when they told reporters they didn't know something about a particular incident (when it was obvious that they did), when in fact they just could not comment on it. My policy was if I can tell you, I will. If I can't, I'll tell you I can't. The gauntlet of microphones and cameras continued right up to the closing of the elevator doors inside the federal building.

The courtroom itself was fairly large. Immediately past the entrance doors was the spectator's gallery that consisted of about five rows of benches. They extended left and right of the center aisle all the way to the walls on either side of the room. The gallery was separated from the front portion of the courtroom by a wooden railing with a hinged gate in the center. The jury box was located on the right side of the front half of the room. The prosecution table was just in front of the railing, a little right of center. The defense table was to the left side in front of the railing. Our table was L-shaped with the short portion along the left wall. This was necessary to accommodate five defendants and five attorneys. The judge's bench was at the extreme front of the room with the witness stand on the right side (as viewed from the rear of the room).

Judge Michael A. Telesca would be presiding over the trial. He was a well-respected, no-nonsense kind of judge who had been on the federal bench in Rochester for a long time. My seat at the table was on the short side of the table facing the jury. John Speranza sat to my left. Jim O'Brien and his attorney were on John's left. Greg Raggi and his lawyer were seated to my right, facing the judge. Mike Mazzeo and Scott Harloff, with their lawyers, were to the right of Raggi. Before long, all the participants were in the courtroom, and the gallery was filled to capacity. The three Justice Department attorneys sat at the prosecution table. Sitting with them was Lt. Berkow, Bill Morris's tape-recording buddy. But, apparently due to the defense's objection to his presence, he was replaced with Agent Bill Dillon of the FBI. Let the games begin.

Scott, Greg, and Mike had their wives and other family members there for moral support. Jim O'Brien was staying with his former neighbors, Dick and Jean Jubenville, and they were there on his behalf. I chose not to have anyone else there with me. In the days to come, supporters of mine would be there, but for the time being I felt like I was walking onto a battlefield, and I didn't want the distraction of dealing with people I cared about when things got ugly. I can't explain it any better than that.

Day one was consumed by jury selection. The previous day's newspaper headlines had already set the tone for racial arguments: "Jury's diversity likely to be a factor." Comparisons between our trial and the Rodney King situation, as well as the murder trial in the Crown Heights section of Brooklyn, were made. Both of the latter were completely different types of juries with respect to their racial composition, yet both rendered opposite verdicts that touched off social turmoil (riots) in the localities where they occurred. Prospective federal jurors came from a pool of registered voters in the ten-county area surrounding Rochester. Three hundred and fifty prospective jurors were randomly selected, and, after some were automatically excused, the judge interviewed twenty-eight people at a time to narrow the list to about one hundred and fifty. Five of the seventy-nine possible choices who showed up the first day were black. Federal rules allow the prosecution to disqualify up to six people, and the defense can disqualify ten. After six hours of questioning, a jury of nine women, one of whom was black, and three men was selected. And while the lone black juror was our choice, Mr. Gennaco objected to the defense disqualifying two black alternates. With the jury excused, attorneys argued back and forth over the process. Mr. Gennaco believed our lawyers were required to come up with a racially neutral reason for striking the alternates. Greg's lawyer, David Rothenberg, argued that case law did not give the government the right to a jury of *its* choice, but did grant the defendant's right to a jury of *his* peers. After all arguments were heard by Judge Telesca, he said he was satisfied with the jury and the process by which it was selected.

The judge set the time lines for the trial. He had decided we would be in court Monday through Thursday with Fridays off. Each day would begin at 8:30 a.m. and conclude at 1:30 p.m. He felt this schedule would be beneficial for two reasons: First, it wouldn't be too much of a burden on the members of the jury, some of whom had a long drive each day. Second, some of our attorneys were not members of large law firms and had other clients they were responsible for. This also worked out well for me. I still had a standing four o'clock date with a mop bucket each weekday. Referring to the following day, Judge Telesca asked the prosecution how much time it would need for opening statements, to which Mr. Gennaco replied, "The government will take no more than half an hour." When he asked the defense, John Parrinello said, "We will take the balance of the day." Well, that didn't go over too well with the judge or Mr. Gennaco. Instead, Judge Telesca told us that since the prosecution needed only thirty minutes, that is all each of the defense attorneys would be allowed. Any of them could, if they so desired, yield the balance of their time to other members of the defense team. With that, court was adjourned until 8:30 a.m. the following day.

The next morning, January 20, at Perkins, while I waited for my oatmeal to arrive, I noticed a few people giving me more than just a casual glance. You know that "where have I seen you before" look. Some would look away when I locked eyes with them. Others would just smile or nod their heads. Apparently, not everyone caught our court debut on the six and eleven o'clock news the night before. I thought to myself, "Give them a couple of days. They'll figure it out." When I got downtown, the scene outside the federal building was the same as it had been the day before and as I expected it would be every day thereafter.

Prior to the jury being brought in, Scott's lawyer, John Parrinello, the lead attorney, attempted to exclude some members of the city/federal investigative team from the courtroom. It seemed that a few RPD investigators had secured front-row seats for themselves. Perhaps they were there to get a firsthand look at their handiwork or document any presence of support for us in the form of other members of the department. While the chief could not prohibit any of his officers from attending a public trial on their own time, he could be advised of it, especially if anyone showed up in uniform or, God forbid, had contact with any of us. In any event, the judge allowed them to stay.

After the jury was ushered in and polled, Judge Telesca began giving them his instructions. I have to give Parrinello credit. He waited all of about one whole minute before lodging his first of what would be numerous objections. It went like this:

| The Court: | Thank you, ladies and gentlemen, for getting here on time. I am going to give you some preliminary instructions now to give you an overview of what is going to happen so that you will know what to expect. What not to expect. After I do that, the attorneys will then give their opening remarks to you. Now that you have been sworn in, I will give you some preliminary instructions to guide you in your participation in this trial. These instructions will be very short. First, it will be your duty to find from the evidence what the facts are. You and you alone are the judges of the |

	facts. You will then have to apply those facts to the law, as the court will give it to you. You must follow the law whether you agree with it or not.
Mr. Parrinello:	Objection, your Honor.
The Court:	You can note that objection. It's a standing objection and I don't want to hear it again. I will use the term "follow."
	It is synonymous with what you want.
Mr. Parrinello:	I move for a mistrial, your Honor.
The Court:	Denied. [And the judge continued with his instructions.]

We all knew that John was a real fire-breather in court. I was just kind of hoping he would wait until the chill from the outside had left me before he pissed off the judge.

Upon the completion of the judge's instruction, Mr. Gennaco announced that one of his cocounsel, Cathleen Mahoney, would deliver the opening statement on behalf of the government. She proceeded to tell them that HIT represented "a squad of police officers who abused their authority by beating people with blackjacks and two-by-fours, by stealing money from people, and even by framing people for crimes they did not commit." She went on to say how Captain O'Brien put the unit together by choosing me to run the day-to-day operations. (Wrong! Tony Cotsworth picked me over O. B.'s objections. But maybe Bill Morris never knew that.) Ms. Mahoney went on, saying that the captain picked Harloff, Raggi, and Morris, that he knew there would be citizen complaints of excessive force. That the HIT Team was violating people's civil rights, but that he didn't care, and we shouldn't worry because he would take care of any complaints that came along. Then she said I, as their supervisor, let them have free rein to abuse people. That I didn't stop assaults when they occurred in my presence and, from time to time, I even set the tone by hitting and kicking unresisting people.

Remember I said when the unit was formed there were concerns about the department's Three-in-Eighteen rule? O'Brien asked Chief Urlacher if IA could red flag HIT complaints due to the number of contacts we were likely to have. This is how the government tied these two men into the "conspiracy" counts of the indictment. Ms. Mahoney told the jury that O'Brien disregarded concerns raised by both citizens and RPD members for the two and a half years HIT roamed the streets of Rochester. Let's see, according to the prosecution, for two and a half years complaints were coming in from citizens and members of the police department. You might think if nothing was being done about these complaints, some other legal authority, like the district attorney's office or local politicians, would be informed. There are always some representatives looking to champion the rights of their constituents. And let's not forget about the news media. It's not too hard to whet the appetite of an eager newspaper or television reporter with a story of police corruption. Yet with all these complaints coming in, nobody else heard about them.

Ms. Mahoney told the jury there would be a lot of witnesses in this trial, including police officers. They would also hear from Billy Morris his accounts of the brutality that occurred over the course time HIT was in operation. She concluded her opening remarks by telling the jury this had not been a war on drugs, but that we were a bunch of officers who couldn't be bothered with rules.

John Parrinello was the first defense lawyer to address the jury. The purpose of the opening statement is to tell the jury what the defense believes will be presented as evidence. It's sort of a preview of what's coming with whatever positive twist the defense attorney can put on it to give the jury a slightly different perspective. John explained that this was the second of three opportunities he would have to speak directly to them. The first being jury selection, and the third would be his closing arguments. He told them they were the ultimate fact finders. That no one can question their verdict, nor did they have to explain their verdict to anyone. He reminded them the government bore the burden of proof and it never shifted from the prosecutor's table to ours. As the lead attorney, John spoke for all of us, though he frequently referred to his client, Scott, by name. This was to make a personal connection between the jurors and the man named Harloff seated with the other defendants. He cautioned the jury about believing the testimony they would be listening to. John described the nature of our job and the conditions in which we worked every night. When he spoke of the government's conspiracy theory, John told the jury how after putting the core group of HIT together, the first thing Jim O'Brien did was invite strangers (rotating patrol officers) to participate. He mockingly paraphrased O. B. with a fictitious quote by saying "Let's go get strangers in, people from the districts. We're going to have this plan to beat people up. We don't want anybody to know about it, and we're going to go out every thirty days and get six new people to come in. We don't even know who they are." Then John emphasized to the jury what a pretty poor conspiracy that would be, adding that it was such a poor conspiracy, we even took pictures of all the people we brutalized. Every time we raided a drug house, photos were taken of the scene, the suspects, and any evidence as it was located.

In June of 1989, after fourteen months in existence, our unit received an award from the mayor. John asked the jury if it made sense to them for the mayor to be giving us an award after fourteen months of brutalizing people. He went on to explain that we received so much attention and recognition, film crews from the television stations rode with us. John said, "I guess according to the government's theory what they wanted to do is they wanted to document this conspiracy so they took TV crews with them on their raids. Logical? Hardly."

After about an hour and a half of talking (so much for thirty minutes apiece), there was an exchange between John and Judge Telesca. Parrinello had 150 pages of notes and was a little more than halfway through them. Cathleen Mahoney objected when John told the jury he felt pressured to rush through his opening remarks.

The Court:	Who is pressuring you?
Mr. Parrinello:	Your Honor, you keep making references about my opening and the time everybody's giving up. My client is looking at fifteen years in jail and I would ask for unlimited time.
The Court:	[To the jury] Ladies and gentlemen, let's take a recess. Please go into the jury room.
[Jury not present]	
The Court:	Mr. Parrinello, I know this case is important. This is your opening statement. This is not summation. I have allowed you a great deal of latitude. Nobody is picking on you and nobody is pressuring you. You have been on your feet since eight minutes after nine.
Mr. Parrinello:	Your Honor, I will stay on my feet all day if I have to—with your indulgence.
The Court:	In fairness to everybody I have to allocate the time.
Mr. Parrinello:	Why? Why are we in a hurry in this case? This case is a serious criminal case. Why are we doing assembly line justice in America? Why do things have to roll along so fast in a criminal case? These men spent seventeen to twenty years fighting crime. Their lives are at stake. Their families are here.

The exchange went on for a few more minutes with the judge telling John he had a sworn obligation to keep the trial moving along. Parrinello answered by saying, "We have the rest of our lives to do these cases." Judge Telesca told him he would have to yield to the rest of the defense at eleven o'clock. Then the jury was brought back into the courtroom. John went into detail about how Bill Morris had worked a deal with the prosecution for his cooperation and testimony. He told the jury to weigh that testimony very carefully and to note things that contradicted it.

At the end of his statement, John made a reference to the movie *A Few Good Men*. It's about two marines on trial for murder. John related a statement of Demi Moore's character to her fellow lawyer where she says she likes the two marines because they stand on a wall and protect her. Parrinello told the jury, "Those two defendants were assigned to Guantanamo Bay, Cuba, and ladies and gentlemen, these men [pointing to us] stood on a wall and protected us."

David Rothenberg, representing Greg Raggi, was the next defense attorney to address the jury. Again, while speaking on behalf of all of us, David alluded to elements of the indictment that pertained to his client. He walked the jury through the counts, location by location, and just as Scott's lawyer did, added just a little more information for the jury to consider.

Next, it was Carl Salzer's turn to speak on behalf of Mike Mazzeo. Like his two predecessors, Carl went into detail about specific charges against his client. Unlike the previous speakers, though, he was fairly brief in his statement. Carl started out by letting the jury know that contrary to Ms. Mahoney's statements, Mazzeo was not a seasoned narcotics investigator. He joined the unit as a permanent member in October of 1988. Then he broke down the charges against Mike. He told the jury they would hear testimony from a Brockport police officer by the name of Mark Cyr, and Gates police officer Gordon Whitehair. Both these officers rotated through HIT. Carl told the jury these officers from suburban police departments would testify that Mazzeo had threatened two different people with his service weapon. Mike was accused of putting his empty gun to a suspect's head and pulling the trigger. Carl said while Cyr can't be specific as to when and where this occurred, Whitehair would testify that Mazzeo threatened a drug suspect by the name of Alonzo Jackson in the back of our raid van. This was supposed to have happened on January 30, 1990. Just as in my case, it was important for the government to nail Mazzeo with a gun charge because it carried a five-year-minimum mandatory sentence. The problem with this charge is that the alleged victim said in his interviews with investigators that he never was threatened with a gun, but he was beaten up. Carl told the jury the evidence would show it was Cyr and Whitehair who beat Mr. Jackson.

Carl wrapped up his opening remarks by telling the jury about an informant by the name of Timothy McNulty. This was someone who supplied Mazzeo with drug information. McNulty was getting out of control: He'd show up for a meet stoned out of his mind on coke. He threatened to kill a police officer, and one night he showed up with a starter pistol. Mike grabbed him and went off on him, shaking him, and screaming at McNulty in an attempt to straighten him out. Mazzeo was indicted for assaulting his snitch.

Next up, defense attorney number four—my guy, John Speranza. The first thing John did was ask if the jury needed a break. They did. They had been sitting for more than four hours listening to legal arguments. Hell, it was all I could do to keep from nodding off, and it was my ass on the line. The break accomplished two things: First, it ingratiated John to Judge Telesca for his consideration of the jury. Second, it allowed the jurors to refresh themselves and be alert for John's remarks.

Speranza explained to the jury that he believed the prosecution would present its case on the conspiracy charge by working backward through the overt acts. He also reminded them that HIT had not been formed until April of 1988, and one of the overt acts of the conspiracy charge against me as a member of HIT took place in January of 1988. Then John created an interesting analogy for the jury to consider. Referring to comments made by the previous lawyers—specifically John Parrinello's because he had alluded to bad acts admitted to by numerous officers during the investigation—Speranza compared the five of us to drops of water separated from a large rain barrel. He said, "What the government has done in this prosecution, conceptually, the evidence will show, is taken a rain barrel and taken out three or four drops of water, and you say these drops of water are not fungible. [As with many of the words that came out of John's mouth, I have no idea what that means.] They are not the same as the other drops of water. We are going to remove those from this rain barrel and we are going to show you that these drops are somehow different.

"Mr. Parrinello talked about this at length when he talked about the Jamaican Organized Crime group, when he talked about the Hotel Motel group.

"That's really what he was talking about, the selective parsing out of this large rain barrel of several drops to say we condemn these drops; these drops are different; they're of a different nature; they're of a different constituency than the rest of the water in the rain barrel."

Speranza proceeded to name the charges against me. As John went down the list, Judge Telesca interrupted him by asking if his remarks would be concluded by 1:30 p.m. That not being the case, the judge said he was not going to keep the jury beyond that time. He advised the jurors to return to court at 8:30 a.m. the following day, at which time Mr. Speranza would finish his opening statement, and they would then hear from Jim O'Brien's attorney, Tony Leonardo. Before sitting down, John told the jury he hoped they would remember at least half of what he had just said.

The next morning, January 21, an artist's sketch of Mike Mazzeo and me appeared on the front page of the local section of the newspaper. Above it, the headline in half-inch bold type read, "Accused: Protectors or Abusers?" The articles associated with the picture gave a brief summary of the previous day's courtroom activity.

After the jury was seated and the usual morning pleasantries had been exchanged, John Speranza picked up where he had left off the day before. He told the jurors he was certain the government would not be able to provide evidence that I had been involved in a conspiracy over a two-and-a-half-year period to violate anyone's civil rights. He explained that the conspiracy count of the indictment was like an umbrella covering all the overt acts, and if there was no conspiracy, then the overt acts were meaningless.

John went on to talk about 65 Prospect Street, where I was alleged to have kicked a suspect in the face. Before he moved on, John made sure to inform the jury that during the investigation, the suspect was shown photographs of everyone involved in the raid. He also mentioned the suspect picked Billy Morris, not me, as the kicker. He mentioned 880 East Main Street, where it was alleged that I struck a suspect in the head with my service weapon, and 20 Barons Street, where the government said I failed as a supervisor to intervene when another suspect was assaulted.

Speranza ended his remarks by telling the jury they would hear numerous contradictions in testimony by many witnesses. He reminded them I was cloaked in the presumption of innocence and, if they didn't find the evidence believable, they shouldn't hesitate to find me not guilty.

Tony Leonardo, representing Jim O'Brien, was the final defense attorney to speak to the jury. He was a large, imposing figure dressed in a perfectly tailored double-breasted suit. Tony didn't speak long. He didn't have to. Leonardo was known for his photographic memory and for addressing the jury in a booming voice without notes. He gave an opening statement that would make an evangelical minister proud. For that reason, I'm going to reprint his entire speech, word for word, right out of the trial transcript.

The Court:	Mr. Leonardo.
Mr. Leonardo:	Good morning. I sat over there yesterday and listened to these fine people talk. I'm trying to think of what I'm going to say to you people to put it all together and to start the journey. I'm going to call it a circus, but we'll get to that later. Isn't everybody saying the same thing here, the government, the defense? Let me say it in simple words. There's a slogan that Monroe County came out with a little while ago and it's on

billboards. The slogan I put over my kid's bed. It says drugs lie. It's a heck of a message. It's what the government said. There's a war on drugs. Every one of these fine men said it, drugs lie. The government said and every one of these fine men said to you, the HIT team tried. I want to put one of those signs here. Drugs lie. They tried. Didn't hear about what the law is. Mr. Parrinello is a great lawyer. He objected to what Judge Telesca said about the law. I don't know. They're both right. The Supreme Court of the United States, they still don't know what it is. They're arguing every day about it. You see that little book that was written two hundred years ago that he holds up? I'll tell you one thing as this trial starts, if those fine men who wrote that book two hundred years ago knew what was going on today, they'd have tears in their eyes that this government interprets that book to prosecute these men for trying. It's simple. It's plain. It's honest and it's true. That's the defense. I should talk about this case with my head and not my heart. I should just talk about him [pointing to O'Brien] and separate him from everybody else because he's only got one count in this case, but I can't do that because that's not in my heart. They tried. They [pointing to the prosecutors] know it. And they're twisting the law. I'm sorry. Who is this guy? I don't want to get emotional. Who's Jim O'Brien and how did all these men get here? Forty-six years old married twenty-seven years, four children in college, solid citizen. The lawyers got to say something good about him. Bah, sounds nice. Twenty-one years old started with the Rochester Police Department. Walked the beat for five years. A lot of street experience, a lot of savvy dealing with people like you and me every day. Twenty-five years old, Sergeant O'Brien. Youngest in the history of the Rochester Police Department. Started the Crisis Intervention Unit. Every police officer in the City of Rochester from the chief on down had to take the course, how to deal with family problems, how to help officers deal with problems. Victim's Assistance Program, federal grant, Jim O'Brien. Help the people, the victims of crime, talking with them, dealing with them, understanding their problems, that's his strength. Twenty-nine, he got lucky. Lieutenant O'Brien. Youngest in the history. Thirty-three, Captain O'Brien. Youngest in the history of the Rochester Police Department, this big conspirator. Five people in the history of the Rochester Police Department—five—got the Medal of Valor. Guess who's one of them? The big guy on the end. Twenty-three years he was head of the hostage negotiation team. You've seen it on TV. Every time there's a life and death situation, they call the SWAT team. They've got all the police cars surrounding the building because some idiot is robbing a bank, holding people hostage. Whether it's some guy up on a building, whether it's some distraught father who wants to kill himself and his kids, he'd go in, talk, listen, reason, stop an explosion from happening. You've got to be a doctor to save more lives in this community than he did. No scalpel. Sometimes just with an ear. 1985, lo and behold, war on drugs. President Reagan, Bennett, [drug czar William Bennett] all over the United States—not just here. SCIS needed a new commander, somebody that could do something, somebody that could fight these animals selling death all over the streets—everywhere not just here, all over the country. Who did they get? Jim O'Brien. Oh, you're going to hear Billy Morris. He's diabolical. I was reading—he's got some notes. His notes said all the men loved Captain O'Brien. He hated drugs. He hated drugs not because he was a cop. He's got four kids, and he tried to do something about it. He took over this unit, Special Criminal Investigations—whatever that means, organized crime, gambling and prostitution and narcotics. He said uhn-nn. We're changing the unit. The men working gambling and prostitution, no more. You go work on drugs. He started the Monroe County Drug Enforcement Task Force. There's a million people in Monroe County. I want a cop from every town in this county to get down here and work with us to fight death, to fight destruction, do something about drugs. All that work, it didn't help. It didn't help anywhere in the United States. So in comes—and they didn't tell you this—the federal government. Remember all the TV programs with Bennett, all the drug sales on all the streets in the United States? The HIT team concept was a federal grant. The federal government—we the people—came up with the money for this grant. Jim put it together. He wrote a plan. He submitted it to the federal government. They approved the money to set up the plan to get police officers to go out on the streets and take back the streets from the animals. That's what he did. He got the plan. He got the money. Now, what was he going to do with it? Well, here's what the concept was: Four seasoned officers from the Vice Squad who knew about the city, knew about drugs, knew about officer safety, knew what it would take to make a drug arrest. Give me four seasoned guys. He wasn't looking for pencil pushers. He wasn't looking for investigators. He was looking for real men. Does he look like a pencil pusher? These are real men. He didn't pick these guys because he went out drinking with them. He didn't pick them because they were his friends. He picked them because he knew they knew the streets and they could get the job done. None of them wanted the job. Who in their right mind would want the job? Here's what it was supposed to be: Bulletproof vests, semiautomatic weapons and shotguns, black shirts with POLICE on it, black hat, and they get seven rookies for thirty days every month to go out with them. They've got to train them, take the streets back. That was the plan because all the people in the community, all the people living in the city didn't have any faith in the police anymore. Drugs were everywhere being sold on their street, next door, drug houses, all night long. Nobody had faith in the police. This whole problem, visibility. Take the streets back, get the confidence of the people. I don't know about you, but all I heard in the opening statement from the government was sparks and fire. Yes, that's what he said. We've got to take the streets back. We're not dealing with choirboys. There's going to be force. Everybody knew that. Go by the book. Do it the right way. There's going to be force. There's going to be problems. Ladies and gentlemen—don't get mad at me—shit happened. It happened. It had to happen when you're dealing with what they were dealing with. Sit back and judge. That was the HIT team. That's what this case was all about, and that's what you're going to see in this courtroom. Thirty months. You people, every day you get up, five days a week. You put aside your family. You put aside your personal problems and you go to work. I do the same thing. At five o'clock at night, five-thirty, we go home. The HIT team, they left their homes. They left their families and their personal problems every day at five o'clock and they went to work, took their clothes off and put on a black outfit—instill in these people—bulletproof vests, POLICE on it, put the hats on, checked their weapons, got ready to go out. The hotline, that hotline was ringing off the wall. All the people in the community, they looked out their windows. They saw animals dealing death. Who are you going to call? The HIT team. Yeah, there was trouble in the neighborhoods. They were animals. These men were out there every day in their face stopping them, trying to stop them. That's what this case is about. That's what you're going to hear. Drugs lie. The HIT team tried, and shame on the

United States of America. Shame on them. Shame on the people at this [prosecution] table. Shame on all of them for putting the judge, everybody else in this courtroom here through this. It's a circus. It's not right. It's not fair, and it's not what those people two hundred years ago had in mind when they wrote that book. Thank you.

About the time the echo from Tony's voice subsided, Judge Telesca ordered a ten-minute recess.

Street corner drug arrest in April 1988 at Jefferson and Columbia Avenues. Greg Raggi is second from left. Billy Morris is center rear. Courtesy of WHEC-TV News 10 NBC.

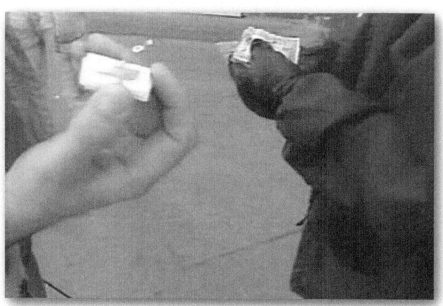

Heroin and cash recovered from the suspect arrested at Jefferson and Columbia Avenues in 1988. Courtesy of WHEC-TV News 10 NBC.

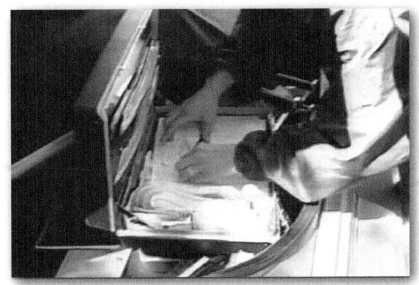

Arrest reports are completed at the scene, and the booking copy is sent with the patrol officer who transports the suspect to the city lock-up. The rest of the report is added to the arrest package, which is completed later back in the office. This process is repeated for as many arrests as are made during the shift. Courtesy of WHEC-TV News 10 NBC.

Billy Morris. Note his salt-and-pepper long hair and beard. Kind of like the description from Varian Hogan as the person who kicked him at 65 Prospect Street. Courtesy of WHEC-TV News 10 NBC.

The author describing the arrest process to a local TV news
reporter. Courtesy of WHEC-TV News 10 NBC.

An active, vacant drug house (covered porch) at 65 Prospect Street in
April 1988, which was fortified with a steel door. The windows were
covered with steel grates on the inside and three-quarter-inch plywood
on the outside. This is the location where Varian Hogan said he was
kicked in the face. Courtesy of WHEC-TV News 10 NBC.

An active, vacant drug house on Seward Street in Genesee Section where a city school teacher was arrested after buying cocaine in April 1988. Courtesy of WHEC-TV News 10 NBC.

The HIT Team receiving an award from the City of Rochester in June 1989. Left to right: Scott Harloff, Billy Morris, the author (recovering from knee surgery), Greg Raggi, and Mike Mazzeo. Courtesy of the author.

The author and his attorney, John Speranza, hugging outside of the federal building following a unanimous acquittal of all charges on March 26, 1993. Courtesy of Rochester *Democrat & Chronicle*.

Twelve

The government was ready to call its first witness. Ann Marie Hoffer had been the secretary in SCIS for about seven years. She would be the first of "our own" the prosecution would call to testify against us. Before she was brought into the courtroom, there was a brief, albeit lively, discussion as to the relevance of her anticipated testimony.

Ann Marie was basically called to do in Jim O'Brien. He was charged with only one count of conspiracy to "injure, oppress, threaten, and intimidate" suspects between 1988 and 1990. The crux of Annie's testimony was that suspects were abused in the interview rooms located near her reception desk. While she mentioned Raggi and Harloff with respect to "noises" coming from the interview rooms, she could not provide any specific time frames. She said the noise coming from the interview rooms was so bad at times that she had to leave the area. The nail she was expected to provide for O'Brien's coffin was that she had brought these perceived abuses to his attention, but he did nothing about it.

The objections flew fast and furious during her direct examination. The first one, by John Parrinello, came after the tenth question asked by Mr. Gennaco. The majority of the objections were based on the fact that Ann Marie's testimony was not specific to anything in the indictment as it applied to us. After using a large diagram to give the jury a perspective of the layout of the SCIS office, Mr. Gennaco had Ann Marie identify all of us sitting at the defense table. Then, in what can only be described as a broad-brush attempt to paint a picture for the jury, she was asked about the beatings in the interview rooms that she had told investigators about. Of course now, no names were mentioned except Captain O'Brien's. Apparently, the jury was supposed to infer it was us who were administering the beatings.

Parrinello would be the first to cross-examine Ms. Hoffer. John focused his questioning around interviews she'd had with RPD investigators. With documentation of the meetings, he began with her first interview on October 23, 1990, when she gave a statement to Investigators Boccardo and D'Ambrosia. First, John asked Annie if she saw Scott Harloff's name anywhere in the statement. She answered no. Then he got her to talk about a specific incident she had told the investigators about—an incident where she said a suspect had been beaten.

> Q. And you were talking about witnessing that beating in the SCIS office, weren't you?
> A. A particular beating are you asking me?
> Q. Yes, by a particular person. Remember that interview on October 23, 1990, about a beating in the SCIS office…
> A. Uhm-uhm.
> Q. —and a particular person who did the beating?
> A. Yes.
> Q. Who was the particular; wasn't it Rob Aponte? [Narcotics Officer not in HIT]
> A. Yes.
> Q. Do you see Rob Aponte sitting at this [defense] table?
> A. No.
> Q. Where is Rob Aponte working today?
> A. Which police precinct? I don't know.
> Q. No, is he working with the Rochester Police Department?
> A. I believe he still is, yes.
> Q. Did you tell Mr. Gennaco that Rob Aponte beat a person in the SCIS office?
> A. Yes.

Q. I see. And, Rob Aponte is still a police officer, right?
A. Yes.
Q. As far as you know he hasn't been charged with anything, right?
A. To the best of my knowledge.
Q. Yes, and Scott Harloff's name isn't in this document about beating anybody in SCIS, is he?
A. No.

Then John moved on to Ann Marie's second interview, on October 29, 1990, when she told Investigator Rob Wetzel and Sergeant Mark Gerbino about a Jamaican who was beaten in the SCIS office. She said Officers George Markert, Joe Celorio, and Kenny Mann were present along with Billy Morris. Then Parrinello got Annie to point out to the jury that the first three were still with the RPD, the first two still in Vice. And that none of them were sitting at the defense table.

When John was finished, David Rothenberg questioned Ms. Hoffer about the accuracy of the diagram of the SCIS office the prosecution had admitted into evidence. She had indicated in her testimony that it was not true and accurate to her knowledge. David wanted the chart removed from evidence, but the judge denied his request.

Tony Leonardo cross-examined Ann Marie next. He asked the secretary about the one and only complaint of missing money she had been aware of. The point of his questioning was that in all the time Ann Marie had been in SCIS while Jim O'Brien was in charge, there was only one complaint of missing money. With the help of the witness, Leonardo explained to the jury how O. B. had referred the individual to Internal Affairs to file a formal complaint, and that contrary to allegations in the indictment, he did not try to cover up the incident. Tony ended his questioning by having Ann Marie explain to the jury that the office is completely separate from the rest of the police department. And, even with hundreds of suspects brought there over the years, she never saw any members of HIT strike a single one. John Speranza and Carl Salzer had no questions for witness number one. After an hour and forty-five minutes on the stand, she was excused and the judge ordered a brief recess. Annie left the courtroom crying.

The prosecution called their second witness, RPD Investigator James Dean Thomas. I never knew him to use James as his first name. Mean Dean, as he was often called, was brought in specifically for me. He joined the department six months after I did, and we ended up working together in Genesee Section. In December of 1985, I made sergeant and went to Lake Section while Dean went to the Vice Squad to work narcotics. He was later promoted to investigator.

Jessica Ginsburg, one of Mr. Gennaco's assistants, handled the direct examination for the prosecution. After the usual witness background information was provided for the jury, Ms. Ginsburg had Investigator Thomas lay out the makeup of the HIT Squad as he knew it to be. Again, working from a large chart, the government wanted the jury to see our names in large print to remind them who the bad guys were. The problem was that they were referring to the chart as the "permanent members" of HIT during the relevant time period, January 1988 through October 1990. The fact was there were other permanent members over the years not reflected on the chart. And, as it had been stated before, HIT wasn't formed until April of 1988. Numerous objections were made, most of which were overruled, but the judge did refuse to let the government use the chart because it was not accurate. It was a moral victory if nothing else.

Then Ms. Ginsburg got to the real purpose of Dean's testimony: the raid at 65 Prospect Street on January 15, 1988. This was the heavily fortified drug house we raided three months before HIT was even established. It was the reason I was charged with Overt Act #2 in Count I (the conspiracy), and Count III.

On this particular raid, after experiencing considerable difficulty gaining entry to the house, three people were arrested. We had to go through a window, and once inside it was almost pitch black. As we fanned out through the vacant building, officers went to various locations. I went directly to the basement along with one of the uniformed officers assisting us. A short time later we were joined by Bill Morris and Roy Hopkins who helped with the search of the basement. Two suspects were found hiding in a dead-end stairway and were taken into custody. Upon initial entry, Dean Thomas had gone to a small room on the first floor. There he found a suspect named Varian Hogan hiding and took him into custody. In the process, Mr. Hogan received a split lip and a broken tooth. Guess who got indicted for it three years later? Interestingly enough, Mr. Hogan went to Internal Affairs thirteen days after the raid to make a formal complaint. He described the officer who kicked him in the face: white male about six feet two inches tall, skinny, thirty-five, long salt-and-pepper hair, beard, and mustache, wearing brown cowboy boots. With the exception of the boots, he described Billy Morris to a T. It was the boots that would provide Morris the opportunity to shift the blame to me. Our since-convicted drug dealer would repeat his recollection of the incident to the FBI a few years later.

Dean Thomas was interviewed in Internal Affairs on June 14, 1988, and never even mentioned my being with him when he arrested Mr. Hogan. When he was interviewed by the FBI on July 29, 1991, during the civil-rights investigation, he said he was "reasonably sure" I was one of the officers kicking Mr. Hogan. On August 14, 1991, in another interview, he said I *was* (my emphasis) kicking Mr. Hogan in the head. The following day, Thomas told the grand jury I was kicking Mr. Hogan in the head wearing some type of dress boot. It's amazing what a witness letter from the Justice Department, not to mention a grant of immunity, will do for a person's memory.

It's time to set the record straight with respect to "the boots." In 1987, I bought a pair of Frye western boots. I still had them years later, and you would never believe they were as old as they were. They're in mint condition because I never, ever wore them in the winter. I didn't even wear them in the summer, because they made my feet sweat. Basically, I wore them only in the fall or spring. Some years I didn't wear them at all. But I sure as hell wasn't wearing them on January 15, 1988, during a raid at an unbelievably filthy drug house that I had been to before! Billy Morris knew I owned a pair of western boots. My guess is he convinced his handlers, in spite of Mr. Hogan's description of his assailant, that since I did own a pair of boots, it must have been me doing the kicking. Since Morris told the feds about Dean's unnecessary force, which Thomas would later admit to under the protection of immunity, he may as well corroborate Billy's version of the raid. Especially since that's the only way Dean would be immunized.

The first day of testimony ended with Investigator Thomas's direct examination by Jessica Ginsburg. At 1:15 p.m. she ended an hour of questioning, and since there was no court on Fridays, Dean would have to go home and wait three more days to be cross-examined. I can only imagine what it must have been like for him trying to fall asleep knowing John Speranza and the rest of our Dream Team were waiting to chat with him.

Thirteen

Friday's newspaper headlines were predictable: "Interviews were like beatings, says secretary. Witness turned up radio to escape noise." In reference to Dean Thomas's testimony, the headline read, "Witness hints at police beatings." Keep in mind, some people read only the headlines. The story recapped the previous day's events in the courtroom. After relating Ann Marie's description of what she heard emanating from the interview rooms, the reporter saved anything positive for the very end of the quarter-page, two-column article. It said, "During cross-examination, however, Hoffer admitted that when she initially testified before a grand jury she did not implicate any of the officers on trial. Instead, she implicated four other vice officers. Further, she testified that she never saw any of the HIT officers strike a suspect."

In Saturday's paper there were two articles. One referred to the "legal theatrics" employed by our attorneys. The reporter felt Tony Leonardo deserved the best performance award for his opening statements. The second article had to do with the memo Chief Irving issued that outlined conditions RPD Officers were to adhere to when dealing with our attorneys. Leonardo told the reporter the bottom line was that a lot of people were afraid to talk to our lawyers for fear of reprisals by the department.

On Monday, January 25, I ate my usual breakfast of oatmeal and coffee at Perkins while reading the morning paper. The first article was headlined "Defendant's lawyers get lesson in etiquette. Judge issues call for more decorum." In addition to prefacing Dean Thomas's upcoming testimony, the article described the mood in the courtroom as it had thus far been observed: "restrained and combative." We, the defendants, were described as wearing dark suits and no expressions. John Parrinello was said to have voiced an objection to nearly every sentence spoken by the first two prosecution witnesses. It was also noted that there had been forty-five objections in three hours and about a dozen requests for a mistrial, all of which had been denied by the judge. The attorneys had also been admonished by Judge Telesca to conform to commonly recognized standards of courtroom behavior. The article mentioned a little tension between Mike Berkow and me on the first day of the trial. "During a break, Berkow walked through a set of swinging half doors. Alessi was behind him and Berkow stopped to hold the doors open. Alessi scowled. He waited for Berkow to clear the entrance, and then thrust opens the doors, smacking them into the wall. A friend came over and took Alessi's arm, quietly ushering him out of the room."

I found the second article to be a little more thought provoking. "Defense asks: Why were members of HIT singled out? Witnesses indicate wider problems." The reporter pointed out that the first witness, Ann Marie Hoffer, had told a grand jury that four officers—but not those on trial—were responsible for slapping and bumping suspects in the police interview rooms. Dean Thomas admitted to striking a suspect and said he witnessed another officer—again, no one at the defense table—put the same suspect's head into a toilet to retrieve two packets of cocaine. The article further related that prosecutors had said dozens of officers would testify about witnessing and taking part in similar acts, suggesting this kind of behavior, or at least knowledge of it, was widespread. The reporter asked how the five of us were distinguished from our colleagues. "'The question in my mind,' said lawyer David Rothenberg, who is defending Gregory R. Raggi, 'is how did these five officers get selected out of the dozens of officers, then prosecuted criminally, when everybody else got a pat on the back or a finger wagged in their face?'" With breakfast and the newspaper both finished, it was time to head for the federal building. As I got up to leave, one of the two men sitting at the next table smiled at me and said, "Good luck today."

Before the jury was brought into the courtroom, Judge Telesca admonished the lawyers on both sides for their conduct since the beginning of the trial. "Ladies and gentlemen, this case is very emotional and volatile. Emotion, however, cannot dominate our actions as professionals and affect the orderly conduct of this trial. This trial, like any trial, is a search for the truth. It is not combat. I have on a number of occasions suggested to counsel that they conduct themselves in a professional manner and refrain from yelling at witnesses or at each other, and to have appropriate respect for each other and this court and its proceedings. That is not asking too much, because it is a sworn duty of all attorneys. I am no longer suggesting this course of conduct, but instead I am insisting on it. Therefore, I will not hesitate to resort to the imposition of sanctions for improper professional courtroom behavior including the ultimate removal of counsel from further participation in this case if necessary. I am committed to move this case along in an orderly, professional manner."

The jury was produced, and Dean Thomas was called to the stand at 8:40 a.m. After some minor clarification of his prior direct testimony by Ms. Ginsburg, the witness was tendered to my attorney, John Speranza. John's preliminary questioning concentrated on the investigator's prior interviews and statements, starting with Thomas's first appearance in Internal Affairs approximately four and a half years earlier on June 14, 1988. During the investigation, Dean had seven interviews between November 6, 1990, and July 31, 1991. He was called to Internal Affairs again on August 14, 1991, and into the grand jury the following day. That's the day he received his witness letter. In federal jargon, that's the one that says you can either be on the bus (with everyone else who cut a deal for immunity) or you can be left behind (with all the other targets of the investigation) as the bus passes you by. Dean's letter of immunity was dated January 7, 1993. Prior to his trial appearance, he had three meetings with Mr. Gennaco, Ms. Mahoney, and Lieutenants Duffy and

Berkow. He also met three times with Ms. Ginsburg, who would guide him through his direct testimony.

Once John had established for the jury just how much attention had been paid to the investigator in preparation for his court appearance, he began to take Dean down memory lane. Back to January 15, 1988, and the raid at 65 Prospect Street. Keep in mind the only reason for Dean Thomas's testimony was to convince the jury I had kicked a drug dealer in the face at that location with my much-celebrated cowboy boots—a story first related to federal investigators by none other than their star witness, Billy Morris, who, as you now know, matched the drug dealer's description of the officer who kicked him.

Like an artist starting out with a blank canvas, John began to paint a picture for the jury, all the while eliciting affirmative responses from the witness. Speranza started with the time of the raid, late afternoon in January, to establish diminishing daylight and temperature conditions. Then he described the fortifications of the house with its steel door secured by angle iron. The windows were covered with three-quarter-inch plywood and steel mesh grates. He mentioned that it took an estimated five minutes with a battering ram to get through the window. John referred to it as storming a medieval castle. He talked about how once we were inside the house it was pitch dark with the exception of a few small candles in the kitchen.

After the backdrop had been established, John began to illustrate for the jury the state of mind of his witness, and of the rest of the raid team, amid all the chaos at the time. Anticipation, nervousness, and fear all came into play, while our primary goal was to get out of this operation alive. Speranza went through a litany of possible hazards waiting for us inside the drug house including armed sociopaths, vicious dogs, and booby traps. These were the easy questions. After all, even though it had occurred five years ago, all the things Dean described were pretty standard conditions on most drug raids. Now came the hard part. John began to test the investigator's memory as to the names of the officers present and what they had been wearing, specifically on their feet. John shifted gears, going back to Dean's Internal Affairs statement, which he gave six months after the raid. In that statement, he said it was just him and Greg Raggi in the small room with Mr. Hogan. Now he says he doesn't remember Greg being in the room, but I was and so were Bill Morris and Roy Hopkins. Then came the following exchange:

Q. Now let's jump it up five years to last Thursday when as of Thursday you testified that it was you, Morris, Hopkins, and Alessi in this room, right?

A. Yes.

Q. All right. What was Morris wearing in this rendition, do you remember?

A. No.

Q. Do you remember what Hopkins was wearing in this rendition?

A. No.

Q. Do you remember what you were wearing?

A. No.

Q. What kind of clothing did Tom Alessi have on?

A. Other than the boots that I saw?

Q. Yes.

A. Don't know.

Q. You don't know. But the only thing you remember were the boots that he was wearing, right?

A. Yes.

Q. You don't remember anything else but boots, correct?

A. Right.

Q. You are here to deliver two things: you shone the light in this guy's face and there were no injuries and Alessi was wearing boots. That's your mission, isn't it? That's what you have to do in this courtroom to get your deal, isn't it?

A. No.

Q. It's not? Is not, OK. Five years ago you remember nothing. You remember events from day to day, from testimony to testimony, but yet of all the things—can't remember Sensabaugh's

boots. Raggi, I can't remember what he was wearing; anybody
else who was there, I don't what they had on, what this guy
had on for a jacket I don't know; what did he have for pants, I
don't know. He [pointing to me] had boots on. The only one
with boots, right?

A. That's what I—

Q. Did you check everyone else's feet? You said you didn't, right?

A. Right.

Q. What were you wearing?

A. Sneakers.

Q. Sneaks in the middle of January?

A. Right.

Q. Was Hopkins wearing sneaks?

A. I don't know.

Q. You don't know. He was in the room with you, right? Billy
Morris, was he wearing sneaks?

A. I don't know.

Q. You don't know. He was in the room with you. Could Billy
Morris have had boots on?

A. Sure.

Q. Sure, he could have. How about Hopkins, could he have had
boots on?

A. Yes.

Q. Sure, he could have. How about Greg Raggi, could he have had
boots on?

A. Sure.

Q. Sure he could have. So now in your second rendition of who was
there, out of all the people who were there—four—three of 'em
could have had boots, right?

A. Uhm-uhm.

Q. You're the only one with no boots?

A. Right.

Q. You can't have boots on because you might have kicked him in
the face. So you've got to have no boots, but everybody has got

to have boots. Now you didn't say on direct-examination that you thought, well, all these other guys, they might have had boots. You said Tom Alessi had boots because you've got to nail him, right?

A. No.

Q. Excuse me a moment. OK. Last Thursday under direct-examination you indicated to Ms. Ginsburg that your testimony in 1988 was a lie, right?

A. Yes.

Q. OK. Now, this morning you told me that maybe it isn't a lie because you said that's the way you remembered it when you testified in 1988, correct?

A. Uhm-uhm.

Q. Isn't that what you told me? Yes or no.

A. Yes.

Q. You did. So in point of fact you remembered it this way in 1988 as you testified to here under oath then it may very well not be a lie, correct?

A. What I testified to in 1988?

Q. Yes. You said it to me moments ago that's the way I remembered it when I asked you about Raggi and yourself in the room. Didn't you say that?

A. Regarding that, yes.

Q. Oh, just regarding that?

A. Yes.

Q. OK. So that was the only thing that you remembered that may have been accurate, correct?

A. I'm just basing that on—

Q. Correct?

A. Yeah.

Q. OK. So there's no question about it that it may have been correct then when you said just you and Raggi were in the room, right?

A. It may have been, yes.

And so went the cross-examination. John asked Dean about all the meetings he had with members of the prosecution team. In five or six conversations with different investigators, he never mentioned 65 Prospect Street. He had even initiated some of those meetings because he feared he would become a target of the investigation due to his involvement in certain cases. In one such case, Thomas was named in a lawsuit for kicking a defendant. During these meetings, Dean was asked if he had assisted HIT on any cases. He testified that he told the feds of two operations where he worked with us: once on Wilkins Street and another time on Weiland Road. As late as July 17 of 1991, there was no mention of Prospect Street. Then John got to the meat of the testimony. It wasn't until July 29, 1991, three years and seven months after the infamous drug raid, that Dean Thomas decided to tell federal investigators about it. It also just happened to be after he found out Billy Morris had become the government's star witness.

Back in 1988, prior to giving statements in Internal Affairs, Billy and Dean told each other what they were going to say. Basically, it was that Varian Hogan, the dope dealer who received a split lip and chipped tooth, had fallen while trying to flee the police. Now that 65 Prospect Street figured prominently in the indictment, and knowing he had dovetailed his Internal Affairs statement with that of Billy Morris, Dean apparently came to the conclusion that it would be a good time to once again go with the Morris version of what happened to Mr. Hogan. That version being me kicking him with the boots Billy said I was wearing. And, for his cooperation, Investigator Dean Thomas received federal immunity. Also, let's not forget, after all the time that had passed and all the cases Dean had worked on, the only thing he definitely remembered was what I was wearing on my feet that day.

John reiterated for the jury the numerous meetings the witness had with the prosecution team in preparation for his testimony. Speranza got Dean to explain that in addition to having been granted immunity by the government, he was also given a free pass by the Rochester Police Department. John had a copy of the investigator's Internal Affairs Career History Report. It showed an entry dated

August 14, 1991, with Chief Roy Irving as the complainant in a departmental investigation. The date of the incident was January 15, 1988 (the date of the Prospect Street raid), and the disposition of the complaint read, "Sustained, w/no discipline." The details of the complaint read, "Failed to document SRR." SRR stands for Subject Resistance Report. Before the days of political correctness, it was simply called a Use of Force Report and was to be completed whenever an officer had to use more force than you normally would just handcuffing a suspect who wasn't resisting arrest. The bottom line was they said Dean used force on Mr. Hogan and didn't document it. Funny thing, though, there was no mention of all the times he was untruthful in the numerous statements he gave prior to July 29, 1991. You see, that's the difference between being on the bus and watching it pass you by.

John finished his cross-examination of Investigator Thomas with this exchange:

Q. Now, they didn't tell you, but maybe you knew that their informant Morris had put the finger on Alessi and they needed a guy like you to come in and finish it off, another witness to support their informant Morris and they got you, didn't they?
A. No.
Q. No? Immunity, lie, no discipline, you don't lose a dime of pay. They bought you lock, stock, and barrel.
   Ms. Ginsburg: Objection, your Honor.
   The Court: Sustained.
Q. And you went into that grand jury and you delivered exactly what they wanted you to deliver and you did it here. I have no more questions for you.

After three hours and twenty minutes, John ended his cross-examination at noon. For the next ten minutes, David Rothenberg, Greg's attorney, questioned Dean about all the reports and documents he had reviewed during his many meetings with the prosecutors. David asked Dean if it was his understanding that all those meetings and the reports he had been shown had been for the purpose of helping the prosecution get at the truth. Thomas answered yes, and Rothenberg attempted to show Dean a report in which Varian Hogan had identified a photograph of Billy Morris as the person who kicked him. Ms. Ginsburg objected on the basis that there was no foundation that Dean had ever been shown the report. BINGO! That was David's whole point. They never did show Dean *that* report. While he wasn't permitted to read the document to the witness, the judge did allow David to ask if the contents were ever brought to his attention. When Dean answered no, Rothenberg ended his questioning by asking him if he had any explanation why he hadn't been shown the report in this search for the truth. Again, the answer was no.

Waiting in the on-deck circle was Scott's lawyer, John Parrinello. The very first question out of John's mouth was, "Do you have a nickname?" Dean looked a little surprised, which I'm sure was Parrinello's intention, and quickly answered, "No." After asking the question again and without waiting for a response, John told the witness to look at the jury and tell them what he was sometimes referred to by his fellow officers. Dean said he was given the nickname Mean Dean in high school but that he objected to it. I remembered when guys would call him that when we worked in Genesee Section together. What I couldn't remember was him ever objecting to it. Not then or when anybody called him that in SCIS.

Parrinello then grilled the witness about the numerous meetings he had with the prosecution team. John would give Dean a particular date then ask the location of the meeting, who was there, how long it lasted, and if anyone took notes. Then John went through a number of issues inherent to drug trafficking. This included the use of dangerous dogs, the use of juveniles, prostitution, and AIDS. When he touched on the subject of drug-related homicides, there was this exchange:

Q. With respect to murders, sir, your experience that there were murders over drugs?

A. Yes.

Q. And what year did we set a record for murders in Rochester; wasn't it 1991?

A. Yes.

Q. And what year did the HIT Squad stop?
   Ms. Ginsburg: Objection, your Honor.
   The Court: If he knows.

Q. What year did the HIT Squad stop operating; wasn't that October of 1990, sir?

A. Yes.

It's funny how every now and then one of life's simple pleasures puts a smile on your face when you least expect it. While I sat there, I remembered being on suspension during the summer of '91. I heard about an interview from a homicide investigation. While questioning a young man, an RPD investigator asked why there were so many guns on the street. The guy replied, "That's easy, there's no more HIT Squad. You never knew when they would come around a corner and jump out of a van. Nobody wanted to get caught with a gun by those guys."

John went over with Dean all the dangers associated with narcotics investigations. He touched on the shortcomings of the criminal justice system and the demoralizing effect it has on cops. Parrinello has a way of sneaking up on a witness with a question right out of the blue. He had been talking about how we'd received an award from the mayor and that we'd had television crews riding along with us. He asked Dean if he was aware of the chief playing videotapes at section roll calls reminding officers not to have contact with us and what to do if they were subpoenaed by the defense. Then without breaking stride, John asked the witness if he knew Billy Morris and did he know of any reason Billy Morris would put Dean's name on a "big hitters" list. "Objection, your Honor!"

Apparently, Ms. Ginsburg didn't see the question coming either. The judge allowed the question and Dean said he could only speculate, but that it would be a lie. John's last question:

Q. Sir, you don't know whether or not any of the conduct performed by Sergeant Alessi in sixty-five Prospect Street caused any injury to Varian Hogan, do you?
A. No.

Tony Leonardo, like many defense attorneys, doesn't always ask a witness a direct question. Instead, his questions begin as a statement of what he believes (and would like the jury to believe) is a fact that requires only a yes or no answer. It's one way of having some control over what comes out of a witness's mouth. If anything else is about to be volunteered, the attorney can quickly cut the answer off with something like, "Please, sir, just yes or no."

After confirming that Jim O'Brien had been Dean's commanding officer for about five years, Tony said, "Now, you've testified about this incident—and I'm not going to get into any of the details at sixty-five Prospect Street—but you never once told that guy [pointing to O'Brien] what happened inside sixty-five Prospect Street, did you?"

"No." The witness answered.

After a couple more positive statements on his client's behalf, resulting in confirmatory responses, Tony ended his cross-examination.

Carl Salzer's only question of Dean Thomas was to confirm that Mike Mazzeo had not been at 65 Prospect Street or 391 Norton Street. On redirect, Ms. Ginsburg brought up the question of my footwear again. She asked Dean how he knew it was me wearing the boots. He said he had seen them before the raid and recognized my legs and feet when he saw them. Amazing. But my attorney wasn't about to have the jury left with that impression. Speranza pressed Dean again about the raid briefing where he said he recalled seeing my boots.

Q. Do you recall testifying that you don't even remember being at the briefing? "I do not remember the briefing. I honestly don't remember the briefing." Remember that?

A. Yeah. I didn't remember where it was.

Q. Now, I asked you at this briefing—you didn't remember having the briefing, correct?

A. Right.

Q. You didn't remember where it was, correct?

A. Right.

Q. You don't remember who was there, correct?

A. Right.

Q. You don't remember when it was, correct?

A. Right.

Q. You don't remember anything about it, correct?

A. Correct.

Q. The only thing you remember—of all the things you don't remember—one thing comes out in your mind, and it's Tom Alessi's legs and the fact that he had boots on, correct?

A. Yes.

Q. It's fair to say then that's the only thing that stuck in your mind about this whole briefing, correct?

A. Yes.

Q. All right. Now, in this testimony on August the fourteenth of '91 where you testified in the PSS [Internal Affairs] just one day before you went into the grand jury, you didn't mention anywhere in this testimony that the only thing you remembered of all the things that happened in that briefing were Tom Alessi's legs and feet, did you?

A. No.

Q. You didn't say that there, did you?

A. No.

Q. You said you didn't remember anything, right?

A. Correct.

Q. So somewhere between August the fourteenth of '91 and today you remember—of all the things you don't remember, you remember Tom Alessi's feet and his boots, right?

A. Correct.

Judge Telesca had already declared it had been a long day, and shortly after the witness's last answer, he announced we were in recess until 8:30 a.m.

Fourteen

Surprisingly, the next day's newspaper didn't have as much coverage of Dean Thomas's testimony as I'd thought it would. "Prosecution witness admits he had lied about '88 raid." It would have been great if they had just printed that and not the rest of the article. Dean was quoted as saying, "I made the decision that it was time to stop lying," and the article went on to say how he watched me kick a drug suspect in the mouth while wearing cowboy boots. I thought the reporter could have balanced it a little by citing John Parrinello's final question and Thomas's answer. Remember the one about not being able to say that I caused any injury to Mr. Hogan? The article did, however, note that the witness was not prosecuted or disciplined for his actions during the raid. It even had John Speranza's quote, "They bought you—lock, stock, and barrel."

The prosecution's first witness of the day was the physician's assistant who had seen Varian Hogan at Saint Mary's Hospital. Hogan had been brought in for treatment prior to being processed for arrest. Jessica Ginsburg questioned Mr. David Elio for the first fifteen minutes of his testimony. She had him explain to the jury where he worked and for how long. Mr. Elio went through all his training and qualifications. Eventually, Ms. Ginsburg asked the witness if he had been working at Saint Mary's on January 15, 1988. The purpose of Mr. Elio's appearance was to describe the injuries to Varian Hogan when he was brought to the hospital after the raid. Mr. Hogan had refused treatment, and about all the PA could do was recommend he get his lip sutured and visit the dental clinic for his chipped tooth.

The defense raised several objections because the witness was testifying as to how Mr. Hogan was injured, based on the notes from the triage nurse. Hogan never did respond to any of Mr. Elio's questions that night in the ED.

John Speranza cross-examined the witness first. He went through a list of possible scenarios that could have produced the injuries Mr. Elio observed that night. Things like falling against the edge of a bed frame or into a doorknob. Mr. Elio concurred that the injuries were consistent with getting punched, kneed, or elbowed in the face. John Parrinello and David Rothenberg also briefly questioned the witness. When Tony Leonardo got up, the only thing he had the witness clarify for the jury was that Mr. Hogan's injuries were indicative of a single kick to the face, but they certainly weren't consistent with numerous kicks by several people, as he claimed was the case. They weren't even consistent with the "several kicks" Dean Thomas attributed to me.

Next, the prosecution called Rochester Police Captain Robert Dewey to the stand. Mr. Gennaco conducted his direct examination to explain the department's official policy on the use of force. As usual with "expert" witnesses, we had to listen to his vast years of experience. He started with joining the RPD as a trainee, through his days as a supervisor in the Communications Unit, Court Liaison, Internal Affairs, and finally, to his current assignment in Research and Evaluation. Not much of a street cop, but he certainly had a lot of mileage in administration.

Captain Dewey was asked to read aloud the oath one takes when becoming a police officer. He went on to explain the department's table of organization, the hierarchy of command. The intent was to show the jury that Captain O'Brien reported directly to the chief of police. I suppose it was to help enhance the link between those two "coconspirators," Urlacher and O'Brien. Then came the Rochester Police Department General Orders. They, along with the rules and regulations, provide written guidelines to which members of the department must adhere. What was difficult to understand was why they were focusing on departmental issues when this was a federal trial. Mr. Gennaco was asking the witness to read GO #335, which dealt with use of force. Of course there were several objections from our table, primarily because the jury might be led to believe a violation of departmental policy was proof of somebody's constitutional rights. The judge allowed the testimony, stating that at the end of the trial, he would charge the jury as to the applicable law concerning excessive force. Great, let's hope by the end of the trial Judge Telesca's instructions will still have a bearing on inferences drawn now.

An hour after he took the stand, Captain Dewey began answering questions for John Parrinello at 10:20 a.m. John centered his questioning around the captain's tenure as commanding officer of the Maple Section while HIT was in existence. Dewey was asked about numerous drug locations and the problems they caused. Specifically, Parrinello asked about the time an entire street had to be shut down due to the heavy volume of drug trafficking. The witness was also asked how many raids he had participated in with our unit and if he ever had to write anyone up for misconduct. All in all, John helped the captain illustrate for the jury just what an asset HIT proved to be for cops in his command and residents in his section.

Tony Leonardo and Carl Salzer cross-examined Captain Dewey for about fifteen minutes each. Then, after a brief redirect by Mr. Gennaco and recross by John Parrinello, Dewey was excused and the government called its next witness.

Officer Dan Gleason was assigned to the Genesee Section and had rotated through HIT three separate times. He came through in April and October of 1988 and again in September of 1989. Unlike Dean Thomas, who was a permanent member of the Narcotics Unit, Gleason was the first police witness who had been temporarily assigned for a thirty-day period out of the Patrol Division. Also unlike Investigator Thomas, who pretty much testified against only me, Dan Gleason was brought in to nail me, Harloff, and Raggi.

One of the stories Billy Morris had regaled the feds with to sweeten his deal was that Scott and Greg stole drug money. On April 22, 1988,

Harloff and Gleason were watching a drug house on Seward Street in the Genesee Section. At one point a car pulled up in front of the house, and a guy came out and approached the driver's side of the vehicle. After a brief conversation with the female driver, the man from the house went back inside and reappeared a few minutes later. When they observed what they believed to be a dope deal, the two officers, along with other members of the raid team, converged on the vehicle. Both the dealer and the driver of the vehicle, who just happened to be a city schoolteacher, were arrested.

Back at our office, the dealer, in an effort to get out of a jam, said he was a resident of the house on Seward Street, and he would give consent to search it, which meant we didn't have to get a warrant. He also gave us information on a house around the corner on Champlain Street where there was supposed to be a large amount of money. Returning to Seward Street with a signed consent-to-search form, a fourteen-year-old kid was found to be the sole occupant of the house. Naturally, he wouldn't disclose the whereabouts of any dope in the house, but after a thorough search we found about an ounce and an half of cocaine in the form of eighty-two dime bags ($10 each). We also found $490 in cash. Having learned from our newest informant that the house was supplied from the Champlain Street location, we really didn't expect to find much, but it was a start.

Prior to returning to Seward Street, we obtained a search warrant for the house on Champlain. The informant said a female out of New York City was supplying the house to the tune of about three kilos of coke a week. The dope would then be cut and distributed to Seward Street and at least three other houses on the east side of Rochester. He also said there were guns in the house, including an Uzi submachine gun.

When we hit the house, only one male dealer was inside, and he was grabbed as he made his way to the bathroom in the rear of the house where we recovered a loaded .380-caliber semiautomatic handgun. Although there were no other weapons in the house, we did find a box of .45-caliber ammunition, 236 dime bags of cocaine, 4 hypodermic needles, and a shoebox containing a little over $20,000 in cash. All in all, it was a pretty good raid. Afterward, I was asked if we could give our informant $50 to get back to New York City. He had legitimate concerns for his health and safety after burning his former employers. I gave the OK to take the money from the seized drug profits, and he was gone.

I don't know why the feds didn't charge me with larceny. Especially when Bill Morris tried to whet their appetite during his second debriefing on May 3, 1991, and again on May 11. He told Special Agents Harding and Dillon and Lieutenants Duffy and Berkow that I was very interested in confiscated money and was always trying to count it. No shit. If I accounted for the money and the amount counted was the amount turned in to the property clerk, nobody could come back and say their money was stolen. He told them I was never personally observed stealing money, but he assumed I must have, due to the fact that in a very short period of time, I, who previously had very little money (I'm not quite sure how he was privy to my financial status) did now own a boat worth $45,000 and was living a high-end life. What a dickhead. I guess I forgot to tell him my boat payments were equal to the combined payments of my truck (which I sold because of the take-home car) and the smaller boat I traded in. Come to think of it, I neglected to inform Morris of my wife's salary, which helped provide a nice house for us to live in.

One sentence of the May 11 debriefing notes read, "Although CS#1 [confidential source] did not personally observe Alessi stealing money, he states Alessi had too many bills [again, I'm not sure how Morris knew how many bills I had] and too many toys not to be stealing." I guess since he was stealing money, it was just easier to figure I was, too. Or perhaps it was just something juicy to give them. Still, given all the other horseshit he spoon fed his handlers, I don't know why they didn't just go on Morris's assumption.

Maybe they didn't charge me with authorizing (or stealing) the fifty dollars from the Champlain Street cash because nobody would claim it and they didn't have a victim. Gennaco sure made a big deal out of it when he had Dan Gleason on the witness stand. Gleason told the jury he overheard a conversation back at the Public Safety Building where I told Morris I gave the informant fifty dollars. Never happened. I don't know what Gleason thought he heard, but I never gave the guy any money—I authorized the payment. Call it his severance pay. One thing Mike Gennaco did was to get the witness to lay the foundation for future testimony regarding the seized drug money. Gleason actually found the money on a shelf in a closet. Scott told him to put the shoebox back on the shelf. Why, so he could help himself to it? No, because it hadn't been photographed yet. More on that later from Mr. Morris.

Officer Gleason also testified that while the dealer from Champlain Street was on the floor, Morris, Raggi, and Harloff all stepped on the guy's back while stepping over him. I'd like to see what they would have done if he had reached the gun in the bathroom in time. And, in an attempt to make his testimony credible, Gleason admitted to slapping the guy in the head when he tried to get up.

Now it was time for Officer Gleason to stick another skewer in me. Count IV of the indictment charged me with pistol-whipping a suspect at 880 Main Street. In addition to being a separate indictment count, they used the same incident as one of the overt acts in the conspiracy charge. And as if that wasn't enough, the same thing was used for count XIII. That one said that I "knowingly used and carried a firearm during and in relation to a crime of violence." I remember when I first read the charges and came to this one, I couldn't believe my eyes. Like I've said all along, I pretty much know all the things I've done, but I sure as hell know what I didn't do.

It was April 11, 1988, the very first month of operation for HIT. We were all up on North Street in Goodman Section around 8:30 p.m., outside the Club Domino. Officer Bill Lawler, a rotating member who normally worked that area, spotted a known dope dealer coming out of a store across the street. When Lawler called to him, the guy jumped into the passenger side of a waiting car and the chase began.

Twenty-eight-year-old Ivan Hawley was the driver of the vehicle, and he took off down a side street. I was driving my Thunderbird with a five-liter engine, and he had a '76 Buick, so Mr. Hawley was not about to get away. It was just a question of where and when he would give up. Dan Gleason was next to me in the passenger seat, and Officer George Markert was in the back. After pulling alongside Hawley's car several times with Gleason showing his badge and yelling for him to stop, the car finally pulled to the curb on Prince Street near the corner of East Main. This is where some people's version of the incident gets a little fuzzy. Officer Markert, who would also give incriminating statements to the prosecution team, said he was next to me in the car. In his testimony, Gleason never even mentions Markert being in my car. In his grand-jury testimony on August 29, 1991, Officer Markert said, "I think I was a passenger in a car driven by Sergeant Alessi, but I'm not positive." No wonder he wasn't called as a trial witness.

After Mr. Hawley stopped, I approached the driver's side of his vehicle. Gleason went to the passenger side. Initially, Hawley refuse to open his door. When he finally did, I grabbed him by the left shoulder using my left hand. My gun was in my right hand. While Officer Gleason dealt with the passenger, Markert and I pulled Mr. Hawley out of the car and took him to the ground. At some point he ended up with a minor injury to his head that was bleeding. I don't know if he whacked it on the car door during his extraction or if he hit when he went to the ground. And, to be honest, I didn't care. You run from the cops and resist arrest, you deserve what you get. The guy's got an injury and we'll get him to the hospital for treatment. The first I heard about the driver claiming to have been hit with a cop's gun is when the indictment came out three years later. Interestingly enough, Mr. Hawley never lodged a complaint in Internal Affairs after the incident. He also refused medical treatment at the hospital that night. And there's one more thing to consider: Bill Morris was there. If I or anybody else at the defense table had hit a suspect in the head with a gun, it wouldn't have been a big secret, and yet during his five tape-recorded meetings with Berkow, his four debriefings with the feds, or his grand-jury testimony, Morris never said a word about me hitting Mr. Hawley with my gun. That definitely would have been worth extra points.

Mike Gennaco ended his direct examination of Officer Dan Gleason with questions related to leaving early. He had Gleason explain to the jury how an officer can take either cash or compensatory (comp) time after working overtime. Then, when an officer takes less than a whole day off, the time is deducted from his comp banks. It was explained to the jury that when rotating members of HIT were released early, they were never docked the appropriate amount of comp time.

After an hour and a half on the stand, the witness was excused with instructions to return the following day at 8:30a.m. The jury was released and trial day number five was over.

Wednesday morning, January 27, a brief recap of both Officer Gleason's and Captain Dewey's testimony was in the newspaper. The reporter, Leslie Sopko, made sure she mentioned that Gleason testified how "Alessi *stole* [my emphasis] fifty dollars from a drug house on Champlain Street and then gave it to an informant for a train ticket." But even she couldn't understand his version of how Ivan Hawley got injured. After quoting a portion of his testimony, she wrote, "Gleason, however, provided no other details. It was unclear how the suspect was injured." Too bad she hadn't been on the grand jury.

At 8:40 a.m., Officer Daniel Gleason took the stand for the second time and was greeted by John Parrinello. First, John revisited all Gleason's interviews with the prosecution. Parrinello had them all laid out for the witness—all ten of them. Then, for the remainder of his two-hour cross-examination, John queried Officer Gleason about a number of things, including the raids on Seward and Champlain Streets. Gleason responded with affirmative answers when John discussed being dismissed early during in-service training, something that still goes on today. That's the one they demoted me for.

During Parrinello's cross-examination of Officer Gleason regarding the money found at 292 Champlain Street, the subject of photographs came up. Gleason had testified on direct examination that he found the money in a shoebox on a closet shelf. After stating he had put the box of cash back on the shelf because it hadn't been photographed yet, Mike Gennaco had asked if he had done that on his own or had he been told to do so. Gleason said Scott Harloff told him to replace the evidence. I'm not sure what sinister impression that was supposed to have on the jury, but Parrinello was not about to just let it go. When John recounted Gleason's statement relative to the money, he had the witness confirm for the jury that Scott was complying with standard operating procedures by telling him to replace the box until it was photographed. "Nothing out of the ordinary about that?"

"No, sir," replied Gleason.

Then John asked Gleason where the photos were and if he had ever seen them. The response was that he didn't know where they were and had never seen them. Addressing the court, John said, "Do we have the photos? Mr. Gennaco says we don't have the photos." A short time later, Judge Telesca announced it was time for a break.

Recess was over, the jury had returned to the courtroom, and John was about to resume his cross of Officer Dan Gleason. That's when prosecutor Mike Gennaco told the judge he would like to set the record straight on a request made before the break. He said, "After that request was made, I consulted with my esteemed cocounsel to learn there are photos that had been available to the defense relative to this location [292 Champlain Street]."

I thought I saw the artery in Parrinello's neck explode. Nah, that can't be. There would be blood all over the place. John bellowed, "Is there some reason I couldn't know that during the break? With that, the judge excused the jury. Here we go again.

At issue was whether the government had made the photos available to the defense in accordance with Rule 16 of the federal rules of evidence. Cathleen Mahoney insisted they had, mentioning a defense request earlier in the month or in December. John argued that our request was made in January of '91, and the response came in January of '93. He also argued that he would have prepared his cross-examination differently with the photos in hand. After several minutes of citing paragraphs, subparagraphs, and sub-subparagraphs of Rule 16, Judge Telesca sided with the government and denied Parrinello's request for a dismissal. After the jury reentered the courtroom, John said he had no further questions of Officer Gleason.

For the next eighty-five minutes, my attorney, John Speranza, would carefully dissect not only Dan Gleason's direct testimony but his numerous interviews as well. John pointed out how in all his initial contacts with members of the investigative team, he never mentioned the pistol-whipping incident at 880 East Main Street in April of 1988. After reviewing hundreds of reports, there was nothing said about Ivan Hawley being injured after a brief but fast car chase. Speranza reminded Gleason of his grand-jury testimony January 9, 1991, when asked by Mike Gennaco, "Did you ever see Sergeant Alessi engage in physical abuse?" To which he answered, "No, I did not." And finally, after replaying the incident like a movie frame by frame, John ended his cross-examination with two questions: "You did not see Sergeant Alessi strike Ivan Hawley with a gun, correct?"

"Correct."

"Nor did you hear him hit Ivan Hawley with a gun, correct?"

"Correct."

Before he was excused from the witness stand for good, Officer Gleason answered questions from Messrs. Salzer, Rothenberg, and Leonardo. A brief redirect by Mike Gennaco, and witness number five was heading for those big double doors at the rear of the courtroom. We were in recess until 8:30 the following morning.

Fifteen

This is probably as good a time as any to put your mind at ease as to how much actual testimony I've put in here for you to read. At the beginning of the trial, the government had a witness list that numbered around one hundred. Relax. They didn't put that many on the stand, and I'm not going to recap every one they did. But try to keep this in perspective. A trial lasting ten weeks with five defendants, each with our own attorney, plus three prosecutors and numerous witnesses. That's six opening statements (one prosecutor and five defense lawyers), one direct examination and five cross-examinations per witness, and six closing arguments. When you're the one sitting in the box seats, you tend to hang on every word. Even when rereading the interviews and sworn testimony, there is so much that is important and relevant in terms of the "big picture," but if I put it all in, this book would end up as thick as the Manhattan yellow pages. So I've got to parse (as John Speranza would say) the right amount of material to show what they tried to do without putting you to sleep. Remember, this was never supposed to go to trial. In fact, several police witnesses were assured their Internal Affairs or FBI interviews would never become public domain—with all the evidence against us, we would surely plead guilty to whatever deals we were offered. OK. Having said all that, let's continue.

As I said earlier, Mr. Hawley never made an Internal Affairs complaint regarding his encounter with the police. He did, however, file a lawsuit. Exactly six months to the day following his arrest, he was testifying in a civil hearing, giving his version of what happened that night.

During cross-examination, Michele DiGaetano, attorney for the city, asked Mr. Hawley if could see any of the officers. He answered, "No." She continued. "So then they were both behind you, right?"

"Yes."

"You obviously didn't see somebody hit you, is that right?"

"No."

"You had a sensation of somebody hitting you in the head."

"Yes."

"Some*thing* hitting you in the head."

"Yes."

When questioned about any conversations, he had a vague memory of somebody saying, "I will teach you to run from us." With respect to the hospital, all he said about who drove him was, "Two of them had taken me down to the hospital." Keep in mind this is six months after the incident.

Three years later, on July 24, 1991, Sgt. Ed Knaak of the RPD and FBI Agent Tim Weir interviewed Ivan Hawley about the incident. Quoting from their report, "He said he got out of the car and *officers* [my emphasis] grabbed both of his arms to handcuff him. He thought his hands were in handcuffs behind his back when he saw a hand with a gun come down and hit him in the head. He says he fell to the pavement and was eventually carried over to the curb." Later in his statement, Mr. Hawley mentioned a plainclothes officer with a scruffy beard who "talked like the Godfather" and took him to the hospital. For the record, the cop he referred to was Bill Lawler, the officer who started the chase when he recognized Hawley's dope-dealer friend. It was Lawler and George Markert who took him to the hospital. The investigators showed Mr. Hawley two photo arrays. For the uninitiated, a photo array is a spread of six photographs of people with similar likenesses. In the array that included my photo, Hawley picked out two possibles: One was me, who he said resembled the one who talked like the Godfather. The other was not a police officer.

Fast-forward to January 28, 1993, almost five years since the incident on East Main Street. Mr. Ivan Hawley was sworn in on the witness stand at 9:25 a.m. and began his direct examination by Ms. Mahoney. After providing some personal background, Mr. Hawley was asked about the events of the night in question. He described how we chased him and his friend from North Street until he stopped his car near Main Street. Then he said "a gentleman with a handgun pointed it at me and ordered me out of the car. He told me to face the passenger side of the car." In this testimony, unlike his statement to investigators back in 1991 when he "thought" he was handcuffed, now he's certain of it. "He took one of my arms and put it behind my back, clipped the handcuff on, took the other hand, put it behind my back, clipped the handcuff on; therefore, I was handcuffed."

Our attorneys made several objections—most of which were overruled—because all through his testimony, Mr. Hawley did not identify anyone he had been referring to. It was all "he," "they," "the gentleman." Finally, Judge Telesca cautioned Ms. Mahoney that if her witness was not able to connect any of the defendants to the incident, his testimony would be stricken. What happened next can only be described as unfuckingbelieveable. This is one you have to read play by play.

By Ms. Mahoney:

Q. Mr. Hawley, let me ask you, do you see anyone in this courtroom who you are sure was present that evening?

A. I remember some…I remember…I see somebody who's familiar that night.

Q. OK. Will you tell us who that person is?

A. Do I have to?

Q. Yes. If you want to tell this jury what happened that night you have to say if you recognize anyone who was there that night.

A. It was a long time ago. It was five years ago. I'm trying to put it behind me.

Q. Are you afraid, Mr. Hawley?

Mr. Parrinello: Objection.

Mr. Leonardo: Objection, your Honor.
Mr. Parrinello: Move for mistrial.
The Court: Sustained.
Mr. Speranza: Motion for mistrial?
The Court: I'm not granting the motion for mistrial. I am merely sustaining the objection.

By Ms. Mahoney:

Q. Can you identify anyone in this courtroom as being present that night?
A. I remember the gentleman over there. [Pointing to me]
Q. Which gentleman are you pointing to?
A. The fourth gentleman down from this end.
Q. Can you describe his facial characteristics?
A. He has a mustache; he has glasses on; a little gray hair.
   Ms. Mahoney: May the record reflect he's identified the defendant Thomas Alessi.
   The Court: So ordered.

WHAT? I'm almost falling off my chair. I couldn't believe the ludicrous dog-and-pony show I just witnessed. Then Ms. Mahoney asked Ivan Hawley what he remembered about me. His answer: "I remember him being extremely aggressive. I remember him saying comments. He was the one that made the comment 'I'll teach you to run from us.' He was the one who made the comment. He was the one who was coming up behind me when I was struck in the back of the head." Back in '91, Mr. Hawley told investigators when he "thought" he was in handcuffs he saw a hand with a gun come down and hit him on the head right after he got out of the car. During this same interview he was shown a photo array with my picture in it and misidentified me as Bill Lawler. Perhaps my face all over the television and newspaper, along with details of the allegation, refreshed his memory five years later.

Satisfied with the identification, the judge allowed the circus to continue. Now feeling the relief of having wrestled this awful nightmare from the depths of his tortured memory, and with the spotlight upon him, Hawley began to embellish. Asked what happened after he was handcuffed, he said, "OK. I was led toward the back of the car. The gentleman that I pointed out...I was walking toward the back of my car, and a gentleman had his hand on my arm. I was in handcuffs, and I looked over to see what was happening with the person that was in the car with me, Mike. I saw the gentleman I picked out over here coming toward...coming toward me. And there was a streetlight above us. I pulled over and it happened to be beneath a streetlight. So you could see very clearly and I have good eyesight. I'm observant and I saw this gentleman coming toward me and then I was struck on the back of the head and I was told to get down." And just to add a little flare to this epic tale, he says that I pushed his face into the pavement and held him down with my knee to the back of his neck. Strangely enough, he never mentioned that part to the investigators three years before, or, for that matter, the convenient streetlight.

By now I was in shock, but it got better. Ms. Mahoney asked if he was ever taken to the hospital for treatment. "Did the defendant take you to the hospital or did other police officers take you to the hospital?" Mr. Hawley's answer: "There was another officer and the defendant also." It was all I could do keep from standing up and screaming at him, "It was Bill Lawler [Godfather voice] and George Markert who took you to the hospital, you idiot!"

According to the prisoner custody log from the arrest, between transporting him to Saint Mary's Hospital, where he refused treatment, and back to the Public Safety Building to finish the paperwork, Mr. Hawley was in the company of those two officers from 8:45 p.m. until 9:30 p.m. I saw him maybe all of ten minutes at the arrest location, and he didn't name me as his assailant from a photo array in 1991, but miraculously he did so five years later in court. Why did I have the feeling the witness had been well coached?

The investigator's report of the initial interview mentioned only two photo arrays: one with my picture and one with a picture of Greg Raggi. I wondered why they didn't show Mr. Hawley photos of all the officers who were involved in his arrest. In any event, three months after his lawyer gave the OK for the interview, Hawley received a check for $7,500 from the City of Rochester as settlement of the lawsuit. He should have been given twice that amount and an academy award for his performance on the witness stand.

For the next two hours, John Speranza cross-examined Ivan Hawley in what is best described as an exercise in futility. Not in the sense that the gifted attorney was unable to illustrate the witness's inconsistencies for the jury, because he did. It's just that when a lawyer has a witness on the stand who has given prior inconsistent statements under oath, he really wants the person to admit what he's saying at the present time is different from what he said before. This means one of the statements is untrue. In Mr. Hawley's case, every time John asked him if he recalled a specific statement from either his civil hearing or his interview with the investigators, the response was, "I don't recall my exact words." At times, John became noticeably exasperated but managed to maintain his composure.

John Parrinello subjected himself to the frustrating experience of questioning Mr. Hawley for only about fifteen minutes. He concentrated on the witness's relationship with his passenger on the night of the chase and how often Mr. Hawley had been in that part of the city. He also questioned the witness about his prior drug use. During John Speranza's cross, the issue of the witness's criminal history came up. The jury and Mr. Hawley were excused from the courtroom while both sides argued relevance. At the end of her direct examination, Ms. Mahoney asked Hawley if he had ever been arrested for drug use, and he stated he had not. The jury had also heard that the witness lived at home with his mother and worked full time for a printing company. John Parrinello argued that because he had six prior contacts with police involving petit larceny arrests, it wasn't fair for the jury to be left with the impression

Mr. Hawley was just a law-abiding citizen in the wrong place at the wrong time. The judge disagreed, and the subject of the Ivan's criminal record, including that he had run from police before, was off-limits.

The next witness was Officer Mark Mariano. He had gone through HIT in May of 1988 and was brought in to do Jim O'Brien and Greg Raggi. Mariano was on for less than an hour. Judge Telesca cut the jury loose early just as another argument between our table and the prosecution was developing. In that short time, though, he told the jury that O. B. had given certain instructions to Mariano's group relative to the treatment of suspects. While it was a typical precautionary speech any boss would give new members of a specialized unit like ours, the prosecution put a sinister twist on it to advance their conspiracy theory. As for Greg, Officer Mariano told of an arrest he and Raggi were involved in where the suspect was alleged to have been struck a number of times by both men. He also spoke of a number of arrests his group was involved in where he didn't think there was enough probable cause. Mariano would be the first witness called the following Monday. As he left the federal building, television cameras caught him as he attempted to light a cigarette. I like to believe it was his nerves that caused his hands to shake the way they did. But then again, maybe it was just the January cold.

When the next morning's paper came out, there were only excerpts from Officer Mariano's testimony. Ivan Hawley didn't even get an honorable mention. Not one line from reporter Leslie Sopko describing the inconsistencies between his statements of six months after the incident and those five years later. I would have thought she'd at least mention how Mr. Hawley pointed to me as he told the jury how it was me that he saw, with the aid of the streetlight, just before he was struck. It's a good thing he got the $7,500 from the city because he missed out on his fifteen minutes of fame.

When court resumed on Monday, February 1, Ms. Mahoney called Officer Mariano back to the stand to resume his direct examination. She began by asking him about an arrest on May 10, 1988, in which a young man named David Reardon and his girlfriend had been stopped on Jefferson Avenue. Reardon was in possession of a small amount of marijuana and was taken into custody. At the scene, he began ranting and raving and at one point slammed his own head on the hood of one of our cars. Reardon was placed in the backseat of Bill Morris's car to be transported to a parking lot a short distance away to await the paddy wagon, and he would not stop rambling. Mariano was in the rear of the car with Officer Matt Sands. Reardon was between them. Morris was driving, and Greg Raggi was in the front seat. Mariano testified that in an attempt to shut the annoying arrestee up, he slapped Reardon in the face two or three times after making lewd comments about the man's girlfriend. When asked what happened next, the witness said Greg reached down into a small bag in front of him, took out an object, and struck Reardon on the knee twice. Ms. Mahoney asked Officer Mariano to describe the object. He said, "The object was six or eight inches long. It was cylinder [his mispronunciation]. It was black. It was round—tubular, I guess. And then he put back into the little bag that he had with him." Then Ms. Mahoney asked Mariano, based on his training and experience, what he believed the object to be. "I believe it to be a black-jack." This was count five against Greg in the indictment. Mariano went on to describe incidents involving Raggi at other locations. All designed to paint a picture for the jury of Greg using excessive force.

The day after his arrest, Mr. Reardon made a formal complaint to Internal Affairs regarding his arrest. The complaint was primarily about the way he was physically treated during the arrest. He also said that while he was in the unmarked police car, the officer with badge #663 (Mariano with a badge holder on a chain around his neck) hit him with a fist three times on the left side of his face and made comments about what he'd like to do to his girlfriend. About halfway through his statement, Reardon said, "The guy in the front passenger seat turned around and he whapped me on the knee with this little—it was like a leather thing with a piece of metal on the end of it, and it was real flexible. He just whapped me. It didn't really hurt that bad, you know." When asked if he had received any injuries, Reardon answered, "No, I didn't. I don't have any injury on my knee. Like I said, it was only a light tap, it wasn't all that bad." Then he was asked how many times he was struck. "One. That was the only one."

Oddly enough, when Sgt. Ed Knaak and Special Agent Tim Weir interviewed Mr. Reardon three years later on July 18, 1991, their report stated that he said, "The officer in the front passenger seat hit him with a blackjack about ten times." That's the first mention of a blackjack. Because the investigator's report doesn't quote Reardon verbatim, it's not known if the term was suggested to him or if it was his term for the object he was allegedly struck with.

After about an hour of questioning by Ms. Mahoney, Greg's attorney, David Rothenberg, began his cross-examination of Officer Mariano. Eventually, David got to the subject of Mr. Reardon and the "black-jack" incident. Referring to the use of undercover vehicles, Rothenberg had the witness concede that such vehicles do not have police radios permanently installed in them for the obvious reasons. Mariano stated that officers carry portable radios when using these vehicles. Then David went on to describe a significant part of the radio: the antenna. As Rothenberg cited each characteristic of the antenna, Officer Mariano concurred. "A portable radio has a black antenna on it, doesn't it? About six to eight inches long, right? Flexible, right? Cylindrical, right? Then when David asked the witness if it wasn't a radio Greg was holding and didn't he snap the antenna across Reardon's leg, Mariano responded, "He could have."

He went on to say the investigators who questioned him had suggested the word blackjack. But he was all too willing to repeat it in the grand jury in August of 1991, where he even embellished when asked if Reardon appeared to be in pain. "Yes. He definitely was reeling from getting hit with that thing. He was shocked." Remember Reardon's statement in Internal Affairs? "No, I don't have any injury on my knee. Like I said, it was only a light tap, it wasn't all that bad."

During his cross-examination, David discussed Mariano's Internal Affairs career history, a total of nine pages. There were six complaints

stemming from the Reardon incident alone. He used it as an introduction to the informal agreement Mariano and dozens of other police
witnesses had with my old friend Lt. Duffy. It was also during Officer
Mariano's testimony that the issue of immunity came up. You'll hear
more about that later. Suffice it to say the investigators didn't have too
much trouble getting Mariano to believe what he saw in Greg's hand
that day was a blackjack. Here's more food for thought: in the entire
investigation—which covered more than three years and hundreds of
interviews—this was the only allegation of its kind. You'd think if someone was in the habit of whacking people with a blackjack, it might have
come up more than once in a twenty-year career. One of the last questions asked of Officer Mariano was, "You didn't actually see a blackjack,
did you?" His answer was no.

Think about it. Greg Raggi was indicted by a federal grand jury for,
among other things, tapping a guy on the knee with the small rubber
antenna of his portable radio because a cop with an extensive Internal
Affairs history looking to save his own career let them believe Mr.
Reardon was beaten with a blackjack. Incredible.

Tuesday, February 2, would be another day on the witness stand for
Officer Mariano. John Parrinello had to finish his cross-examination.
Then David Rothenberg and Tony Leonardo would have a chat with
him. But before any of this could begin, Mark Mariano had to cool his
heels in the waiting room for more than an hour while Judge Telesca
heard arguments and rendered a decision on the question of witness
immunity.

Earlier I mentioned that during the investigation, then lieutenant
Duffy (he rose through the ranks to eventually become chief of police)
had been authorized to grant police witnesses departmental immunity
for what was termed low-level, unjustified uses of force and prior false
statements. At the end of the previous day's testimony, the judge ordered
the prosecution to give the defense team any documentation relative
to the matter. The letter faxed to our lawyers indicated that sometime
after December 7, 1990, Lt. Duffy gave witnesses immunity verbally.

There were a number of problems with this. First and foremost, we were never notified of this prior to the fax. The law requires that the defense be made aware of any benefit granted to a witness. The prosecution's reasoning was that since the immunity was of a departmental nature given by the RPD, it didn't apply to the government's case; therefore, Mr. Gennaco did not feel compelled to reveal the information to the defense.

After hearing arguments from both sides, and defense motions to dismiss the indictment, Judge Telesca went to his chambers to formulate a decision. When he returned to the bench about thirty minutes later, he basically disagreed with the prosecution's argument and agreed with ours. And while he did not grant the motion for dismissal, he did express his displeasure and concern over the whole immunity issue. One reason being since the government had not granted the witnesses immunity from federal prosecution, cops were testifying in open court and, to quote Judge Telesca, "They have admitted to federal crimes on the stand." This would not be the last we would hear of the issue of immunity. The jury was brought in and Officer Mariano was recalled to the witness stand to resume cross-examination by John Parrinello and Tony Leonardo.

And so the parade of witnesses continued. For the remainder of that day, through Thursday, and up through Tuesday of the following week, the jury would hear testimony from four more people. There were RPD officers Robert Johannson and Robert Jobe, and civilians James Pilato and Willie Brown. Johannson spoke of incidents where Greg Raggi was alleged to have used excessive force. During his direct examination by Jessica Ginsburg, he was asked about a particular raid he had participated in. In this incident, the above-mentioned Mr. Pilato had thought it would be a good idea to bring an illegal handgun to a known drug house in the inner city where he wished to purchase cocaine. To make a long story short, we discovered the gun after we hit the house, and Mr. Pilato was strongly admonished for his poor judgment.

The specific allegation was that Greg had slapped James Pilato after it was determined the found gun belonged to Pilato. Asked why he didn't report what he had observed at 20 Barons Street, Officer Johansson stated he wanted a positive career with the police department. He said there were ample opportunities for things of that nature to be taken care of by supervisors, people with more experience and more time on the job than he had. A few minutes later he was asked why he lied in a report to Internal Affairs. In an unsuccessful attempt to hold back the tears, Johansson sobbed out his answer. "I was afraid. I didn't want to make waves. I just wanted to get along and do my job and not…not become a person on the outs, so to say. I'd always dreamed of becoming a police officer, becoming a narcotics officer. The department had some very powerful people and I felt if I did that, I wouldn't be able to become a part of the narcotics team at that time or in the near future." I remember thinking to myself, "Sleep easy Rochester, you're in good hands." Officer Johansson explained how he had been interviewed on Thursday by the civil rights investigators and promoted to Sergeant Johansson the next day. Talk about passing your career interview.

The next two witnesses were civilians. James Pilato gave his version of what happened at 20 Barons Street. He identified Scott Harloff as the person who had "smacked" him the night of the raid. An argument arose over his identification when it was learned he had been shown a color photo array containing Harloff's picture two days before his court appearance. Two problems went along with this: First, Mr. Pilato had just testified he believed he had identified Scott from a photo array in Internal Affairs the day after the raid. But in fact he was never shown a picture of Harloff back then. Second, in the color photo array he viewed, Harloff was the only person with blond hair. Now the witness sees the blond guy from the array sitting at the defense table. What do you think, just a little suggestive?

Willie Brown, the government's next witness, had been arrested after a brick was thrown at our people on Joseph Avenue in September of 1988. Mr. Brown was accused of throwing the brick and almost hitting

167

Officer Elsie Martinez in the head during a drug bust that didn't involve him. He was brought in as just one more of our "victims." It was alleged that he had been kicked in the groin during his arrest, and Bill Morris credited Greg Raggi with this act. When asked if he recognized anyone in court from the night of his arrest, Mr. Brown stated he didn't. He did, however, say he saw the officer who gave him the finger one day while he was walking down the street. When asked to describe that officer he said, "He had long gray hair." The only guy in our group with long gray hair was Bill Morris.

John Parrinello briefly cross-examined Mr. Brown, the main point being that the witness had pleaded guilty to disorderly conduct, the charge he had been arrested on by our team during the raid. Mr. Brown claimed he didn't know what he was pleading guilty to at the time, but he did it because his mother told him to.

At 9:50 a.m. Monday, February 8, Sgt. Robert Jobe was called as the government's next witness. This was another shot at Greg Raggi. Jobe had rotated through HIT in October 1988 as a patrol officer. One of the alleged "victims" of our three-year rampage of terror was a well-known dope dealer named Kenny Smith a.k.a. Meatball. Jobe's group was involved in an arrest of Mr. Smith. In his direct examination by Jessica Ginsburg, Sgt. Jobe testified that during the transport of Mr. Smith to the Public Safety Building, Greg slapped the suspect because he was verbally abusive to the officers in the car. The witness related how worried he was that Meatball would make a complaint, but he said Raggi told him not to say anything to Internal Affairs. He also testified that another rotating officer with them, Dominick Perrone, was so upset by this incident that when he emerged from the car at the PSB, he was "ashen in color."

Back on November 6, 1990, then officer Jobe gave a written statement to an RPD investigator. In it, he said our unit would drive around and just pick people at random to jump out at and chase down. If they happened to have dope on them, a reason for probable cause was conveniently created. He went on to say this bothered him so much that he went out of his way to not find dope on people. On the one occasion he did encounter a suspect holding drugs and had to arrest him, he said he was lucky the charges were later dropped. He then stated he was so upset because of the way things were done, his heart would pound when he had to go to work. For the life of me, I just can't remember anyone forcing him to stay in the unit. All he or anyone else had to say was, "You know, sarge, this really isn't what I thought it would be. I'd prefer to be back in patrol." There'd be no questions asked and no hard feelings. Some cops like it, some don't.

During his cross-examination of Sgt. Jobe, David Rothenberg went over all the meetings the witness had with members of the investigation team. At one point, David asked Jobe if he had been granted immunity, to which he responded that he had not. This had not been overlooked by Judge Telesca. Then Rothenberg got into the area of probable cause. A concept that, based on his testimony, seemed to be a little fuzzy to the witness. David cited various case laws relative to probable cause and asked Jobe if he remembered any of them from his academy training. "And do you recall a Supreme Court case law to the effect that probable cause is a flexible common sense standard? Do you recall that language?"

"Not specifically," replied the witness.

David moved on to Sgt. Jobe's four-page deposition given to investigators. Specifically, David talked about the part where Jobe said he had gone out of his way to not find drugs on people when he searched them. The witness was reminded that in both his deposition and his grand-jury testimony he had admitted he didn't look for drugs when searching suspects. Then David asked Jobe if it ever occurred to him that he was failing to carry out his duties as a Rochester police officer. When the word no came out of the witness's mouth, the judge stopped the cross-examination.

Judge Telesca asked both David and Ms. Ginsburg to approach the bench. After a short conversation, the jury was told they were being excused so that legal issues could be discussed. The judge directed his attention to the witness. Telesca advised the bewildered-looking officer that his testimony and admissions might amount to a violation of law. The judge went on to explain that Jobe had Fifth Amendment rights and was entitled to a lawyer. The witness was asked if he had been given any formal immunity by the city, the state, or the federal government. After hearing that no such immunity had been granted, the judge ordered a recess so that Sgt. Jobe could consult with an attorney. Arguments over immunity erupted as soon as the witness left the courtroom. The prosecution contended they had complied with the judge's earlier direction that it be on the record as to whether a witness had been granted immunity. Our guys didn't see it that way. I didn't go to law school, but it seems to me when a witness is on the stand giving incriminating testimony, and it's a big surprise when he says he wasn't given immunity, then maybe the prosecution didn't comply with the judge's direction.

When Sgt. Jobe returned to the stand, he was in possession of a letter of immunity from the federal government. Oh no. Another pothole. Judge Telesca advised the witness that his letter did not protect him from state prosecution. Again, there was a difference of opinion as to whether federal immunity protected a witness from state prosecution. Lead prosecutor Mike Gennaco began citing case law where such a precedent had been set. The judge was not familiar with the case and ordered the citation delivered to him. Judge Telesca also wanted Sgt. Jobe's attorney, Charles Crimi, to come before the court. After another short recess, Crimi was standing at the podium explaining to the judge that he had not fully explored the circumstances of the immunity issues as they pertained to his client. With that, Telesca adjourned the court until 8:30 the following morning.

Tuesday, February 9, would turn out to be a short day. Sgt. Jobe was recalled to the witness stand, but not before Judge Telesca informed him and his attorney, Charles Crimi, that the witness was in fact protected from state prosecution by virtue of his federal immunity. After citing the statute that guaranteed such protection and advising both attorney and client that refusal to testify would result in contempt charges against Jobe, the judge ordered him to the stand.

David Rothenberg resumed his cross-examination from the previous day, and his line of questioning focused on the arrest of Kenny "Meatball" Smith. Before Rothenberg was finished, he elicited from the witness the fact that he never actually saw Greg Raggi slap the suspect. Tony Leonardo and David Salzer also briefly questioned Jobe before rendering him back to prosecutor Ginsburg for a short redirect.

That was it. All done for the day. The jury was excused with Judge Telesca advising them we would have a very full day tomorrow and from here on in. Waiting in the on-deck circle was none other than the government's very own star witness, Billy Morris.

Sixteen

William F. Morris, self-professed liar and convicted criminal, entered the courtroom the following morning wearing a navy-blue pinstripe suit. His hair was cut short, and he was clean-shaven except for a mustache. This was a strikingly different look from his Vice Squad days. Gone were the long curly locks and full beard, the blue jeans and sneakers, as well as his usual Boston Celtics shirt or jacket. Yes, sir, Mr. Morris looked very professional, a paid professional informant. I don't know if his handlers told him how long he would be on the stand. This would surely be his easiest day, with the possible exception of the incident that occurred outside as Morris was making his way to the federal building.

As played out on the news that night, our star witness was walking past the regular group of media people outside the court. As one of the photographers attempted to get a close-up of him, Morris pushed the cameraman aside and told him, "I'm bringing you up on assault charges." Why so testy, Bill? He entered the building and was once again in the safe harbor that was Mike Gennaco and company.

Even though Morris's appearance on the stand this day would be all direct examination by Mr. Gennaco, John Parrinello had asked the judge for permission to request a meet with the witness prior to John's cross-examination. Judge Telesca told Parrinello he could ask Morris himself before the jury was brought in. Now you would think this would be fairly simple. "Hey, Billy, can you and I have a chat before I cross you on the stand? No? OK, thanks." But nothing is simple with John. After a brief discussion regarding his immunity, John set Morris up by politely saying how they had known each other for a long time, and that they had done this before in terms of cross-examination, and they never had any problems. Maybe if Billy had just agreed, everything would have been cool, but he had to ask, "What's your definition of problems?" To which Parrinello replied, "Well, I've had problems with what you said under oath before in cross-examination, but in terms of our personal relationship, we've never had any personal problems, have we?" You could actually see the color leave Morris's face. John just fired the first shot in a war with the witness that would last for several days. Knowing he had just been accused of prior acts of perjury, the witness responded by saying it was a misleading statement. After Mr. Gennaco asked the court for a simple question of the witness, John asked Morris for a meeting, which he declined. The jury was brought in, and the witness was tendered to Mr. Gennaco for direct examination.

Since Bill Morris was on the stand for nine days—eight of them being cross-examined by our attorneys—you can imagine how much information was covered. In addition, those days were filled with numerous objections, some of which led to excusing the jury while legal issues were argued and decided. Out of respect for you as the reader, I have no intention of putting you through the tedious process of reading all of his testimony. That plus the fact he doesn't deserve that much attention. I will give you the *Reader's Digest* version of Mr. Morris's journey through fantasyland.

After the usual witness background summary, prosecutor Gennaco began his line of questioning with an incident Greg Raggi was charged in. In this raid, a Jamaican dope dealer had been struck in the groin, and this suspect had referred to that part of his anatomy as his "seed." The thing I remember most was for a long time after the raid, Morris would joke about the guy, imitating his accent. "Oh man, you hit me in my seed." Strangely enough, he left that part out of his testimony. From there, Gennaco moved on to the raid at 65 Prospect Street, the infamous cowboy boots incident where I was supposed to have kicked a suspect in the face. And for the record, I'm going to clear up the whole

Prospect Street matter in the very near future when Parrinello cross-examines Morris. At one point, the prosecutor asked the witness about his grand jury statement with regard to my whereabouts in the house. John Parrinello objected on several grounds, which caused the judge to make a statement to both sides. "Let's lay down some ground rules right here and now. You [Parrinello] have an obligation to object. He [Morris] has a *story* [my emphasis] to get out. We have had some understanding as to the parameters of that to move this along. You [Gennaco] may use leading questions. You [Parrinello] may object when you think it's necessary to do so in the protection of your individual client. OK. I understand what the issues are. Let's move along. It serves no great purpose to have constant interruption. That is not to say your objections don't have any merit whatsoever, but I have to put down some ground rules. I expect everybody to cooperate. Let's move along." From where we sat, it seemed the last sentence had been and would continue to be the judge's primary concern throughout the trial.

Then it was Scott Harloff's turn. In response to Mr. Genacco's question, Morris related an incident on Lake Avenue in October 1998 when a drunk driver cut him off as he pulled out of a Wendy's parking lot. Harloff, Morris, and one of the temporary officers, John Kompanijec, had gone to pick up food to bring back to the office. Using his "Kojak light," Morris pulled the driver over, but the guy refused to get out of his car. After his hands were literally pried off the steering wheel, the driver was brought back and spread-eagled on the side of Morris's car. The witness went on to state it was then that Harloff grabbed the intox by his hair and slammed his head down on the top of the unmarked police car, knocking some of his teeth out. Morris said Scott then brushed the teeth off the car with his hand.

In his grand-jury testimony on July 18, 1991, Morris's exact words were, "In doing so, he really slammed his head down and his teeth came in contact with the car and his front teeth fell out, I mean like Chiclets gum all over the top of the car and his front teeth were all over the car." It was Morris who made the comparison of the guy's teeth to Chiclets gum. Now at trial, Mr. Gennaco asked the witness if there were any subsequent references to the teeth by himself or any other permanent members (namely Harloff) of HIT. Morris said that he, Harloff, and Kompanijec all referred to the teeth as Chiclets. It was a clear-cut attempt to paint Scott as finding humor in the drunk driver's misfortune.

Strangely enough, of all the material I have relative to the investigation, including all recorded statements of police officers to RPD and FBI investigators and the grand jury, there is nothing from Officer Kompanijec corroborating Morris's testimony. I guess when you think about it, it's not really that strange after all, considering all the uncorroborated testimony the prosecution accepted. Here's the best part. In his statement to investigators on July 23, 1991, the driver himself said that while he was being handcuffed he became "very mad." He said he turned around and pointed his finger at the officers and demanded to know what he was under arrest for. For those of you who don't know any better, this is not something you want to do while being handcuffed. The driver went on to tell investigators that the larger of the two officers (Harloff, whom he picked out of a photo array along with Morris) spun him back around, and with Scott holding one of the driver's arms behind his back, Harloff grabbed the driver by his shirt collar and threw him up on the roof of the car. That's when his mouth struck the roof, two teeth were broken, and one tooth was chipped. This was a far cry from Morris's "Chiclets gum all over the top of the car" version of the incident. And for the record, the driver had an extensive dental history of decayed teeth, which may account for why they broke so easily.

One of the incidents Morris testified about was a search warrant raid at 405 Hayward Avenue. Harloff was accused of threatening to shock a suspect in the house with an electrical cord from a radio. This would be typical of some of the ball busting that went on regularly. Like the time I told a dope dealer during one of our numerous raids at a drug house on Lake Avenue that I'd throw him out a third-floor window if he didn't tell us where his stash was. Even though I obviously wouldn't, just as

Harloff would not really electrocute someone, all that mattered was that the bad guys believed it.

Here is Morris's exact testimony. See if you can figure out what the hell he's saying. "There was a radio that was in what appeared to be a dining room area off to the right of the hallway in the house. The radio was pulled out of the plug and the wall, and there was some frayed plugs on the end of the radio that were not in the plug jack but attached to the radio. And Investigator Harloff went over to the subject with the wires and pointed the wires at him and wanted to know where the drugs were." Yeah, I know. Read it again and it still won't make sense.

That's OK. Here's what the government's star witness dazzled the grand jury with two years earlier to get his good friend indicted: "Scott goes into the side room with him [the suspect] and rips a radio *out of the wall socket* [my emphasis]. While he rips the radio, the radio comes out and there are two frayed ends of the electrical cord, and I believe the plug is still plugged into the wall socket. [Refer to his first sentence. Which is it, Billy: plugged in or unplugged?] And he tells the guy, 'You are going to tell me the truth; you are going to tell me where the dope is or I'm going to electrocute you.' He comes after the guy with the frayed ends of the wire. Never touched him with it, but petrified the guy." Oh well, it was good enough for the federal prosecutors. Remember that this was never supposed to go to trial.

Before he was finished, Bill Morris would recount thirty incidents of alleged physical abuse and theft between 1988 and 1990. The following day, the morning newspaper recapped his testimony: "By the end, the cumulative nature of the testimony almost had a numbing effect. It became hard to distinguish between the alleged February 1988 beating with a shovel, the alleged May 1988 assault with a blackjack, and the alleged February 1989 threat to a suspect with live electrical wires." I wonder how many readers took note of the word "alleged." Another part of the article said, "His manner was polite, although his testimony at times seemed rehearsed." No shit, you think?

As I read the paper over my morning oatmeal before heading for court, I almost laughed out loud when I got to the end of the article. "Gennaco asked Morris why he decided to cooperate in the civil rights investigation."

"Because I had done something wrong," Morris replied. "There may have been other reasons [I repeat, no shit!], but that was the primary reason. The only thing to do was to stand up and do the right thing." Imagine how soon Diogenes could have ended his search for an honest man if he had run into Bill Morris in ancient Athens.

The reporter described the witness as "unflappable," as he answered the prosecutor's questions. We'd see if Morris flapped a little when John Parrinello cross-examined him.

Day two of Bill Morris's testimony began at 8:35 a.m. on Thursday, February 11. Mike Gennaco questioned the witness for the next forty minutes and during that time another half-dozen or so allegations were discussed, as well as a review of some of the prior day's testimony. There was a lighthearted moment just before the prosecutor finished his direct examination. Mr. Gennaco asked Morris, "Did you ever see Mike Mazzeo use unreasonable force?" This brought Mike's attorney, Carl Salzer, to his feet. "Object to the form. Without specificity, your Honor," Carl shouted. Judge Telesca asked, "When?" Mr. Gennaco added, "At any time." The witness replied, "I never saw Mike Mazzeo do anything wrong." Carl then rather sheepishly said, "I'll withdraw my objection, your Honor." The jury, the gallery, and even those of us in the box seats got a chuckle out of the exchange.

At 9:15, John Parrinello stepped to the podium to begin his cross-examination of Bill Morris. Having already set the tone the day before, John did not want any doubt in the witness's mind that he was in for a rough time. There were no social pleasantries exchanged. To assist in his attack and provide a visual for the jury, Parrinello laid out printed copies of Morris's interviews with the prosecution. There were twenty-six in all, plus his tape-recorded meetings with Lieutenant Berkow where he negotiated his deal. As he spread the papers out, John began questioning

Morris about the plea agreement he had entered into with the government. Parrinello reminded him how just yesterday he had said that he knew he had done something wrong and was now standing up and doing the right thing. Then John set him up for another sucker punch. Parrinello asked, "And part of that was assaultive behavior. Part of the things you had done wrong was assaultive behavior, correct?"

"Yes, that's correct," was the response.

"And before delivering the testimony yesterday you engaged in assaultive behavior," referring to the pushing incident with the news cameraman outside the federal building. This brought Mike Gennaco to his feet with a loud objection as once again the color left the witness's face. After a short sidebar, there was a brief back-and-forth between Morris and Parrinello over details of the pushing incident before Judge Telesca ended it.

Having accomplished his goal, John moved his line of questioning to the various incidents Morris had testified to being involved in. With each location, eighteen in all, when asked the date of occurrence, the jury heard the response, "I don't recall." Each time he answered, the government's star witness put another dent in his own credibility. For the remainder of the day, Parrinello covered the numerous interviews Morris had with the prosecution team. Before he ended, John brought up the question of Billy's exposure to prosecution. While he had been granted federal immunity, Morris was of the belief that he was also safe from state prosecution. Then John asked him, "As far as you know now, that was not accurate, correct?"

"Yes, sir." Morris went on to say Mike Berkow, as well Mike Gennaco and his entire staff, had misled him. With that fresh in the jury's mind, John asked the judge if they could end on that note.

The next day's headlines reflected the difference between John Parrinello's cross-examination of Bill Morris and his questioning by the prosecutor: "Star witness takes a raking." The article went on to say how even though he admitted to thefts and numerous assaults, Morris was allowed to plead to a single misdemeanor charge.

With no court on Fridays, and Monday the fifteenth being President's Day, we had four full days off. Well, from the trial anyway. I still did my mop-and-bucket routine at Kodak on Friday and had my Saturday-night bartending job at Hemingway's. The weather had been brutal, with blowing snow and near zero temperatures, and now on Tuesday, February 16, I found myself walking back into the uncomfortably cold courtroom. This would be the second full day of testimony for Bill Morris, but he would have to deal with Parrinello the whole day. In fact, for the remainder of the week, John would attack Billy like a pit bull on a rabbit.

The highlight of this day, at least for me, came when John got into the raid at 65 Prospect Street. Remember the cowboy boots? This is what followed. Parrinello asked Morris, "And were you accused by anybody of kicking the person in the face?"

"Yes, I was."

"And did you deny that?"

"Yes, I did deny it."

"And sir, with respect to that location, what you're willing to admit is that you slapped the suspect, right?"

"That's right. I didn't...I kicked the suspect. I don't deny kicking him." Finally! After five years, he admits what the suspect said right after the incident. Remember Mr. Hogan's description of the guy who kicked him in the mouth? He said, "White male, six feet two inches tall, skinny, thirty-five, long salt-and-pepper hair, beard, and mustache."

Now, indulge me just a bit longer so I can show you what a lying weasel Mr. Morris really is. Keep in mind he just admitted to kicking the guy on Prospect Street. His proffer agreement with the government was signed and dated May 3, 1991. All he had to do was give truthful information, which included his own involvement, and he would be granted immunity from federal prosecution. Yes, sir, a free pass. So why then did he go into the grand jury two months later on July 18, sweetheart deal in hand, and lie? After describing how he remembered a pair of cowboy boots kicking the guy and how I was the only one wearing

179

cowboy boots, he makes this statement: "Ironically, the guy blamed me in Internal Affairs that I had kicked him. I don't believe I touched the guy, and I don't own a pair of cowboy boots." *I don't believe I touched the guy!* Morris could have admitted dragging the suspect to the brink of death and gotten away with it. Now he's on the stand two years later admitting he did kick the guy in the face. He then goes on to tell the grand jury that when Mr. Hogan was brought into the Public Safety Building, he needed to be cleaned up. "The guy that Tommy did the kicking on—Tommy Alessi—was a mess. He has got blood on his face, can't bring him into the building like that."

The last sentence of paragraph seven of his agreement reads, "The agreement is contingent only upon Mr. Morris' complete and truthful cooperation and testimony." Part of paragraph nine is a section that says, "Any giving of false information, perjury [keep this in mind because perjury is exactly what he committed in the grand jury], or failure to testify in any judicial proceeding in connection with the individuals, matters, and transactions referred to in this agreement, as well as all other matters related thereto, would: permit the government to proceed fully with prosecution on any charges arising from the matters referred to in this agreement; permit the government to initiate and proceed with the prosecution of any other offenses arising from a breach of this agreement, including perjury."

When I was first questioned by Internal Affairs six months after the raid, I said that after entering the location, a couple of uniformed guys and I went right to the basement to search for suspects. Officer Glenn Hoff and his FTO (field training officer) Pete Brunett of the Genessee Section assisted in the raid. After a complaint was made, both officers were ordered by IA to write special reports detailing their involvement in the operation. Keep in mind that Hoff is new to the job and still in training. This is some of what he wrote in his report: "This officer then entered the building after the SCIS personnel and did proceed to the basement with Sergeant Alessi. Sergeant Alessi and myself did locate two suspects at the top of a dead-end stairwell at the farthest corner of the basement. SCIS personnel then took both suspects and took them upstairs while Sergeant Alessi and myself remained in the basement checking for additional suspects and contraband with negative results."

In his report, Officer Brunett wrote, "Reporting officer went into the basement and assisted SCIS personnel apprehend two black males who were hiding in the basement. Reporting officer handcuffed an unknown black male in the basement after SCIS personnel apprehended him on the southeast side of the basement. Reporting officer escorted the suspect up the stairs and into the front room where SCIS personnel told reporting officer to lie the suspect down face first on the floor. At this time another suspect [Hogan] was lying on the floor. Reporting officer did observe blood coming out of the suspect's mouth but it did not appear to be serious."

I was still in the basement with Glenn Hoff when Officer Burnett arrived upstairs to find Mr. Hogan already handcuffed on the floor. The investigation team had this information and apparently chose to disregard it. What the hell, why let the truth get in the way of a good prosecution? Besides, they had Billy to rely on.

John Parrinello grilled Morris for the next two days before we recessed for the weekend. He covered a number of topics, many of which were designed to show the jury the self-serving motives of the cop-turned-informant. John went over Morris's cooperation agreement in detail, paragraph by paragraph. He got into the tape-recorded meetings with Mike Berkow where Morris expressed his anger at the possibility of having to take a polygraph test. John also read for the jury the part of the conversation with Berkow when Billy said, "I don't give a fuck about anybody else. I only care about me." Then there was Morris's list of "bad acts" from his original notes, which he had prepared for the prosecutors. John went through the list and read off names of several officers and the incidents they were involved in. Interestingly enough, with the exception of Mike Mazzeo and work hours, no other defendant's name appeared on the list.

The following Monday, February 22, Bill Morris was greeted by Jim O'Brien's lawyer, Tony Leonardo. For the two hours that he cross-examined Morris, Tony covered many of the positive changes O. B. had made when he came to SCIS. Leonardo also talked extensively about everyone's concern over the department's Three-in-Eighteen policy with respect to use of force. The government had tied O'Brien's role in the conspiracy to his "taking care" of complaints that arose from HIT-related jobs. You're going to have to bear with me for a bit here. I was going to just skim over this issue, but it's one of the key points that helped make this "search for the truth" the witch hunt it really was.

Count I of the indictment was the conspiracy followed by thirty-six overt acts. The first paragraph referred to Jim O'Brien and included the sentence, "and that he would 'take care of' any complaints regarding excessive uses of force which resulted from this course of action." Remember that phrase. In his very first debriefing on May 3, 1991, Morris related his concerns over the use-of-force complaints that were sure to come along. This debriefing included FBI agents Gene Harding and Bill Dillon, as well as RPD lieutenants Duffy and Berkow. When Morris told them O'Brien said, "I'll take care of all the problems," not one of these experienced investigators asked Billy what he thought that meant specifically.

When he testified in the grand jury in July 1991, Morris said O'Brien's response to his concerns were, "Don't worry, I am going to take care of it for you." So without ever trying to find out what sinister plan O. B. had for "taking care" of complaints, or if in fact he ever did, they drew their own conclusion that it meant the captain would somehow make them disappear. That would be impossible because, as I said before, citizen complaints come in to Internal Affairs. Lt. Frank Frey, who was second in command of IA, appeared in the grand jury on March 20, 1991. This is the same genius who wanted to videotape all SCIS raids and was overruled by Capt. O'Brien. Frey helped the feds conclude that this must be another link in their conspiracy chain. Nowhere in his grand-jury testimony, though, did the lieutenant mention anything about Jim O'Brien squashing a complaint. Again, for the record, a computer-generated analysis for the thirty-month period of April 1988 to October 1990 showed that non-SCIS personnel received 721 citizen complaints while the Vice cops generated 49.

Now we have Morris testifying in a trial that was never supposed to happen. When Tony referred to his direct testimony regarding O. B. "taking care" of the use of force concerns, he asked the witness, "It's pretty clear now what he meant, wasn't it?" Morris responded, "It's very clear now." The bottom line is that Captain Jim O'Brien, a decorated veteran with twenty-five years of service to the community was indicted, and had his career destroyed, because of a comment he made. A comment meant to assure his men he would protect them. Not for doing anything wrong, but because he wouldn't let them take a hit for doing the job he asked them to do.

At 10:25 a.m., Greg Raggi's attorney, David Rothenberg, got his turn at bat. In his cross, David pointed out the discrepancies in a number of Bill Morris's statements that pertained to Greg. One in particular had to do with the suspect from 65 Prospect Street. Morris had told the investigators that when Mr. Hogan (the guy *he* kicked in the face) was brought to the Public Safety Building, Greg Raggi struck him. He said that while they were walking Mr. Hogan through the garage, Greg Picked up a telephone book from a stack that had been delivered for distribution, and hit the suspect in the face. The problem was that in each interview he related the story, it was different. While each version had Mr. Hogan being cleaned up, only one had Greg hitting him. Here's the best part: at no time in any of his interviews did the suspect say anyone hit him while he was at the PSB. Not even in his original complaint. In fact, when he was asked how he was treated when he got downtown his answer was, "Nice."

Rothenberg questioned Morris for the rest of the day and for another two hours the following day. At 10:55 a.m., my attorney, John Speranza, took over, and the first thing he got into was 65 Prospect Street. John went over how the suspect had identified Morris as the kicker and not me. He recreated the various aspects of the raid as to who was where in the house. Speranza went through a list of names and asked the witness if he remembered what each person was wearing on their feet. Of course, while he could not recall the footwear of anybody else, he specifically remembered that he was wearing sneaks and I had on boots. John then asked about the suspect's injuries. Remember his grand-jury testimony? He said the guy's face was a mess. Now, in response to Speranza's question, he says he knew he had blood in his mouth but didn't know his tooth was broken. Then Morris stepped on his dick again when John asked if Mr. Hogan had to go to the hospital and stay very long. "He didn't even go to the hospital," was the reply. Oops. Yeah, Billy, according to his own testimony, not to mention the custody log entry, Mr. Hogan did go to the hospital for treatment.

A few moments later, Bill Morris made one of his more memorable statements. When John got into the area of Billy's expertise as a narcotics officer, he talked about the witness's abilities as a persuader and a manipulator. John said there was no question Morris was a survivor, to which he replied, "I don't know about that."

"Well, you're sitting there and not over there [pointing to us]. So I mean that's one good sign." Then Morris kind of smirked as he looked at us and said, "They may very well have the best seat in the house. It's in the eye of the beholder." I remember wondering at the time if Billy was now regretting his decision to cooperate.

As the morning progressed, the many hours of questioning were beginning to take their toll on Bill Morris. If John Parrinello had made him flap before, John Speranza was about to cause him to come completely unglued. John asked him numerous questions regarding his interviews and the information he provided with respect to 65 Prospect Street. Billy didn't realize it but the soft-spoken, eloquent attorney was killing him with kindness. There was no shouting or animated theatrics in John's cross-examination. What he did was read the reports written from notes the investigators took during the debriefings. In many instances, according to Morris, the reports didn't accurately reflect what he had told them. At one point John attributed a statement to Morris that said the suspect at 65 Prospect Street was "severely beaten at the scene, which caused serious facial bleeding." This was where the witness really began to show signs of stress. When Morris denied making the statement, John said, "I know these are not your notes." Billy then said, "I don't think anybody realizes the impact of that though; that they're not my words. In most instances, the words that are contained in these reports are not my words." At one point a few moments later, Morris actually cracked and had to ask the judge for time to regain his composure. John read from one of the investigator's reports that credited Billy with saying the suspect was a bloody mess. Obviously exasperated, Morris replied, "We had a guy with blood on his face, and quite frankly, I've answered a thousand questions about these guys' notes and I'm...I sit here and get beat up about them and they're not what I said. It's...I apologize, but it's really starting to have an effect on me. Why does this continually happen? Your Honor, could I have five minutes please?" Unflappable, my ass!

After a brief recess, Speranza questioned the witness until 12:20 p.m. when Carl Salzer took over. Mazzeo's attorney asked Morris several questions relative to incidents in which Mike was named in the indictment. For the most part, Billy was not able to corroborate the accusations. Carl then mentioned several incidents where other officers, from RPD as well as other departments, had committed acts of misconduct. His point was to remind the jury that those individuals were not seated at the defense table. Carl ended his twenty-minute inquiry by reaffirming that the witness never saw Mike Mazzeo do anything wrong. "No, I never did," was the response.

John Parrinello stepped to the podium to finish out the day. I'm sure that made Billy feel warm all over. John used the opportunity to capitalize on the fact that the jury had just heard the government's witness disavow being the source of much of the information contained in their reports. As you might expect, the day ended in a confrontation where at one point Morris called Parrinello a liar. Well, that got the judge's attention, and he declared the day finished.

After Morris's third day on the stand, a local newspaper reporter interviewed Billy's wife. She had called the *Democrat and Chronicle* to dispute some of the characterizations in an article the previous Thursday. In it, Dan Aureli, a former assistant DA, referring to Morris, said, "He's testifying because he's saving his ass." Also quoted was Capt. Jim O'Brien, calling Billy a "thief" and a "coward."

In the article, which appeared in the morning paper on Tuesday, February 16, Mrs. Morris said, "We truly agonized over this together." She said how they discussed it at great length and that it was the hardest thing Billy had ever had to do. "But we did what we thought was morally the right thing to do. It was the only thing to do." Morris's wife went on to say, "It's hard when the people were your friends…because you don't want to hurt anybody." No? Remember his taped conversation with Lt. Berkow? "I don't give a fuck about anybody else. I only care about me." Believe me, the only thing hard for her husband was that he had to testify in open court. His handlers had convinced him all he had to do was give them the information they wanted, and he could go on his merry way.

The article ended with Billy's wife saying, "If it wasn't for our family and friends, we'd be having a hard time. But we just hold each other and talk about the day, and we get through it."

Much to his dismay, the witness would have to put up with Parrinello's go-for-the-throat technique for the entire next day. Wednesday morning's headline read, "After several days of testifying against ex-colleagues, witness' stress showing." On this, his eighth day on the witness stand, Morris was questioned at length about the money thefts he attributed to Greg and Scott. John brought up the numerous tape recordings Morris made while wearing a body wire. Even though Billy repeatedly denied it on the stand, his mission for the government was to capture incriminating conversations, including admissions of theft. Actually, the part Morris denied was that he had attempted to elicit admissions, even though on the tapes it is always he who brings up the subject. John then suggested Billy's actions were more like him sitting with his friends and hoping someone would say something about money thefts so it could be captured on tape. Finding this explanation more palatable, the witness conceded to it.

The fly in the ointment was that in the more than seventy hours of tapes Morris made, not one of them contained incriminating statements. As you might expect, it didn't take long for tempers to flare and shouting to begin. At one point, Mike Gennaco objected and asked the judge if everyone could calm down. Parrinello pursued his line of questioning over the prosecutor's objections. John had been trying to get Billy to admit that it was he who led the taped conversations to the subject of thefts. Then, referring to the fact that there was no evidence, he screamed at the witness, "There's the tapes right here, Mr. Morris. You play one for the jury with a theft admission on it. You go ahead and do it." Morris having already stated there wasn't one, Judge Telesca told Parrinello the witness had previously answered the question, and there was no need to yell.

During one of their question-and-answer duels, John told Morris to just answer his questions without gratuities. When the judge told John to just ask the question, Parrinello asked the judge to instruct the witness. By that time, Judge Telesca had just about had it. He said, "I've had all the instructions I need. It has been a long day for all of us. Then he said "Ladies and gentlemen, [referring to the jury] eight-thirty tomorrow morning. You may step down, Mr. Morris." The judge brought the day to an end with this declaration: "I have something else to say. Mr. Morris will be finished tomorrow come hell or high water. Come hell or high water you will see the last of Mr. Morris in this trial tomorrow."

Even though Thursday, February 25, was another cold, blustery morning, the one bright spot for Bill Morris was that it would be his last day on the witness stand. Only five more hours and his obligation to the federal government would be fulfilled. Billy's sweetheart deal would be cinched and, after his sentencing, he could get on with his life. But for the next ninety minutes, John Parrinello would make him flap just a little more.

John's attack began at 8:40 a.m. with questions pertaining to Morris's allegations of theft by Scott and Greg. Citing specific dates and locations from Billy's debriefing notes, Parrinello presented for the jury documentation that contradicted the allegations. Morris had Greg assaulting suspects and splitting stolen drug money with Scott on dates that payroll records showed he was on vacation. Morris had previously testified that Scott had deposited stolen money in a bank on a particular Saturday. We had a letter from the bank stating the branch in question had never been open on Saturdays. Some of Billy's more noteworthy testimony would come at the end of Parrinello's cross-examination.

Remember the guy who had his teeth knocked out on the roof of the car? John asked Morris if, while at the hospital, he recalled the doctor saying the teeth were chipped off because they were decayed. "I don't know if that's what he said. That's not what I saw," Billy answered. Then Parrinello directed Morris's attention to the use-of-force report regarding the incident. In the report Morris wrote and signed, in his writing, was this last sentence. "Dr. Ewing stated the defendant's teeth appeared to be rotten and that fact contributed to the teeth being cracked off." When John said Billy had just testified that he didn't know anything about the rotten teeth, Morris answered, "That's not the question you asked me, and that's not the answer I gave you."

In his direct examination by Mike Gennaco, Morris said he asked Scott why he did it, but said Harloff didn't really have an explanation. Parrinello then asked Billy to read for the jury what he said in his proffer debriefing regarding what Scott said to him. "I didn't mean to hurt him like that," was the quoted response.

Now for the best part. Remember when Morris said Harloff threatened a suspect with electrical wires? I'm going to give you Billy's testimony verbatim, but before you read it, go back to page 176, paragraphs 2 and 3 and reread his direct testimony and grand jury versions. Ready?

Parrinello referred to 405 Hayward Avenue as "the electrical wire incident."

Q. When I say electrical wire incident, we have a whole lot of people here, and what you're claiming is that Scott went at this guy with electrical wires to have him give up where the drugs were.

A. No. I think I defended Scott on this.

Q. OK. Well, let's defend him on the wire thing.

A. I'd like to do that for him.

Q. You do it. I won't ask any questions. You defend him on the wire thing.

A. Sure. It was indicated to me that Scott tried to electrocute somebody to say to give up the drugs.

Q. OK.

A. Scott never did that nor did Scott…he never would have done that.

Q. OK.

A. He took the cords out of the wall. There was nothing hooked up to the electrical circuits in the house, and if anything, in my opinion it was a joke.

So here we have the government's star witness saying an incident his best friend was indicted for—because of the witness's statements—was just a joke. Oh yeah. The suspect in that case was released from state prison after the DA's office threw out his two-count felony conviction. And just to show there were no hard feelings, the City of Rochester paid him $600,000 in one of its largest settlements ever.

At 10:10 a.m., Judge Telesca notified John Parrinello that his time had expired and the witness was tendered for redirect examination. Mike Gennaco revisited some key points of Billy's trip down memory lane with the defense team. Including a brief recess, the redirect lasted until noon. David Rothenberg then recrossed Morris for a few minutes, but much of what he was trying to cover was objected to by the prosecution and sustained by the judge. When David finished, Parrinello advised Judge Telesca that the other defense attorneys were waiving the remainder of their time. When John said he should get the balance of their time, Telesca said no. That prompted a "Thank you, sir," from Morris. In an apparent reference to Cinderella's coach, which also had a time limit, the judge told John, "You're still a pumpkin." And true to his word, at 12:20 p.m., in the middle of an objection argument, Judge Telesca said, "Mr. Morris, I have an announcement to make. You are excused." After a futile attempt by John to continue, the judge said, "You are not going to ask any more questions," and dismissed the jury until Monday morning.

The government played their trump card with the appearance of Bill Morris, and the trial had now reached the halfway mark. Beginning Monday morning, other police officers would get a chance to honor their agreements to testify for the prosecution. They too would get to tell the world about all those little conversations with the investigation team—conversations they never thought would be made public.

Seventeen

Over the weekend, the newspapers recapped some of Morris's testimony and described how the judge brought his appearance to an abrupt end. Saturday's edition featured an article about one of Judge Telesca's rulings. It said he had restricted our lawyers from using the argument of selective prosecution in their summations. The crux of the argument was that numerous other officers had admitted using excessive force but had escaped indictment. Hopefully, the jury would be able to draw that curious conclusion for themselves at the end of the trial. Monday, March 1, and the guest of honor was Officer James VanBrederode of the Gates Police Department. Gates is a suburb on the western border of Rochester, and the witness first rotated through our unit in August 1988. He thought the RPD was such a great place to work that he transferred to the department in 1989 (back then cops from every suburban department were trying to do the same thing). Officer VanBrederode did a second tour in HIT in June of 1990. But the glamour must have faded because he went back to Gates two years later.

Jim VanBrederode was brought in to do Greg, Scott, and me. And for the first time, the jury would hear damning testimony regarding Mike Mazzeo. He was also the first prosecution witness whose direct examination would be guided by Mike Gennaco's other assistant, Jessica Ginsburg. While stumbling through questions to elicit testimony about a vehicle stop where cocaine and money was seized, she was inundated with objections, most of which were sustained. Let's try another one.

In August of 1988, we hit a house on Barons Street in the northeast section of the city. This was one of the incidents I was indicted on for "failing to supervise." At this particular location, we split our forces between the house and an occupied vehicle parked nearby. As the raid team rushed the house, a white male emerged from the front door. I had gone with others to secure the vehicle. That done, I proceeded to the house. Upon entry, I saw several people lying face down on the living room floor. As usual, there was a lot of shouting and turmoil. It turned out the individual who had tried to leave as the raid began thought it would be a good idea to bring a gun along with him that night. He figured a white, middle-class young man from a neighboring county venturing in to a high-crime, predominantly minority part of town to buy dope should have protection. There were only two problems with his plan: the little .22-caliber semiautomatic was on his girlfriend's permit, and he got to meet us.

When cops are dealing with a high-stress situation, such as a raid on a drug house, and they discover one of the bad guys has a gun, well, let's just say it tends to make them a little testy. The sum and substance of VanBrederode's testimony was that Greg, Scott, and I were yelling at the suspect, and "someone," he's not sure who, was tightening the handcuffs on him. The witness also testified that Greg and Scott took the guy into a back room, and VanBrederode could hear screaming and the sound of punches and slaps. As for me, he said I was going back and forth between the two rooms.

Then it was Mike Mazzeo's turn. Mike had a crackhead informant by the name of Tim McNulty who would set up dope deals, mainly in the Highland Section of the city. One night in 1990, McNulty got arrested by uniformed officers and started dropping Mazzeo's name, telling the patrol cops he was Mike's informant. Tim wasn't exactly the brightest bulb in the box. Apparently he had been on the pipe for three or four days and was pretty whacked out. Pissed off about being arrested, he had been ranting and raving that he was going to kill a cop. When this got back to Mazzeo, he called McNulty for a meet. Mike,

Greg, and Jim VanBrederode were in Mazzeo's car behind the former Sears building on Monroe Avenue. Needless to say, Michael was not real happy with young Mr. McNulty. According to the witness, when the informant approached the car and stuck his head in the driver's window, Mazzeo grabbed him around the neck and punched him in the head and face several times.

Officer Pete Leach, the fourth man in the car, gave a different account of the incident when he testified before the grand jury on March 20, 1991, and in an interview with investigators the following August. Officer Leach said when McNulty got to the car, Mazzeo grabbed the informant's shirt with both hands and, while they were face to face, screamed at him about his behavior. Pete went on to say that Mazzeo got out of the car and continued to scream at McNulty while poking him in the chest with a nightstick. The pokes were described as not hard and compared to how a person might use a finger to poke someone in the chest. Two rotating officers also there that night were asked by investigators as to their recollection of the incident. Neither Chris Tuttle's nor Tim Fingland's interpretation corroborated VanBrederode's. Once again, the prosecutors chose to use the version that best served their needs.

Officer VanBrederode was cross-examined by four of the five defense attorneys and briefly questioned by Ms. Ginsburg on redirect. In an attempt to place some sense of value on the witness's testimony regarding the McNulty incident, she asked him why he disagreed with the idea that it was no big deal. Keep in mind this is an officer who can't seem to decide what department he should work for, has no experience in drug investigations, and has never used an informant before. He said, "This was a significant officer safety problem for the following drug deals that took place after he was beaten. Mr. McNulty clearly has an opportunity to put an officer in jeopardy during a drug deal involving an undercover police officer at a location behind closed doors. I consider that a significant violation." Always nice to hear from the experts.

In his cross-examination, Carl Salzer put the whole thing into perspective for the jury. He went over not only McNulty's history of weird behavior and the relationship between Mazzeo and the informant but, more importantly, the witness's lack of knowledge of that relationship. Carl finished by asking VanBrederode if he remembered McNulty shaking Mazzeo's hand and apologizing for the way he had been acting. As you might guess, he did not recall that part of the incident. The witness was excused.

The remainder of the week saw three more officers from the Rochester Police Department make their way to the witness stand. All had been granted immunity and related for the jury a number of incidents where a suspected drug dealer had been slapped or punched by those of us at the defense table. Of course they all admitted having used excessive force themselves, but as you know by now, that didn't count. On Tuesday, March 2, Officer Randy Holmes told the jury how, after buying cocaine from a suspect, he, along with Raggi and Harloff, punched the suspect in the midsection to get him to disclose the location of his stash.

Later that day, Officer Jeff Anderson, whose overtime slip Joyce had torn up, admitted hitting someone in the head with his flashlight after a foot chase then lying in the report about the injuries the guy received. Anderson said the suspect ran into some debris during the chase. This came after shocking the jury with testimony of Scott Harloff swearing at a woman. That's right, swearing. She had been taken out of a car registered to a known drug dealer and didn't appreciate the inconvenience. When she got in Scotty's face, he called her a bitch. I guess the part that really made this a federal offense was that when she demanded to know his identity, Harloff gave her a false name.

During his cross-examination of Officer Anderson, David Rothenberg went through the numerous lies the witness initially told the investigators. He was typical of so many who had engaged in, shall we say, less-than-appropriate conduct; thinking they could save their asses by lying to investigators, they now found themselves with their balls in a vice. At one point, David said, "OK. You had been told by Craig [Deputy Chief Robert Craig] and Berkow that here's what you have to do or else your job will be in jeopardy. Right?" To which the witness answered, "Just prior to the grand jury, yes." Shortly after that, Officer Anderson had to take a short break to regain his composure. Hang in there, Jeff. Tomorrow you get to start your day with the tag team of Leonardo, Parrinello, and Salzer.

The first order of business for Tony Leonardo on Wednesday morning was to address a statement Officer Anderson made during his direct examination. Mr. Gennaco asked the witness about a comment regarding Jamaicans made by Capt. O'Brien in January 1989. Anderson was one of the rotating city officers assigned to HIT that month. He said one afternoon in the SCIS office he heard Harloff, Raggi, and the captain making comments about Jamaican drug dealers. The witness said, referring to O'Brien, "He made a statement that Jamaicans, they aren't citizens; don't have no rights. They should just take 'em and ship 'em back home."

Tony began by confirming that Officer Anderson had eight interviews with investigators and two appearances in the grand jury. And even though he had been asked questions about O'Brien, not once did this comment ever come up. The witness said his first mention of it was in a conversation with Lt. Berkow, just prior to the start of the trial. For the next twenty minutes, Leonardo covered Anderson's experience in the drug-fighting business. To be more precise, it was his *lack* of experience that was highlighted. Anderson, who at the time of his rotation had three years on the job, admitted he'd never heard of the Shower or Spangler Posses. These were two of the premier Jamaican drug gangs wreaking havoc in the city. He didn't know what INS (Immigration and Naturalization Service) was. The best part was when Tony asked the officer if he had heard of the JOCs. "That is familiar, JOC," came the response. Really, Jeff? The Jamaican Organized Crime unit was part of SCIS. They worked out of the same office Anderson had reported to every day during his rotation. The point of Leonardo's counterattack was to make the jury understand that Capt. O'Brien was referring to *illegal* Jamaican dope dealers, and that it was not racist in nature, as implied.

For the rest of the morning, Officer Anderson was cross-examined by John Parrinello and Carl Salzer. After a fifteen-minute recess, the prosecution called RPD Officer Lloyd Cuyler to the stand at noon. The witness would be on the stand for all of the next day and the first half of the following Monday. His would prove to be some of the most interesting testimony of the trial. That's because it would be revealed on cross-examination that Officer Cuyler had committed perjury in a trial three years earlier, and the spin he put on that testimony was nothing short of incredible.

Lloyd Cuyler was the undercover who made the confirmation drug buy just prior to the search warrant raid at 405 Hayward Avenue. This is the location where Scott Harloff was alleged to have threatened to electrocute the suspect. In his direct testimony, Cuyler was asked if after the buy, anything further happened between himself or any permanent members of the HIT Squad and Mr. James (the suspect). Remember this answer for future reference. "I...I told Mr. James...I walked up to him and I told him, I said tell us where the drugs are, give us the drugs or whatever. I'm the one you sold to. I saw your face. You saw my face. We were face to face, person to person, you know, and he said it wasn't me, it wasn't me, and I slapped him." The witness also said he saw Harloff slap the suspect.

Now this is where it gets a little sticky for Officer Cuyler. You see, as the buy officer, he was the star witness at the state trial in April 1990 where Maurice James was convicted and sent to prison. In that trial, the defense attorney asked Cuyler, "Now, did you in any way lay your hands on my client that evening? Did you kick him, did you push him, did you hit him? Did you see any other officers doing that?" To all three questions the witness replied, "No." Then Officer Cuyler was asked, "Was there any conversation with my client while he was inside 405 Hayward Avenue?" His answer. "Not to my knowledge, sir." Compare these answers to the ones in the previous paragraph.

Webster's dictionary defines perjury as "the voluntary violation of an oath or vow either by swearing to what is untrue or by omission to do what has been promised under oath. False swearing." New York State Penal Law, Section 210.05, says, "A person is guilty of perjury in the third degree when he swears falsely." It's a Class A misdemeanor.

John Parrinello started his cross-examination at 12:50 p.m. and spent the next forty minutes going over several meetings Officer Cuyler had with investigators and the prosecution. Officer Cuyler was excused, and we adjourned for the day. After what I'm sure was a peaceful night's rest, the witness got to say good morning to Parrinello at 8:35 the following day. John got right into a meeting Cuyler had with Chief Irving in December of 1990 regarding the officer's upcoming grand-jury testimony. Cuyler said the chief told him to just tell the truth and not to worry because nothing would happen to him. But something did happen to Officer Cuyler: he was given a ten-day suspension.

When he'd walked out of the grand jury room after testifying the following July, Cuyler was met by Lieutenants Duffy and Berkow. He was taken into another room where the two command officers laid out what was going to happen to him. John now asked the witness if they had said anything to him that he took as threatening. Cuyler responded, "Yeah. They didn't make it clear that I was going to get a ten-day suspension. They told me something was going to happen to me and they told me don't worry about it—it's not going to be a termination type of thing, and that nobody could know about it; not to go to the Locust Club, the union, nothing like that, and that it would be arranged that I would receive some discipline and it'd come out of my time bank and nobody would know about it."

In an interview on November 30, 1990, Lt. Mike Berkow was among the four investigators who questioned Cuyler, and one of the topics of discussion was Maurice James and 405 Hayward Avenue. In a reference to Mr. James, the investigative report from that meeting says, "Officer Cuyler admits that he smacked him, too."

During his cross-examination, John Parrinello brought up a memo Officer Cuyler had sent to Lt. Berkow. It seems that sometime after the James trial, Cuyler was in a court hearing on an unrelated burglary case. This defendant had the same attorney as Maurice James, and that attorney wanted to revisit some of Cuyler's testimony from their previous encounter. This must have brought little beads of sweat to the young officer's forehead. The matter was adjourned, and, although you might not know it from the answers he now gave Parrinello, it was clear Cuyler had reached out to Berkow for help. When John asked the witness if he did in fact send the memo and was it regarding court testimony, Cuyler responded in the affirmative. "As a matter of fact, Lt. Berkow met you and went over your trial testimony in the Maurice James case regarding an incident that occurred on February 14, 1989, at 405 Hayward Avenue, an incident which you testified to in this courtroom, correct?" Seems like a fairly simple question, right? Well, Cuyler answered, "Correct." Only a few moments later, in response to a question, he said, "I don't recall meeting with Lt. Berkow and going over trial testimony. I would think if I had, this would be unnecessary."

In the memo, Cuyler says, "Lieutenant, I will do my best to explain this thing as best I can, but keep in mind it's from 100 percent memory just as my testimony in the civil rights investigation is. The things Colbert [defense attorney] questioned me on is on page 382." This was a page reference to the James trial transcript where Cuyler was asked if he had laid his hands on Mr. James. After asking the question regarding a meeting with Berkow a third time and getting another ambiguous answer, Parrinello held up the memo and asked, "Do you remember typing this up?"

"Yes, I do," Cuyler answered.

"Does your signature appear on it?"

"Yes. This is mine."

As luck would have it, Officer Cuyler did not have to testify at the court proceeding for the burglary case, because the not-so-lucky defendant died. There was, however, the matter of his forthcoming grand jury appearance. Since he had made the decision to cooperate, Cuyler had to find a way to explain the discrepancy between his state trial testimony and what he had since admitted to the investigators. I'll get to that incredible explanation shortly, but here's an excerpt from his memo to Berkow: "Thanks for taking the time to help me out with this. You have access to my grand-jury testimony for the civil rights case. Can you check it to make sure I'm not screwing anything up?" I'm not going to play back all the questions and answers from our trial. Instead I'll get right to the heart of Lloyd Cuyler's explanation as to why he feels he did not commit perjury in the James trial.

In his memo to Berkow, Cuyler cites page 382 of his testimony: "Line four, the question is did I in any way lay my hands on the defendant. My answer was no. The question was very vague, and I wasn't sure of it referring to handcuffing, transporting, or merely escorting the defendant. I then added, not that I remember because when there is a suspect present he may move or be escorted by any police officer in the house for several reasons including officer safety and discussion of the case." So what Officer Cuyler was now asking the jury to believe is that when Mr. James's attorney asked the question, it never occurred to Lloyd that he was referring to striking the suspect. Stay with me, it gets better.

The next question from Mr. James's attorney was, "Did you kick him, did you push him, did you hit him?" That was followed by, "Did you see any other officer do that?" To both questions Cuyler said "No." Keep in mind he said in his direct testimony in our trial that he slapped Mr. James and that he saw Harloff slap him. His explanation for the discrepancy: "That's a compound question, it's not an *or* question," meaning that he did not do *all three* of those things, nor did he see any other officer do *all three* of those things.

The last explanation showed even more brilliance when John Speranza crossed him the following Monday, March 8. John went through each component of this "compound" question and when he said, "You did not hit him? Is your answer you did not hit him; is that true? The witness responded, "No. I slapped him. So if you want to interpret that as hitting him then yes, but I did not do the other things that he covered in the question." When Speranza asked the officer if he didn't believe there were any differences between his two testimonies, this is what he said: "There is a difference. I was asked specific questions in this trial. In that trial I was asked compounded and vague questions. The questions were poor."

During his cross-examination, Officer Cuyler was asked numerous times by John Parrinello if Mike Berkow had helped him formulate the explanations for his discrepant testimonies. Being a good soldier, he wasn't about to admit that. When asked what he was thanking the lieutenant for in his memo, Cuyler said it had to do with the fact that the defense attorney from the burglary trial wanted to question him about his previous testimony. He knew his credibility was being called into question. The fact is Officer Cuyler never did say exactly what he was thanking Berkow for. Now, think about this in terms of yourself. Say you testify under oath and give definite answers to questions, and later you give different answers to the same questions. Would you really have to ask someone else for help to explain why? Well, maybe you'd need somebody to point out that the questions in the first trial were "compounded and vague." And if that somebody just happens to be a command officer with a law degree helping to spearhead the investigation you found yourself caught up in, so much the better. I'll let you decide if an RPD lieutenant helped a junior officer cover up an act of perjury.

Allow me to interject a little background on Mike Berkow. He received a law degree from Syracuse University while he was on the job. Somehow he managed to convince the chief in a previous administration to let him arrange his work schedule so he could attend school and work his wheel over the weekend. I'm not quite sure how he was able to do that, because Joyce told me when she was dating Mark Gerbino, a good friend of Berkow's, they would often see him out when he was supposed to be working. Berkow then took a leave of absence from the department to clerk for a federal judge. Guess which one. The

Honorable Michael A. Telesca. While we all knew Judge Telesca's integrity and sense of fairness was beyond reproach, from where we sat, their prior association was a bit disconcerting. Needless to say, Berkow returned to the RPD, rose to the rank of lieutenant and, along with Lt. Duffy, cocommanded the witch hunt against us.

The next day's newspaper article included this paragraph: "When Harloff's lawyer, John R. Parrinello, attacked Cuyler's credibility by disclosing the state court dialogue, several jurors turned in their seats and looked uneasy."

When it came to yours truly, Officer Cuyler's testimony was just as inconsistent. On direct, Mr. Gennaco, referring to Hayward Avenue, asked him, "The permanent supervisor [that would be me] of the HIT Team, was he at that location during any of this incident that you've described?" Remember that the incident he just described was Mr. James being slapped. "Not that I recall," the witness responded. Careful, Lloyd, you're getting away from the script. The follow-up question: "During any of the time that you were at that location, sir, did you see Sergeant Alessi present?" That's better. "Yes." With John Speranza going crazy with objections, Cuyler went on to say I even told my guys to stop because the uniforms were coming in.

Fast forward again to Monday, March 8: when Speranza, on cross, repeated the witness's testimony from five days ago when he said I told people to stop, Cuyler denied saying that. John has this look when he's been caught off guard by an answer from a witness. It's a look that says, "Are you fucking serious?" Holding a copy of his direct testimony, he listened to the witness's answer to a very specific question. Cuyler said, "OK. It is my testimony that I do not recall at which time Sergeant Alessi came in. I did not see him there when I saw those things occurring."

After another forty-five minutes of redirect and recross examination, Officer Cuyler was excused, and Brockport police officer Mark Cyr was called to the stand at 12:20 p.m. Brockport is a small community in the northwest part of Monroe County. Mark Cyr began his law enforcement career with the Rochester Police Department in 1985, but after a year and a half he sought the safer environment of a smaller village department. Many believe getting shot at while he was a city cop had a lot to do with his decision to migrate.

Officer Cyr was called to give testimony against Greg Raggi and Mike Mazzeo, but Judge Telesca ruled he would not be allowed to talk about a specific charge against Michael. The essence of Cyr's testimony was that in January of 1990, during a raid on a drug house in the northeast section of the city, Greg Raggi assaulted the suspect in the house by breaking a three- or four-foot-long two-by-four across his back. Under direct examination by Cathleen Mahoney, the witness said the board struck the guy in the upper back by his shoulder blades. Before I get into the specifics of Officer Cyr's version of this incident, I'd like you to try and imagine yourself getting hit hard enough across your shoulder blades to break a two-by-four and what the resulting injury would be like. Or, you could do what the husband of one of the jurors did: take a three-foot two-by-four and *try* to break it on a cement block wall.

His first interview was December 21, 1990, when Officer Cyr told investigators "that at no time did he see any handcuffed persons, persons who were not resisting, struck with feet, fists or any other object." The following February 4, he signed a proffer agreement and was interviewed again. It was at this interview that Cyr first mentioned anything about Greg hitting someone with a two-by-four. On February 20, he accompanied investigators to the house where he said the incident occurred and identified it from the record. Cyr was interviewed again on May 24 and made his grand jury appearance on June 20, 1991.

They must have really liked Officer Cyr because they reinterviewed him the following November. It wasn't until March 3, 1993, that Cyr received his witness letter from the feds. Now he had immunity from federal prosecution relative to anything he already said as well as from his testimony at trial.

After all the interviews he had and the journey to the location where he said the incident occurred, prosecutor Mahoney questioned Officer Cyr for only twenty minutes. John Parrinello and Carl Salzer used only twenty minutes between them to cross the witness. And only two minutes of that time was spent by Parrinello establishing that Scott Harloff was not at the scene.

Greg's lawyer, David Rothenberg, took his turn at bat at 1:00 p.m. and got only about twenty minutes of questioning in before Judge Telesca recessed for the day. David would get to start fresh with Officer Cyr first thing the next morning.

Of course we couldn't possibly start the next day's business without first having read the titillating article in the morning paper recapping Monday's testimony. The article was about Cyr's account of Greg breaking a two-by-four over Orenthal Casey's back. "Cyr said Casey was crying after the attack, but there was no testimony about the extent of Casey's injuries." The next line did two things: it demonstrated just what a compassionate soul Officer Cyr was and it confirmed Casey was never injured. "'I asked him if he was all right, and he said yes,' Cyr testified." As I said before, imagine someone breaking a two-by-four across you shoulder blades and how "all right" you'd be.

For the first two hours of Tuesday's proceedings, Rothenberg used police reports and photos from the night of the two-by-four incident to elicit details from the witness. Who was there, what their positions were, the suspect's location in the basement, how the board was allegedly swung at Mr. Casey. When it came to his final question, David made it a good one. "When you were describing the two-by-four, isn't there a word you left out when you were describing the two-by-four? Think about it."

"No, not that I recall," answered the witness.

David shot back, "How about 'imaginary'? Did you leave that out?"

"Objection, your Honor," was the response from a blindsided Cathleen Mahoney at the prosecution table.

After a brief redirect by Ms. Mahoney and recross by Rothenberg, the judge ordered a short recess. We returned to the courtroom at 12:15 and the government called their next witness. Bear with me, only three more to go. Ex-RPD officer Carl Jefferson walked into the courtroom toward the witness stand for his guided testimony by lead prosecutor Mike Gennaco. I could hardly believe my own eyes when I saw what he was wearing. He had on a purple suit that made him look like the Grand Marshal in some sort of Easter pimp parade. When Harloff's lawyer, John Parrinello, first noticed the former cop's fashion stylings, he leaned over and whispered a single word to Scott: "Bonus!" Jefferson joined the Rochester Police Department in 1987. He had three tours in HIT: February, March, and October of 1989. He resigned from the department in July of 1990 for "personal reasons." The prosecution would get their money's worth out of Carl Jefferson. He would talk about Greg, Scott, and me. I'll save the part about me for last. It turned out it was something I had prepared for since we first began reviewing discovery material, getting ready for the trial.

Jefferson was one of four African-American cops who rotated through my unit in October of 1989. Jefferson, along with Lloyd Cuyler (whom you've already heard from), Kevin Riley, and Randy Benjamin would become known as the Black Assassins, a name given to the four by Bill Morris. On those occasions when a suspected (or known) dope dealer was foolish enough to fight or run, the Black Assassins would make them regret their decision. Back then, they wore the title like a badge of honor. Of course, I'm sure that now, like so many others who drank the Kool-Aid and promised to go and sin no more, they all saw the error of their ways.

The witness first described how at one location we'd hit, the suspect attempted to escape. After Harloff caught him at the door, he slipped out of his shirt and made it out of the building. Jefferson gave chase and ran the guy down. He said that after the suspect was cuffed and returned to the scene, Greg Raggi was so upset over the guy getting away that Raggi kicked him in the chest so hard "his entire body was elevated off the floor." Of course, that's the quote that made it into the next day's paper.

Jefferson went on to tell the jury about a guy stopped on Joseph Avenue who thought coming out with a hatchet would be the intelligent thing to do. Fortunately for him, the hatchet man wasn't shot, but he was thumped pretty thoroughly. When Gennaco asked if a use-of-force report had been done, the witness replied, "Not until afterwards. We received word that a complaint had been filed. The chief [Urlacher] had ordered an investigation to take place at which time we did the PSS forms." Imagine that. The same chief named in our indictment for conspiring with Jim O'Brien to cover up citizen complaints ordered an investigation.

Now it was Scotty's turn. Jefferson testified about a raid where he made the drug buy with a twenty-dollar bill that he had previously marked with his initials. After returning to the car, the house was hit using a battering ram to knock the door down. A search for the marked buy money proved negative. When a large roll of cash was found in the coat pocket of one of the occupants, Jefferson said Harloff told him to just pick one (a twenty-dollar bill) and that Scott marked it with his initials, claiming it to be the money used to buy the dope.

Carl Jefferson also testified that at another location I backhanded a cuffed suspect proclaiming his innocence. This isn't the one I said I was saving for last, but I figured as long as the witness was on such a roll I'd include it, even though I really couldn't remember doing it. Then it was back to Scott. Jefferson told the jury about a search-warrant buy he had made with a confidential informant at a location on February 7, 1989. Two weeks later when the place was hit, the witness couldn't identify any of the occupants as the person who made the initial sale on the seventh. It was then that Jefferson said Harloff told him to "just pick one." So he did.

Now this is the one I was waiting for. Gennaco asked Jefferson if he recalled being at 385 Troup Street on March 14, 1989. The witness acknowledged he did and proceeded to explain how after the house was hit, people were bailing out of windows to get away. One guy managed to break loose and take off running even after he was handcuffed. Jefferson said he and Lloyd Cuyler ran him down and pounded him so bad he had blood coming out of his ear. At that time Bill Morris and

Scott Harloff pulled up in their car and surveyed the damage. The witness then told the jury Morris called me down to the scene because of injuries to the suspect. It was at this point Jefferson said I complimented them for doing a good job. When asked by Mr. Gennaco if I had reacted in any way, his exact answer was: "Agent Alessi said good job, smiled, and walked away." *Agent* Alessi? Who did this nitwit think I worked for?

Remember when John Speranza and I were poring over the six-thousand-plus pages of discovery material from the government, and I told him we would need copies of my travel vouchers? I had been in Myrtle Beach, South Carolina, with Mazzeo and Tony Cotsworth on March 13, 14, and 15 of that year. We were at a seminar where one of the instructors was Capt. Vince Faggiano of the Rochester Police Department. Sometimes the devil really is in the details. You'll love Jefferson's response when Speranza shows him a copy of the travel voucher on cross-examination. After a couple more revelations by the witness, the judge called an end to the day.

I had already left the courtroom when John Parrinello made an off-the-record comment to the folks at the prosecution table. It was something to the effect that they might want to put a trough in the room and wear raincoats tomorrow because it was going to get real bloody.

Wednesday, March 10, the headline read, "Ex-cop tells tale of lies, beatings." Well, at least the reporter, Leslie Sopko, got one part right. It was definitely a *tale*. She had been filleting us in the newspaper from the very beginning. She included Jefferson's testimony about Harloff telling the witness to randomly pick out a suspect for arrest and Raggi kicking an individual so hard that "his entire body was elevated off the floor." Of course, I wasn't excluded. She put in the "good job" comment I was supposed to have made on Troup Street (while I was in South Carolina).

At 8:40 a.m., ex-cop Jefferson was recalled to the witness stand. Mike Gennaco had not finished his direct examination, and in the first thirty minutes, we listened to some genuine pearls come out of Carl's mouth. He testified about a guy with a hatchet whom he, Lloyd Cuyler, and Randy Benjamin thumped. Three-quarters of the Black Assassins jumped this individual so fast and hard he never got the chance to even think about using the weapon in his hand. I remembered they used to pride themselves on how quickly and efficiently they could take someone down. Jefferson told the jury that Morris, Raggi, Harloff, and Mazzeo had been describing to other members of SCIS how they couldn't get in on the guy. They said, "We jumped in there; didn't give 'em a chance to move; didn't give 'em a chance to get his arm down—he was down, boom, real fast and then we beat 'em up real good."

Apparently, Mr. Jefferson had forgotten how proud he used to feel after he and his fellow assassins took someone down. Now he tells the jury, "I began to feel that we were the bad guys. We were doing more damage to the people than the people were doing to themselves." Then came the real gem: "I began to feel that I was just as bad as the bad guys. I mean, I came on the department to consider myself a leader in the community, to set an example for the young coming up, to set an example for the neighborhood." Give me a fucking break! It was all I could do to keep from throwing up. Shortly after that, the witness was excused, the jury was removed, and a vigorous motion argument was conducted by John Parrinello based on eleventh-hour delivery of the substance of Jefferson's testimony. Of course, as with every other motion to dismiss, this one was denied. After a thirty-minute recess, Parrinello began his cross-examination of the former Black Assassin at 9:45 a.m.

After the usual preliminary questions pertaining to the number of meetings the witness had attended with the prosecution team, John got to the meat of his cross-examination. He elicited from Jefferson that at one of his meetings with Lt. Duffy, the witness was promised immunity for his cooperation in the investigation. The significance of this was that the immunity wasn't from state or federal prosecution, but from departmental charges. Why would someone no longer a member of the Rochester Police Department need immunity from departmental charges? Because Carl Jefferson had gone to Chief Roy Irving's office to inquire about getting his former job back. It's too bad Mr. Jefferson couldn't have known it at the time, but he'd have a better chance of being struck by lightning while holding the winning New York State lottery ticket.

By the time John Parrinello had finished with the witness for the day, the jury got to hear a laundry list of names of people Jefferson and his fellow "assassins" had applied their heavy-handed tactics to. They also learned about his problems with his ex-wife and his girlfriend.

John cross-examined the witness for the remainder of the morning. Instead of breaking for lunch, Judge Telesca ordered a late-morning recess at 11:15 a.m. and advised everyone we would be ending the day's activities at 1:00 p.m. Jefferson was being questioned about one of the many use-of-force reports he had filed when the judge announced, "We are going to call it quits for the day. Ladies and gentlemen, please be back Monday at eight-thirty." Parrinello made two more motions to dismiss the case based on the government's failure to produce discovery material. Keeping his record intact, the judge denied these motions as well. Since it was only Wednesday, we were looking at an exceptionally long weekend.

Eighteen

Mother Nature must have thought we needed even more time off because on Saturday, March 13, 1993, what some called the Storm of the Century blasted most of the northeast, so there was no court on Monday. By the time the storm was over, Rochester came in second only to Portland, Maine, with 161 inches of snow.

Carl Jefferson returned to the stand at 8:40 a.m. on Tuesday the sixteenth and was greeted by John Parrinello, who would grill him for most of the morning. The witness was questioned about numerous cases as well as his unsuccessful attempt to rejoin the Rochester Police Department. At 11:05 a.m., Parrinello advised the court he had no further questions for Mr. Jefferson. I wasn't sure, but I thought heard a sigh of relief from the former cop's lungs. His respite would be short-lived because exactly nine minutes later, my lawyer, John Speranza, stood up, took a deep breath, and began his cross.

John focused on the previous testimony Jefferson had given in interviews and in the grand jury. The witness was interviewed twice on October 31, 1990. He went before the grand jury on January 24, 1991. In any of his prior testimony, there was no mention of the two incidents he had just attributed to me. The only thing he did attribute to me was that I had told him and the rest of his group not to use excessive force. It wasn't until Jefferson was asked to review a number of arrest packages in December of 1992 that he suddenly recalled my alleged misconduct at 610 Brown Street and 385 Troup Street. Keep in mind this is someone who wants to be rehired by the police department from which he had resigned. I'll let you decide if Mr. Jefferson had a reason to provide enhanced cooperation. On March 8, 1993, a week before his appearance at this trial, Jefferson was allowed to correct his grand-jury testimony. Guess what? Still no mention of the incidents he tagged me with.

Just prior to finishing his cross-examination, John handed Jefferson defendant's exhibit #83 and asked the witness to read it to himself. The document was a travel voucher from the City of Rochester dated March 13, 14, and 15, 1989. It was for a training conference on drug raids and liability. Under the circumstances, I found this to be just a little ironic. I was there with Tony Cotsworth and Mike Mazzeo in Myrtle Beach. John attempted to have Jefferson reconcile the fact that I couldn't have been on Troup Street on a date inclusive of my time in South Carolina. All Jefferson could respond with was, "I know what I saw." This is how John finished:

Q. You know what you saw?
A. Yes, sir.
Q. And you know you saw it on March 14, correct?
A. Yes, that's correct.
Q. And you cannot possibly be wrong or mistaken; is that right?
A. That's correct.

With that, John advised the judge he had no further questions.

When John offered the voucher into evidence, the lead prosecutor, Mike Gennaco, objected. His objection was based on hearsay, and he said there was no foundation. God forbid they should let the truth interfere with a good hanging. Judge Telesca received the voucher into evidence.

Carl Salzer and David Rothenberg consumed the next twenty-seven minutes with minimal cross-examination, and Gennaco used the same amount of time was on redirect. The witness was excused after a couple more questions by John Parrinello and John Speranza.

At 12:40 p.m. the next-to-last witness was called to the stand. Rochester police officer Wayne Harris was questioned by Cathleen

Mahoney. She had only twenty-minutes' worth of questions regarding Greg Raggi and Mike Mazzeo, and the judge ended the day's activities at 1:00 p.m. Officer Harris would get to face John Parrinello shortly after breakfast the next morning.

The following day's morning paper had only the crux of Harris's brief testimony—that he saw Raggi strike a suspect with a metal pole. This may be hard to believe, but there wasn't a word printed regarding the exculpatory evidence that contradicted Carl Jefferson's statements as to my whereabouts on March 14, 1989.

Wayne Harris took the witness stand at 8:35 a.m. and was cross-examined by John Parrinello for the next two and a half hours. John spent a considerable amount of time going over the specifics of Harris's proffer agreement with the government. Parrinello also pointed out discrepancies between the witness's grand-jury testimony and that which he gave yesterday. At 11:27 a.m., Carl Salzer cross-examined Harris for about fifteen minutes relative to Mike Mazzeo's actions during an arrest. After a brief redirect by Ms. Mahoney and a short recross by Parrinello, the witness was excused.

When asked for their next witness, the government wanted to call Sue Campbell to the stand. She was a city employee who worked in the payroll department. It was the prosecution's intention to have her testify as to how much money the City of Rochester received from the government through federal grants. Counts eighteen and nineteen of the indictment charged us under Title 18 USC 666 with conspiring to and "stealing" federal funds by getting paid for but not actually working a full eight-hour shift. It was at this point that Judge Telesca excused the jury from the courtroom.

After reading the indictment, the judge took issue with those two counts the prosecution was trying to hang on us. Telesca's argument was that the statute was intended for fictitious or "ghost" employees. This would apply to municipalities receiving federal money supposedly used to pay nonexistent workers. The statute makes an exception for bona fide employees. The judge said, "What troubles me is I think this Section 666 (c) precludes the very allegations that are made in this indictment and that it excludes bona fide salary, wages, and so forth. These are bona fide employees. It is alleged in the indictment that they are employees of the City of Rochester, that they are police officers duly appointed during the relevant period January '88 through '90. There is no question they were legitimately on the city payroll. I think this section was meant to cover when a locality puts false employees on a payroll and collects the money and pockets it."

It was the government's contention that because we sometimes left early without documenting it, we were stealing grant money by getting paid for a full forty-hour work week. Part of the flaw in their thinking was that the grant money did not pay our salary. It could however be used to pay overtime, if needed, without supplanting the city budget. In citing an analogy, Judge Telesca said, "The federal government, in a very intrusive posture, becomes a time keeper throughout the country, and conceivably a school teacher leaving work an hour early can be prosecuted for a federal crime." After some discussion on the matter, the judge decided he was not finished researching the statute and would hold off on the testimony of Ms. Campbell for the time being.

The prosecution didn't have much luck on their next choice of witnesses. When the judge asked if they had anybody else ready to go, Mike Gennaco announced the name of Bill Brongo. Telesca's reply: "Well, I have a problem with him, too. I have a problem with Mr. Brongo. Let's talk about Mr. Brongo." The proposed witness had been an assistant district attorney and chief of the enforcement bureau of the Monroe County DA's office. He dealt strictly with narcotics cases and worked closely with our unit as well as narcotics investigators from other agencies.

I have to admit that the back and forth we had just witnessed over counts eighteen and nineteen put a smile on my face for the first time in a long while. But now, with Judge Telesca having a problem with Brongo, my smile was turning into a full-fledged shit-eating grin. I had a pretty good idea where the prosecution was attempting to go with their next witness.

Judge Telesca said after reading Brongo's grand-jury testimony he concluded that all the witness had to offer was information based on rumors and third-party conversations with defense attorneys who were suggesting excessive force was being used by the HIT Squad. Telesca further said that because Brongo had brought this to the attention of Capt. O'Brien, and O. B. hadn't gotten back to him, it would allow the jury to infer that O'Brien had knowledge and acquiescence of excessive force being used.

In response, Mike Gennaco said Brongo had an additional source of information. I had trouble believing this when I heard it. Gennaco said that as part of his duties of a supervisor, Brongo reviewed grand-jury packages and that based on reading accounts of arrests, the witness came to the conclusion that excessive force was being used. In a report from his first interview on October 26, 1990, investigators referring to Brongo wrote, "He states that he has his own feeling that he has formulated that the HIT Team, when making their arrests, are a little too forceful. However, he has never gone out on a HIT Team raid and observed their procedures." In Bill Brongo's grand-jury testimony on February 26, 1991, when asked how he became aware of this excessive force, he responded, "Really, in a couple of ways. The first would be looking at the packages. You see, it seemed like a lot of people were running [yeah, Bill, that's what they do to avoid arrest] you know. In order to make an arrest, I understand that a certain amount of force is to be used. And I don't know how much that is but a lot of people were running away and had to be directed to the ground to be handcuffed."

Also in his grand-jury testimony, Brongo indicated that through conversations with another city police officer, he had heard of excessive force being used. That the officer he was referring to was none other than the malcontent, E. J. Lergner, didn't exactly come as a huge shock.

So it was the prosecution's intention to present a witness already on record saying he never went out on a raid with us, and he had no idea how much force is necessary to affect an arrest under the conditions in which we were working. Judge Telesca to Mike Gennaco: "But he's going to come in now and testify at the time he had this strong hunch and there were conversations and nothing was done about it at the time and infer guilt here? Not in this courtroom. Not in this courtroom, Mr. Gennaco. I'm sorry."

The jury was brought back in, and the judge adjourned for the day. It really would have been interesting to see the assistant district attorney cross-examined by our team on his extensive lack of personal knowledge of the substance of his testimony.

Thursday, March 18, the trial began with my attorney reading to the jury a stipulation agreed to by the prosecution. This referred to the incident on Troup Street where Carl Jefferson swore I congratulated my men for beating a drug suspect. John Speranza read aloud to the jury regarding the facts of the stipulation: "One, that Thomas Alessi, then a sergeant in the Rochester Police Department attended a seminar entitled Drugs, Raids, and Liability held March 12 through March 15, 1989, in Myrtle Beach, South Carolina. Two, that Thomas Alessi is accordingly not present at 385 Troup Street on March 14, 1989."

Judge Telesca clarified for the jury that it was a fact that was agreed to, and there was no need to have any further proof on it.

Nineteen

At 9:12 a.m. on March 19, the government called their final witness to the stand. Officer Steve Rice had rotated through HIT in February of 1990. He had since been assigned to the Technicians Unit—a move some viewed as a reward for his cooperation in the investigation.

Rice's testimony centered around four incidents. At a raid on February 23, 1990, on the east side of the city, a number of suspects were handcuffed awaiting processing. One particular individual who had been a constant source of irritation to our unit was a Jamaican named Ameen McFadden. He had been showing up at several different drug houses. Rice testified that at one point Scott Harloff threatened McFadden by holding a pair of vice grips and asking the suspect how he thought they would feel on his balls.

Regarding a raid the day before at another eastside location, the witness testified that the buy officer got beat in that he had slipped money under the door but no drugs had been passed back. After entering the location, the buy officer found the suspect hiding in the attic. Rice stated he saw Harloff push the guy, who was cuffed, toward the stairs and that he fell head over heels down the stairs. The witness then said when the suspect reached the bottom he saw Greg Raggi slap him in the face. There was considerable objection by John Parrinello during Rice's testimony because the actual address was 66 Ellison Street, and the witness said the incident occurred at 5 Ellison Street.

The third incident involved an arrest on the west side of Rochester. February 24, 1990, had turned into a blustery winter day with heavy snow falling along with the temperature. The road conditions had deteriorated badly enough that I told everyone we were going back to the Public Safety Building after the next arrest. Officer Rice was riding in Greg's car, and, when a second suspect took off running, Greg moved into the area while other members of the unit pursued on foot. One of the team pursuing the suspect was Officer Shawn Brosnan. Because they were on an outer perimeter, Rice and Raggi never got a close look at the suspect. And because the weather was so bad, some on the team were dressed in hooded sweatshirts. This was the case with Officer Brosnan. As Greg responded to the scene of the foot chase, Rice spotted Brosnan running near the street and thought he was the drug suspect. Brosnan was actually chasing the target. At one point Rice pointed to Brosnan and said, "Get him." As Greg turned the corner he hit the brakes and skidded into Brosnan as he stepped into the street. The right side of Greg's car struck Brosnan and he went down. The basis for Rice's testimony regarding this incident was that he had convinced the prosecution as well as Officer Brosnan that Raggi had deliberately struck who he thought was the suspect. Apparently, the goal now was to make the jury believe that in order to catch a suspect for a minor drug offense, Greg was willing to intentionally run him down with a car.

Officer Brosnan was transported to the hospital with minor injuries, and, as often happens in law enforcement, this negative incident became the object of humor within the unit. Whenever Greg saw Officer Rice he would point at him and say, "Get him." This was a reference to Rice's misidentification of Shawn Brosnan as a fleeing drug suspect.

At 9:45 a.m. John Parrinello began his cross-examination of Officer Rice. He questioned the witness about his testimony regarding allegations against Scott Harloff. After about forty-five minutes, Judge Telesca called for a recess and dismissed the jury. It was at that point the prosecutor, Mike Gennaco asked to have a word with the judge, and what he said almost sent Parrinello through the roof. This was the exchange that took place:

Mr. Gennaco: The only thing I have is there appears to be some delay tactics going on here. I think we could be

> finished with this witness by the end of the day
> and I would hope that cross-examination would
> not take beyond today.
>
> Mr. Parrinello: I resent that comment. I'm going to get upset
> with him in a minute if he keeps it up.
>
> The Court: Just a moment.
>
> Mr. Parrinello: And I might engage in some atmospheric-driven
> conduct with him in a minute.
>
> The Court: You're not going to do it.
>
> Mr. Parrinello: I'm going to do it unless he shuts up right now.

The "atmospheric-driven conduct" remark was a reference to a description of our behavior by one of the government's witnesses. At that point, Judge Telesca ordered a break saying, "We can all use it."

After the recess, John Parrinello grilled Officer Rice for another three hours until we broke for a late lunch. When we returned, Greg Raggi's lawyer, David Rothenberg, took his turn at the witness. He questioned Rice about the allegation of Greg intentionally running down Officer Shawn Brosnan, thinking he was a drug suspect they were chasing.

David started by getting Rice to acknowledge for the jury that the incident was a startling event. He even got the witness to agree it made quite an impression on him. Once he had the hook set firmly in Rice's mouth David said, "In fact, it made such an impression on you that when you met with the civil rights investigators the first time to talk about this case, you brought this up right away, didn't you?"

"No, I did not," responded Officer Rice. This interview was on November 23, 1990. Then Rothenberg asked about two subsequent interviews in February and March of 1991. The jury heard how in the first three interviews with the government investigators Rice never mentioned this startling event that made such an impression on him.

What really happened was that when Greg, who was watching the actual suspect on the left side of the street, hit the brakes, the car skidded into Officer Brosnan who was running into the road on the right side at the same time. Rice told investigators in his interview on July 16, 1991, that Brosnan ran into the street. The point David was attempting to make for the jury was that the witness had failed to mention in both his grand-jury testimony and his direct testimony now that Brosnan ran into the street. This would tend to show the more likely circumstances of an accident.

Rice was asked about the weather conditions that night. He didn't recall. Let me point out that Officer Rice is a police technician who testifies frequently in court, and he knows how to prepare for his appearances. Now he's in one of the most significant trials of his career, and he can't recall the weather or road conditions that contributed to a fellow officer being sent to the hospital. Pretty convenient, isn't it? David showed the witness a copy of the accident report, which indicated snow and sleet with icy road conditions—the same report that was available to Officer Rice.

Then David got into the witness's ability to read Greg's mind. That is, to know for sure what Greg Raggi's intentions were at the time. Rice said he could not know what was in Greg's mind but that he formed an opinion. David replied, "And the fact that you don't know that, that doesn't stop you from coming into this courtroom and offering up this testimony, does it?"

"Correct," responded Officer Rice.

I find it hard to believe that a police officer working with a partner in a critical situation would not give that partner the benefit of the doubt under the circumstances as they existed. But then again, if the price for testimony favorable to the prosecution is immunity for one's own indictable offenses, then maybe it's not so hard to believe.

After a few more questions, David tendered the witness to Mr. Gennaco for redirect examination. Five minutes later, Officer Rice, the government's last witness, was excused, and at 3:55 p.m., fifty-eight days after the trial began, the prosecution rested its case against us.

Twenty

The jury was dismissed with instructions to report back to court at 8:30 a.m. Monday morning. Once the jury was out of the courtroom, the judge asked if the prosecution had an application, to which Mr. Gennaco answered yes. It was to dismiss count fourteen of the indictment. This had to do with our alleged embezzlement of government money by getting paid even when we left early. Also, two charges for using a weapon to threaten a suspect were dropped against Mike Mazzeo. The remainder of the afternoon was dedicated to our attorneys filing motions for dismissal of various other counts in the indictment, most importantly, Count I, the conspiracy. One by one, our legal representatives stepped forward and presented their arguments to Judge Telesca as to how the government failed to prove their case. After hearing all arguments, the judge said he would reserve decision and let counsel know of his ruling. Court dismissed.

The next day's headlines read, "Three counts against cops are dropped. Prosecution rests in civil rights case." Surprisingly, Leslie Sopko, the reporter who had more often than not slanted her articles (not in our favor) throughout the course of the trial actually included contradicting evidence relative to Greg Raggi's motor-vehicle accident. While she summed up Officer Rice's testimony, she added that a police investigation concluded the pavement was icy and that the accident was unavoidable.

Even though we did not have court on Fridays, the judge still ruled on the motions that had been filed. It came as no surprise to me that he denied all requests to dismiss the case against us. His decision read in part, "The government has introduced evidence upon which a reasonable mind might fairly conclude guilt beyond a reasonable doubt on each and every element of the offenses charged." At least he did drop the embezzlement charge and the one against Mike Mazzeo for allegedly threatening a suspect with his weapon.

It turned out to be an exceptionally long weekend because one of our lawyers, Tony Leonardo, was sick with the flu. Much of the time was spent polishing summations that were to be delivered by each of our attorneys. By the time we got back into the courtroom it was Wednesday morning, March 24. Our legal Brain Trust had decided not to call any witnesses, and the defense rested. Summations took us to an early recess and would continue the following day.

One bright spot revealed itself as I read Thursday's morning paper over my bowl of oatmeal. After President Bill Clinton was elected, he named Janet Reno as his attorney general. The headline read, "US attorney holdovers asked to quit. Reno's request surprises Vacco." Dennis Vacco, assistant US attorney for the Western District of New York, was losing his job. Too bad he wouldn't get to ride into Washington, DC, with our scalps on his belt. While it may have provided a small degree of satisfaction, at the same time I remember thinking that I didn't want our scalps to be on anybody's belt.

During summations, both the prosecution and the defense get one last chance to address the jury personally. Well, that's not entirely true. The prosecution goes first then the defense attorneys each have a say on behalf of their clients. But then the prosecution gets another opportunity to rebut the defense's remarks. Not quite sure how that's fair, but that's the way it is.

Jessica Ginsburg spoke for the government. She told the jury we wanted one Constitution to apply to us and another to apply to everyone else. "Constitutional rights are the linchpin of the criminal justice system, and they can't be sacrificed to make things easier or more convenient for the police," she said.

Many attorneys like to use metaphors to help get their message across. My guy, John Speranza, is no different. He told the jury that, "Indicting these men is like indicting Vietnam veterans for using too many bullets in the war." He also said, "Not one witness came in here with a clear conscience, a pure mind. The government handed out immunity like it was popcorn."

Greg's lawyer, David Rothenberg, said our only intention was to take back the streets. He said, "The truth is, these men did a dirty job, a dangerous job every night for thirty-three months—and they did a damn good job. But the prosecution does not want you to hear that they were hard working cops, so they stunk up the courtroom with trumped-up charges."

Closing arguments wrapped up the following morning. Regarding the indictment, Tony Leonardo told the jury, "The only message you can send that will save this community is to go in there, read it, rip it up, and throw it away." Remember what I said about the prosecution getting the final say in a rebuttal? One of the last comments the jury heard was from Mr. Gennaco. He told them, "The community has lost its confidence in the police. It will take years to restore faith in the department...because these individuals took the law into their own hands."

When all the closing arguments had been heard, Judge Telesca charged the jury. This is a process where the judge gives the members of the jury explicit instructions as to their legal responsibilities regarding their deliberations, after which they will render a verdict of guilty or not guilty to each and every charge. The twelve-member jury was dismissed to begin deliberations at noon. Now there was nothing more for us to do but wait. The nine women and three men stayed at it until they recessed for dinner, after which they resumed their duties until they were dismissed at 7:30 p.m. This meant they would be back at it at 8:30 tomorrow morning. It also meant that we got to wait even longer to hear our fate. I remember thinking back to when I was first suspended. December 14, 1990. Now it was more than two years and three months later, and I was on the brink of learning whether I would be going to prison. I really didn't have much hope for a good night's sleep.

March 26, 1993, was only the second time since the trial began that I found myself in my usual breakfast booth on a Friday. Throughout the trial, the judge had allowed the attorneys to use Fridays for their other business interests, so we were normally in court Monday through Thursday. The restaurant was pretty much the same as any other weekday. The only major difference was the newspaper headline staring up at me: "Jury gets case in cop's trial. Panel deliberates 7 hours, adjourns." I hadn't even started eating yet, and my first thought was about what tomorrow's bold print would say.

As we had done for eight plus weeks, members of both the prosecution and defense teams assembled in Judge Telesca's courtroom at 8:30 a.m. At this point, it was more or less just a place to leave our coats and briefcases until the long-awaited verdict. We would stand around in the hall outside the courtroom or go downstairs to the cafeteria for coffee. With no idea when or even if the jury would finish deliberations that day, we could not wander too far away. I had not smoked a cigarette since shortly after coming on the job in 1979 but was beginning to have serious thoughts of buying a pack. I never did. My twenty-two-year-old son, Michael, was there to keep me company. He worked construction and was laid off for the winter. My fourteen-year-old daughter, Julie, would have been there, but she was sick at home. Many of our friends were there as well. Most of them were retired police officers who did not have to worry about suffering the consequences of violating the chief's order not to be at court. Others still on the job just didn't give a damn and showed up anyway.

The day wore on through lunch and numerous trips back to the cafeteria for more coffee. At one point, my attorney, John Speranza, was on about his last nerve because the jury had asked to have testimony regarding me reread to them. This had to do with Ivan Hawley, who said I had struck him in the head with my gun. John was nervous because that charge alone carried a minimum mandatory five-year sentence.

As we were all standing around in the hallway around 3:45 p.m., we got the word. Charlie Salvagio, a retired Rochester police officer, was now a deputy US marshal working in the federal building. Charlie told us to return to the courtroom because the jury had reached a verdict. After a total of fourteen hours of deliberation, we were now just minutes away from knowing what the future held for us.

The courtroom gallery was packed. Some were casual observers, but most were our family and friends. We as a group agreed there would be no show of emotion until the verdicts had been read for all defendants. Our reasoning was that we did not want to be happy for ourselves as individuals if acquitted, only to have someone else found guilty. We were truly a band of brothers who the Rochester Police Department and the federal prosecutors had not been able to break in more than two years, even when they offered us misdemeanor pleas just before the trial started. We'd be damned if they were going to break us now.

Jim O'Brien and I were seated with our lawyers at the short side of the L-shaped table facing the jury. Scott, Greg, and Mike, along with their attorneys, were facing the judge and had to turn only slightly to their right to look at the twelve deciders of our fate. As the jury filed into their seats, some of their faces were somber while others were slightly smiling. Talk about a coin toss. Did they find us guilty and the smiling faces were happy about it? Or was it just the opposite? After the jurors were seated, the bailiff took the verdict from the foreman and gave it to Judge Telesca.

For what seemed like an eternity, the judge read the verdict to himself. He then addressed everyone in the courtroom with an admonishment to maintain order when the verdicts were read aloud. With three charges dropped by the government, there were sixteen left to be decided on. The biggest concern was the conspiracy charge.

Then the judge started reading. One by one they fell. "As to defendant James O'Brien on the charge of conspiracy to violate civil rights. Not guilty." He went to the next defendant. "As to defendant Thomas Alessi on the charge of conspiracy to violate civil rights. Not guilty." He continued. Before Judge Telesca got halfway through the verdict I could see Scott Harloff start to tremble and his eyes begin to mist up. Then Mike Mazzeo. As the judge read off our names and charges followed by the words "not guilty," the gallery reverberated with cheers and applause. By this time O. B., Greg, and I were starting to lose our ability to keep our emotions bottled up. When the judge said "not guilty" to my charge of striking a suspect with my gun (this is the one for which the jury wanted testimony reread) my attorney sprawled across the table and shouted, "Thank you, Jesus."

By the time it was over, the sixteen charges resulted in a unanimous not guilty for all five defendants. Most of the jurors were crying, as were our family members. Someone in the gallery shouted, "We love you" to the jury. Hugs all around. For our lawyers, our friends, and our families. It seemed like the only people not rejoicing were those sitting at the prosecution table. After hugging my son, I made my way through the crowd to a phone booth in the hallway where I called my daughter and told her the news. And, yes, she was crying, too.

Outside the federal building, the television news trucks lined the street waiting for their reporters to come out and do live broadcasts. The police department made sure there was a larger-than-normal presence, as well. There was concern that a not-guilty verdict would cause civil disorder much the same as the Rodney King verdict in Los Angeles just eleven months earlier. Mounted police officers rode their horses in front of the federal building while marked cruisers patrolled the streets. While they watched for signs of trouble, they keyed their radio microphones and began spreading the news to cops all over the city. One news organization's police scanner picked up an early transmission: First officer: Any verdict yet?

Second officer: Not guilty all counts.

First officer: Beautiful.

Police cars city wide sounded their sirens in celebration. Well, at least those occupied by our fellow officers who had supported and believed in us. I imagine the ones who didn't were wondering what life was going to be like for them now that we had been acquitted. They would feel the impact of their decision to assist our persecutors for several years to come.

Back inside, as the courtroom was slowly emptying, when all the handshaking and back slapping was over, we had a decision to make: where were we going to go to celebrate our victory? I had still been bartending Saturday nights at Hemingway's, so I called and asked if they could handle a fairly large impromptu party.

As we emerged from the federal building, it was obvious that all the news reporters hadn't left yet. They were waiting to hear us speak for the first time in more than two years. I remember thinking how much different I felt compared to that day ten weeks earlier when I met them on the way into the federal building on the first day of the trial. "Tom, how do you feel now that you've been found not guilty?" I guess I should have been prepared for this moment, but I wasn't. All I could think of was what it had been like living with uncertainty since the ordeal began. That and the running calendar in my head that I kept track of every day. I said, "My life has been on hold for two years, three months, one week, and five days. This means I can leave the Western District of New York without permission. The verdict restores my faith in the system. That's why I never took a plea."

With a half-dozen microphones in his face, Union President Ron Evangelista was asked what he thought of the verdict. He responded, "The government went on a witch hunt...and they found no witches."

One of the reporters handed Jim O'Brien a portable phone so he could call his wife, Cindy, in Florida. "It's over, honey. Did you hear? I'll call you from another phone where everyone isn't listening."

Greg Raggi said for the record, "I just want to put it behind me," as he walked from the federal building with his daughter, Sarah, holding tightly onto his left arm.

As for Scott Harloff, he said to reporters, "I'm relieved. I want to go back to work. All I ever did was my job." As the interviews came to an end, caravans of vehicles began making their way to the restaurant, including some of the news trucks.

When I arrived at Hemingway's, some of the television cameras were already set up and running. They captured the celebration throughout the remainder of the afternoon and provided live feeds to their respective stations for the evening newscasts. Many of our friends and supporters from the general public, after learning where we were, came to the restaurant, adding to the growing crowd.

Not everyone there was celebrating our victory. One customer, who apparently had been in the restaurant before we arrived, was standing at the end of the bar when I went up to get a drink. As I stood next to him waiting to order, the news came on the large screen TV at the far end of the bar. The scene was of us emerging from the federal building while the anchorperson reported the not guilty verdict. Without looking at me, the customer said, "They should have hung those bastards." I said, "Really. Were you at the trial?" As he turned to me he started to say, "No, but..." He stopped short, looked at me, looked back at the television with my image staring back at him. He looked back at me and left the restaurant without another word or finishing his drink. The party lasted well into the evening until there were only a few of us left. Then it was time to leave, and even though we had been blessed with a favorable outcome with respect to the trial, we were still dealing with an uncertain future.

Twenty-One

Saturday morning, March 27, 1993, and the newspaper was filled with articles and photos from the final day of the trial as well as reactions to the verdict. The front page said it all. Across the top of the page over a large picture of Greg Raggi and his daughter leaving the federal building it read, "Acquitted," in one-and-three-quarter-inch bold type. Beneath that and next to the photo: "5 ex-vice cops cleared of civil rights abuses. Police on street rejoice." Under the photo was a slightly smaller caption that read, "Juror depicts verdict: We all had tears." Next to that was an article entitled "Anger, disbelief over decision," with the subtitle, "But some residents say justice prevailed."

As I read through the articles I realized that for many people it really didn't matter what the jury decided. We were just as guilty to them now as we had been when the allegations were announced more than two years before. From the chief of police and the mayor to the "man on the street," everyone had something to say. When I turned to page seven, I was surprised to see a five-by-seven photograph of me hugging my attorney, John Speranza, outside the federal building. Down the left side of the page were pictures of all the defendants with our names, ages, and a list of the charges against each of us. Along the right side of the page were photos of all the lawyers, both defense and prosecution. Under each picture was a short biography with their ages and educations. In the center of the page was a photograph of Judge Telesca with his bio. The remainder of the page was taken up by more reactions to the verdict.

And so it went for the next few days. Opinions were given as to why we won. Some jurors said the prosecution simply failed to prove the necessary elements for a conspiracy. This was echoed by some attorneys who added that most of the police witnesses were granted immunity for bad acts in exchange for their testimony. That left the question in the jury's mind of why us and not them. It probably didn't help the prosecution's case for the jury to know that we were offered deals to plead to lesser charges just before the trial began. Like I said earlier, this case was never supposed to see the light of day; the government had hoped to overwhelm us with the indictment and deal offers instead of going to trial. Some civil rights activists argued it was a miscarriage of justice. Nothing short of a public beheading would have satisfied them. They had to settle for protest gatherings where they vented their displeasure over the verdict with shouts of "No justice, no peace."

The following Tuesday's morning newspaper had only two articles. There was one was on the front page of the A section and one on the front page of the local section. But just to make sure the public didn't lose interest, both headlines were in large, bold type. The first read, "Trial rings up large tax bill. Costs exceed $2 million; include price of officers' defense." The article broke down the various expenses for attorneys, overtime for investigators, hotel bills for the three prosecutors from Washington, etc. Talk about rubbing salt into a wound. Not only did we beat them at what they believed would be a slam-dunk prosecution, but now the city (taxpayers) had to pay for everything.

The second article was entitled "Major protest aimed at acquittals. Black activist calls 5 officers animals." I said earlier that some people in the community tried to make a racial issue out of our ordeal. We never discriminated when it came to busting dope dealers. Several of the so-called victims enumerated in the indictment were white. That didn't matter to the Rev. Lewis Stewart, coordinator of the United Church Ministry and its Peoples Coalition. He said, "There is no justice for people of color in this country, and this trial proves it." Calling us animals who had no business in uniforms, he told about 120 people the night before at a rally that the trial was a setup and a farce played out by conspiring lawyers and a jury that does not know right from wrong. He went on to say, "Look at the makeup of the jury, composed of one black woman. And apparently, she didn't know who she was…Somehow she lost her identity along the way." So not only does this Christian-minded "Reverend" attack us, but he challenges the integrity of the sole minority juror (that we selected) whom he knows nothing about. It was never about race, but just as others like him had done, Stewart used our case to fan the flames of prejudice and mistrust of the police that existed in the minority community.

And the protests didn't just quietly fade away. Not for a while, anyway. The following month on April 17, 1993, two of the four LAPD officers in the Rodney King case were found guilty in a federal civil rights trial. All four officers had been acquitted in a state trial on April 29, 1992, a verdict that had ignited three days of rioting. Lewis Stewart used the occasion to stage a protest march through downtown Rochester. His 150 or so marchers were protesting not only our verdict three weeks after the fact, but also because only two of the four LA cops were found guilty.

The day before the march was also significant. Former Chief Gordon Urlacher, his ex-aide Roy Ruffin, and Bill Morris were sentenced by Judge Michael Telesca. Urlacher, who had already been serving a four-year sentence for his embezzlement conviction, was given two years for his guilty plea in our case. It was to be served concurrently with the time he was already serving. Since it wasn't going to be added to his existing jail time, it made sense for him to plead guilty. It basically meant that this conviction was a matter of record.

Roy Ruffin was given probation, ordered to stop playing pool for money, and told to get a job. He was also ordered to pay the City of Rochester $25,000 in restitution and perform one thousand hours of community service. No jail time.

William F. Morris, the government's star witness, was sentenced to five years' probation and one thousand hours of community service.

No jail time. I was not present for Morris's sentencing, but there were several city police officers on hand to witness his typical self-serving behavior. In a statement to the judge, Morris said, "Carrying the burden of this case alone for the next several years is cruel and unusual punishment. I must carry this burden for the entire community." When I read that in the paper I thought I was going to throw up. I couldn't help remembering one of his tape-recorded statements to Mike Berkow. "I don't give a fuck about anybody else. I only care about me." So much for his "burden."

The sentencing of the former chief of police and the two Judases, who sold their souls for no other reason than to save themselves from the consequences of their own misdeeds, spelled the end of the worst scandal in the history of the Rochester Police Department. That is, as far as the legal aspect of it, anyway. Its damaging effects would be felt both in the department itself as well as by many of the participants for several years to come. And the Rochester Police Department would take another seven months to decide the fates of Greg Raggi, Scott Harloff, and Mike Mazzeo. They would remain on paid suspension until October of 1993. The issue was whether the three should be brought up on departmental charges for basically the same incidents that the government failed to convict on. And while Jim O'Brien and I were already long gone from the police department, the administration would use another forum to screw our former captain. Any citizen complaints that came in to the department relative to our unit were put into O'Brien's Internal Affairs file. He would find out about them when he applied for a job with the Key Biscayne Police Department in Florida. The chief of that agency informed O. B. that the complaints were discovered during a pre-employment background investigation. Of course, Jim didn't disclose this information on his application. How could he? He didn't even know they existed. He didn't get the job.

Scott's lawyer, John Parrinello, had worked out a deal whereby Harloff could resign from the RPD without further discipline and be free to apply at other law-enforcement agencies. The city agreed not to attempt to influence a prospective employing department with negative information. That promise was broken when Scott considered going to a large suburban police force. Harloff was eventually hired by Chief David Dalton of the Palmyra Police Department, a small village agency in neighboring Wayne County.

On the condition that he waive his retirement medical benefits, Greg Raggi was allowed to reach his twenty-year anniversary and leave the department with his full pension. Pensions are paid to retirees by the New York State Police and Firemen's Retirement System while medical benefits are paid by the municipality from which one retires. Greg was assured that if he did not agree to the waiver, he would be fired before reaching his target date and lose both his medical and retirement benefits. Having no other option, Raggi took the deal and retired on October 3, 1993.

Mike Mazzeo was allowed to return to duty without further discipline. It had long been the contention by people both on and off the department that of the five of us, Mike had been the least deserving of a ringside seat in the courtroom. As a welcome-back gesture, Mazzeo was shot at (and missed) by a suspect his first night back in uniform.

Twenty-Two

It's been several years since the formal end of the ordeal that changed so many lives and destroyed careers. Most of the key people involved have long since moved on to other stages of their lives.

Lt. Robert Duffy rapidly climbed the ranks in the Rochester Police Department, eventually becoming chief of police, a position he held for seven years before retiring. In 2005, Robert Duffy was elected Mayor of the City of Rochester. In January 2011, he was sworn in as Lt. Governor of the State of New York.

Lt. Michael Berkow retired and went on to become the chief of police for two California police departments before being appointed deputy chief of the Los Angeles Police Department. From there he went on to become the chief of the Savannah Police Department.

After working in several jobs around the country with his good friend Mike Berkow, Mark Gerbino was sworn in as chief of police of the Americus, Georgia, Police Department in August, 2011.

Lt. Joyce Walsh was diagnosed with cancer and, after a long battle, died in the spring of 2003.

Special Agent Gene Harding (the agent who arrested Chief Urlacher), after retiring from the FBI, pleaded guilty in July 2004 to a federal misdemeanor for accessing personal information from IRS and Social Security records. Harding had been working for hotels in Las Vegas.

And last, but not least, the government's star witness, Billy Morris. No one I know really knows for sure where he ended up. The last I heard, he had bounced around various jobs in the medical field and is supposedly somewhere in Texas. The one thing I do know for sure is that wherever Morris goes, he will always be a convicted criminal. The label he tried so hard to put on the rest of us in an effort to save himself was his and his alone.

As for the five targets of the government's "witch hunt," we've all come a long way to reach our current stations in life. As of this writing, Mike Mazzeo is still employed by the Rochester Police Department but has attained the pivotal position of president of the Rochester Police Locust Club. The post once held for so long by Ron Evangelista is now occupied by Mazzeo, who, along with so many officers, had been the recipient of the club's protection under Evangelista's stewardship. It was now Mike's job and privilege to not only protect the rights of city cops but also battle with the city over the department's labor contracts.

After retirement, Greg Raggi took a job with Valeo, an auto-parts manufacturing company in Rochester. He went to work primarily for the benefits that he was screwed out of by the city. Greg worked his way up to management and retired after ten years with the company. He went on to take a position with Homeland Security Corporation in Nashville for a few years before permanently retiring back to Rochester with his wife, Michelle.

After retiring from the Palmyra Police Department, Scott Harloff moved to Florida with his wife, Debbie, and youngest son, Tim. He eventually took a position as a probation officer on the state's east coast.

Jim O'Brien and his wife, Cindy, moved to southwest Florida shortly after his retirement. The former RPD captain was hired by a small department where he was promoted to chief of police in 2010.

As for me, it has truly been a long and winding road. After working at Kodak for a year, I was approached by a friend who convinced me I could buy the restaurant and bar that used to be Shields, the old cop bar we had all frequented. After scrubbing toilets for more than a year, it sounded like a pleasant alternative. I convinced Denise we could do it together. The bar and restaurant had changed hands and names since Shields closed down, and it was now the Corn Hill Grill. We bought the business in September of 1993 but closed the doors in November of 1994—with the exception of a few good friends, we just never got the needed support from the boys in blue. I had been told by several RPD members that it was felt by many that patronizing my bar would not bode well for their careers. We did, however, host a dinner for the jury, my codefendants, and our attorneys. Meanwhile, I had been hired by the Palmyra Police Department in May of 1994. After rescuing Scott Harloff, Chief Dave Dalton offered me a position with his agency. I would not be the last ex-RPD cop whose law enforcement career was resurrected by Chief Dalton. Three more followed in Harloff's and my footsteps. I worked in Palmyra for nine months before my career took another turn.

I lost my sister, Fay, to cancer in November of 1994, and the day after her funeral, I received a phone call from a good friend in the RPD. Sergeant Lou D'Angelo told me he had run into East Rochester Chief of Police Bill Young. Young had been a Rochester police officer for nineteen years before leaving to take the chief's job in ER, where he lived. Lou said the chief had asked about me and felt he wanted to offer me a job with the ERPD. After contacting Chief Young, I was hired on February 1, 1995. I was now working in the town where I lived with Denise. And I was making considerably more money. Things were indeed looking up.

I won't bore you with the details of my last eight years in law enforcement other than to say that I worked with some really good people in East Rochester and appreciate the opportunity I was given to get my life back on track. By 1998, my relationship with Denise had deteriorated to the point where I had become interested in another woman, and I moved in with her in June of 1999. The day after my fifty-fifth birthday in August of 2003, I retired from the East Rochester Police Department with full benefits.

The following year, Meg, the woman with whom I'd now been in a five-year relationship, decided she could no longer deal with the stress of me, her, and her four daughters living under the same roof. I moved out in June of 2004. One year later I packed up a rental truck and moved to southwest Florida. For years I've known this is where I was meant to be. While I miss my family and friends, I don't miss the endless Rochester winters I endured for so many years. Now, most days I wake up to sunshine, palm trees, and tropical breezes.

I sometimes think back to the trial and what we were facing had the jury voted against us. I even occasionally think of those who turned their backs on us and gave self-serving statements to the prosecution that belied their own conduct—who drank the government's Kool-Aid because they never thought their cooperation would be made public. For the sake of brevity, not all of the nearly forty members of the RPD who helped the prosecutors try to put us away made it into the pages of this book. Most of them went on with their careers in the department, with a few rising to upper levels in the administration. They know who they are, and their cowardly acts of betrayal will live with them forever. I wonder how many, if any, still think it was worth it when they look in the mirror.

Acknowledgments

It would be next to impossible to personally thank all of those whose support helped to make an extremely long and difficult experience somewhat bearable. The list would surely have to begin with the many friends, colleagues, and family members who never stopped believing in us. In addition to Ron Evangelista and the Locust Club, who backed us from the very start, we were defended by an incredibly talented legal dream team. John Speranza, John Parrinello, David Rothenberg, Carl Salzer, and Tony Leonardo proved once again that Goliath could be beaten. Palmyra, New York, Police Chief David Dalton not only hired me and Scott Harloff but also saved the careers of three additional former Rochester Police Department officers. East Rochester Police Chief Bill Young gave me the opportunity to finish my journey toward retirement and a pension. For anyone who has ever attempted to write a book, you know that it's impossible to do it without help. I could never have completed this project without the invaluable resource material provided to me by John DiMartino. My website professional, M. E. Parker, and author Shannon Danford were extremely helpful with technical assistance and publishing advice. Thanks to retired Hamilton Township, New Jersey, Police Chief Jay McKeen for his insight and advice. Two good friends, Pat Purnell and author Patrick Crough, both former law-enforcement officers, also provided regular critiquing and advice. I say this to my son, Michael, and my daughter, Julie: You always believed in me and in the truth. Your love and support helped me to survive one of the most difficult periods of my life. You mean more to me than you could possibly imagine. I love you both very much. Thank you, and God bless you.

CPSIA information can be obtained at www.ICGtesting.com
Printed in the USA
BVOW06s0743231215

430869BV00007BA/41/P

9 780692 406687